Doubt & Certainty

One Woman's Journey Through Her Veiled Heritage

Edited by Mary Dixon and Donald Henry

Photo editing by Gerry Legere

Cover photo - Gertrude, driving her Model T Ford with Arnold, Elma and Anna, 1918

Printed and bound in Canada at PrintPro
450 Provencher Blvd, Winnipeg, MB R2J 0B9
www.printprowinnipeg.com

Cover and Interior designed by McNally Robinson Self-Publishing
www.mcnallyrobinson.com/selfpublishing

Third Edition
978-1-77280-238-2

DOUBT & CERTAINTY

One Woman's Journey Through Her Veiled Heritage

Elma Enns-Kreitzer
&
Raymond Kreitzer

GERTRUDE'S FAMILY TREE FROM 1875

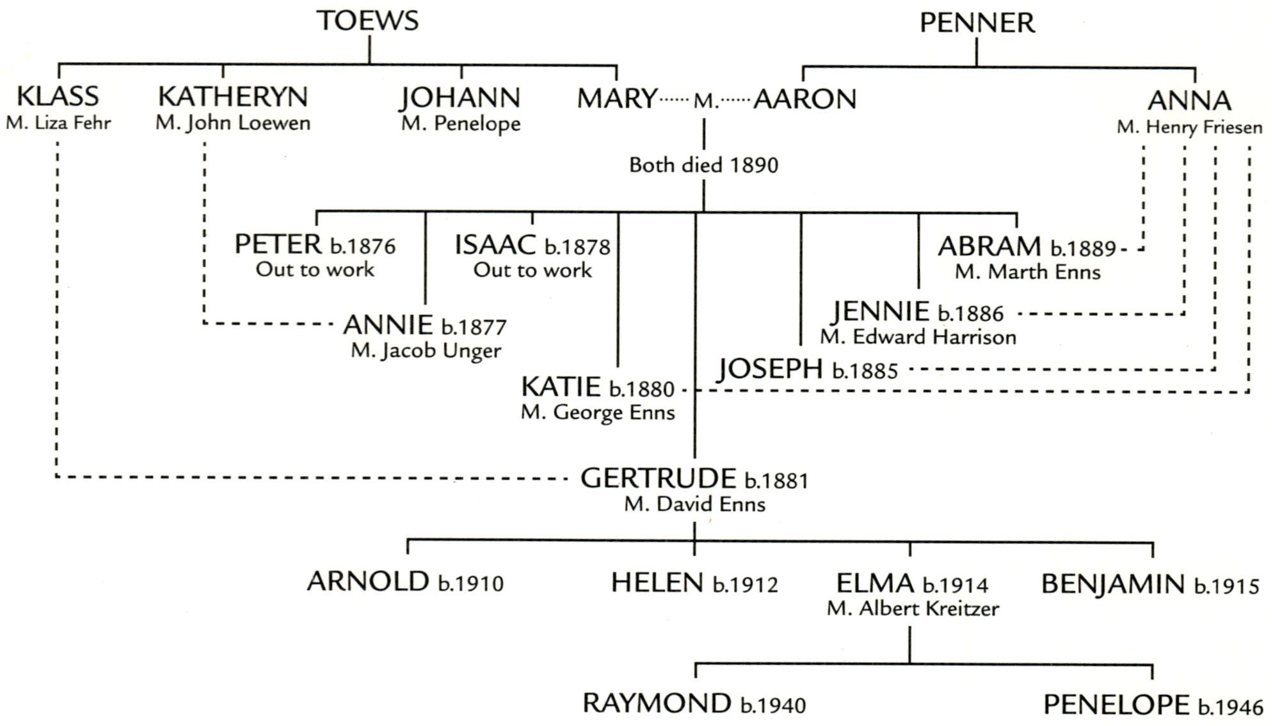

Chapter One

Gertrude groped her way downstairs. It was early morning in late summer. The air was humid and still after the night's torrential rainstorm. She sank into her father's recently vacated, rumpled bed, still warm from his body. Her small frame ached for more rest and with a deep sigh, she reached out to rock the cradle. Her eyelids, heavy with sleep, drooped slowly. Her hand slackened and the cradle's plaintive song stopped. At Abram's loud cry of protest, Gertrude's eyes flew open and she resumed her rocking, once more sending Abram back into a light slumber.

It had fallen to Gertrude to keep watch over her small brother Abram. As she gallantly pumped away, she was dimly aware of the morning sounds of the awakening household. There was the clanging of stove lids and the scraping of the damper as Annie started the fire in the cooking range. She could tell that it was Katie who was banging around the pots and kettles—she thinks she is so much smarter than me, just because she is older! The outside door with its hollow, echoing thump slammed shut, Papa on his way out to the barn. Thinking of Papa reminded her of yesterday and the sickening feeling in the pit of her stomach returned.

* * * * *

Two of their aunts, Kathryne and Anna, had come to give the children a hand. The mending, among other things, had piled up alarmingly since Mama had died. Katie and Gertrude had been happy to escape the house unnoticed. The day was very hot and clammy and they hurried around the house to sit in the cool shade hoping they would not be discovered too soon. They picked a spot beneath the window. They could hear the creaking of their aunts' chairs which they had pulled to the open window to catch what little breeze might come grudgingly in to them. The girls sat without talking, paying little heed to the banal conversation going on over their heads, until suddenly the girls became aware that they were talking about Papa.

"You know," Anna said, "it would be best for the children if Aaron..."

Kathryne interrupted, "You know how much they loved their mother—and now, so soon, for someone to take her place..."

"Yes, but Aaron himself has said that he cannot cope much longer."

"Bah! These men! It's not so much the work as...," Kathryne paused giving Anna a knowing look.

"Kathryne," Anna interjected forcefully. "What if someone heard you?"

"I know, I know," agreed Kathryne, however, not to be

diverted from her point she added, "you know yourself how it is. Remember when Aaron's first wife died? It didn't take him any longer to find a second wife."

Gertrude's eyes widened in disbelief as the conversation revealed to her its ominous story. She tugged urgently at Katie's sleeve. Katie shushed her quickly with her finger across her lips and Gertrude clamped her hand over her mouth.

"Anyway, I do think Elizabeth Froese would be very capable; she's not so young and needs a home of her own," was Anna's response.

At this Gertrude became quite agitated but Katie warningly pressed Gertrude's arm.

"Well, I think it's too soon," persisted Kathryne. "The children might resent her." She knew that she herself might resent anyone taking Mary's place so soon. She had been very close to her sister Mary and the children were very dear to her and looked to her for comfort. She knew that the wounds left by the loss of their mother were still sorely raw.

"This heat is sure to bring a storm," Anna muttered and with a deep sigh, signified that the subject of her brother's pending marriage was best left without further discussion.

Katie and Gertrude quietly hurried away from their misbegotten hiding place. As soon as they were out of ear shot, Gertrude burst out, "It isn't true—it isn't true!"

"What isn't true?" Katie asked more off handedly then she really felt.

"That Papa was married before.....," Gertrude cried out shakily, tears welling up in her eyes, "and that he is going to marry that......"

"Oh Gertrude, you are such a child, of course Papa was

married before—that's nothing.....," her seniority making her so wise. "I have known it for a long time."

"Why did Mama never tell me?" Gertrude asked unhappily.

"You were much too young to know."

"Ach!" Gertrude spat out impatiently. "I don't want to have Elizabeth for my mother.....she's an old maid, and..... and....," she was at a loss for further words.

"I don't either." Katie's bravado fell away. " Maybe Papa won't do it.....," her words faded into the deep recesses of her own private hurt. Then quickly she reverted to her old self. "At least you don't have to worry about it. Children shouldn't concern themselves about such things."

Gertrude did not reply, Katie's constant sniping at her childishness silently rankled her.

* * * * *

Gertrude's father, Aaron Penner, had been awakened during the night to rolling thunder and bright flashes of lightning. Yesterday's heat had not failed to bring the predicted storm. He turned, reaching for the comfort of Mary beside him, then realizing bitterly that Mary wasn't there, he drew back. It was like a physical rebuke. His loneliness and grief took a renewed grip on him.

Even as a child, in the old country, before he had come to Canada, Aaron had had a fear of storms. Age had not lessened its awe. With time, however, the wild, unleashed beauty of summer storms had become more of a fascination and he had made a somewhat uneasy truce with its superior power. Suddenly a jagged, angry streak of lightning followed by thunder crashing through the house shattered his fragile bravery. His tortured soul was left naked, the violence of the elements pressed around him again, threatening to suffocate him. As the storm lessened, Aaron's inner turmoil subsided once more and his thoughts drifted back to the events of the last few months.

* * * * *

The winter of 1890 had been a long and rigorous one. It had seemed endless. He had never felt so deeply nostalgic for the country they had left behind in exchange for this cold, hard Canadian climate. It was a continuous battle with the forces of nature—the winters' chill penetrated all defences, never ceasing to test everyone's fortitude. The summers, because of their very shortness, lengthened the days and poured out oppressive heat and boundless energy in a frenzied effort, as if to atone for the hardships and cruelty of the winter just passed while, at the same time, hurrying them along to the new winter so soon to come.

For Mary, the winter had seemed endless and with the approaching spring, the child within her grew heavy and restless. It too was waiting for release. Aaron and Mary had spent many evenings together in the kitchen near the warmth of the stove. After the children were in their beds the house was still. They had a few moments to themselves. They were sitting, each on one side of the table. The flame of the small coal oil lamp between them sent their shadows flickering to the walls around them making the kitchen seem smaller than it was, giving it an intimacy it otherwise lacked. Mary, her elbows resting on the table, let her black shawl slip down and fall to her shoulders. Her deep sigh drew Aaron's eyes to her. He saw, as if for the first time, the grey showing in her soft brown hair. She wore it parted in the middle and drawn back from her face and rolled into a tight bun at the nape of her neck. He saw the beauty in her deceptively plain face, but he also saw more clearly the tired lines which this past winter had etched deeper into her fair skin.

He rose abruptly and went to the stove. He lifted the lid and prodded the flames to give them more life. He bent to the wood box, carefully picked a few pieces of wood and laid them on the fire. "I hope our wood will last out the winter," he remarked, as he settled himself back on his chair, listening to the cheerful popping and crackling as the wood caught fire.

"Well, I think you and the boys put up enough for us to get through. Don't you think the thaw will be coming soon now?" Mary wondered hopefully.

"Yes, I hope so." The snow had come early and spread its thick, white blanket shamelessly, unthinkingly. "But is it ever much different? In the fifteen years we have been here, has it ever been different? Fifteen years—if we haven't learned in that time, we never will."

Mary murmured comfortable agreement, feeling safe and secure, certain that the burden of their pioneer status was becoming easier, slipping quietly away. She felt they were beginning to be part of this land.

Aaron turned to his wife after they had sat quietly enjoying the renewed heat from the small stove for some time. "Mary.....Mary, how do you feel? I have been worried about you."

"Why.....Aaron." Mary was touched by his concern. "I'm fine, just fine. I've been through this many times before."

"But things seem different this time somehow," Aaron faltered awkwardly. At times Aaron's sensitivity still surprised Mary. He was so strong and self-sufficient, not only as the head of his own family but also as a leader in their community.

"It hasn't been easy," Mary conceded. "But it will be over soon." Mary reached over and patted his hand, knowing she had given him the comfort he sought, reassuring him without taking away from his masculinity. Mary knew from the confidences which the women in their closely knit community shared, that most of their men felt they had no part in the birth of their children. She also knew that, in their turn, the women drew away from their men, shutting them out of a ritual that was best left within the confines of their own private world. Mary looked at Aaron and smiled, knowing that between Aaron and her it was different...... she didn't know why, but it was. Aaron returned her smile. They were seldom more demonstrative than a smile or a touch of the hand. The many generations of holding back as dictated by Mennonite doctrine had shaped their restraint into an ever present trait against which they were helpless. The seeds of their progeny were planted as a God-given duty. Who is to say what pleasure they gained in the planting? The appetites of their young, healthy, virile bodies went into the making of their large families.

Reluctantly, Aaron broke the silence. " Brother John Wiebe came by today." The preachers were generally greeted with a certain amount of awe.

"Oh?" Mary waited expectantly.

"Well, he wants to talk to Peter and Annie. I told him yes……"

"But why? Have they done something wrong?" Alarm in her voice. Her protective instincts were quickly aroused.

"Oh no, nothing like that." He was just as quick to reassure her. "He just thinks it's about time they and a few other of the young people should prepare themselves to join the church and be baptized." Church elders were responsible for ensuring that the younger members of their flock were baptized in a timely manner. If they were too young, they might not fully understand the meaning of the expression of faith that was required of them at the ceremony . On the other hand, there was always a risk that by leaving it too long, they might succumb to outside, more worldly influences and stray from the fold.

"Well!" Mary, as though thinking aloud, continued, " I can hardly believe they are old enough……but, then, look at the way Annie is being such a help to us…..I don't know how I could've managed this last winter without her, She's so good with the younger children too. She will make a fine mother someday, don't you think, Aaron?"

"Yes…..yes, " Aaron agreed absently, thinking also of his sons.

"But, I find it hard to think of our oldest two being ready to join the church," Mary said somewhat wistfully. She recalled their own youth. Without much thought, they had joined the old Mennonite Church. But a number of years back, John Holdeman who had already developed quite a following in Kansas, came into their midst and with a forceful manner, convinced some of their numbers that the old church to which they belonged had become too lax. He claimed that the only path to regain their lost salvation was to follow his teachings. He had revised and tightened up some of the traditional Mennonite practices. He put in place more restrictive dress and grooming codes and more stringent avoidance of anything he defined as 'too worldly'. All musical instruments were banned. Hymns could be sung in church but they must be sung in unison only. To sing in harmony was a sin. The creation and the appreciation of art was forbidden. The bible was the only reading material allowed. Punishment for breaking the rules according to Holdeman's doctrine resulted in swift excommunication followed by shunning. People who had never belonged to their church were by definition sinners but shunning was not to be practiced against any of them; only against excommunicated, former members. Members were not allowed to shake the hand, eat at the same table, form business relationships or, in fact, have any kind of close relationship with the excommunicated. The only escape from the pain of being shunned by family and neighbours was to repent and rejoin the church. Mary had felt, along with many others, that they had managed quite well, living a good Christian life in their peaceful village, without benefit of John Holdeman's teachings. Nevertheless, she had bowed to her husband's wishes but not without a deep sense of loss. So, along with others, Aaron and Mary Penner fell into line with Holdeman's new version of Mennonite dogma and a Holdeman congregation established itself in their community side by side with those who remained in the old church.

"It will be different for our children than when we joined."

"Yes, they have grown up as Holdemans. They don't know anything else," Aaron agreed.

"Yes, that is true. But then, it isn't only the church that has changed since we were young. It's also the people….. they have changed too since the split in the church and the breaking up of our village. Everything is different. There are so many of our old friends and neighbours that we never see anymore…..only when we happen to meet at the village store. Why, you know, Aaron, our children have cousins they haven't even met!"

"The people didn't leave the village because of the split in the church," Aaron began to explain.

"But it helped," Mary broke in quickly. "They wouldn't have been so eager to go."

"You see, don't you, Mary, that we had to go live on our homesteads in any case. We promised the government to build them up, improve them."

Since they were innately an independent people, it was not too difficult for them to move out of the village. They had outgrown the need for the protective closeness of communal life. The rift in the church had merely hastened the inevitable. The main village street which had once been the link that held them together in a new country now lay as the dividing line between two growing farming communities. The Holdemans had gravitated to the north of the village and the Kleine Gemeinde, as the old church members were known, settled to the south. They built their own churches which were the ruling centres of their societies. They became a separated people, with skilfully camouflaged antagonism lurking between them.

"Come Mary." Aaron rose from the table. "Let's go to bed."

The snows melted and April gave way to May. It was a warm, sunny day when Mary knew that her time had come. She stood, looking out the window. The yard was still muddy where the heavy snowbanks had lain. She could see the little buds on the trees, ready to burst into life. She knew she must call Annie, but she felt reluctance at sharing this moment which was still so very much her own.

Although she had never seen a real painting, she imagined that the scene outside her window was like a beautiful, unfinished work of art which was waiting for the artist to add the many colours of summer. She wondered, with a fleeting wistful sadness, whether this time she would see the finished picture. She felt a strange detachment from the world about her these last few weeks. She had looked at the faces of her children with renewed fondness, but a remoteness which she could not shake. And Aaron—their union had grown meaningful even though the marriage into which they had been manipulated by well-meaning others had begun with painful awkwardness. Then her moment of introspection was violently wrenched from her by the sharp gripping pain which coursed through her body. The urgency in her call brought Annie hurrying to her side.

"Mama, Mama." Annie came breathlessly to her. "Is.....?"

"Yes, Annie." Mary gripped her side. "I don't think there's much time. You remember what you are to do?" Annie was shaking at the sight of her mother's agony but she pulled yourself together, proud of her mother's trust in her.

"Don't worry Mama. I'll stop at Aunt Kathryne's just like you said, before I go on for the doctor. Will you be alright?" she called as she hurried out the door. She knew she could not wait for an answer.

"Gertrude! Gertrude!" Annie called. "I have to hurry to the village. Look after Abram. Take him outside and don't let him bother Mama.....but see that he doesn't get his feet wet."

Gertrude took Abram by the hand and Joseph, who was just younger than Gertrude, pressed close beside them as they stood watching Annie running, skirts flying, out of sight. Gertrude then manoeuvred the boys to the sunny side of the house where there was still some straw piled around the house. Papa put it there every fall—he said it was to keep the winter out. They settled down comfortably on it to await Annie's return. The sweet smell as the sun dried it had become an integral part of spring. Its aroma filled the fresh air and penetrated the house. As she leaned back against the house, Gertrude regretted that it would soon all be removed.

Annie clutched her large, woollen shawl which she had carelessly thrown about her shoulders and picked up her long skirts with her other hand so as not to impede her progress as she sped on. It was only about half a mile to the village where Aunt Kathryne still lived but today it seemed much farther. As she reached the Loewen's house the door flew open and Aunt Kathryne stepped outside. "Mama sent me. She told me to hurry," Annie managed to blurt out. Her excitement finally overwhelming her. Suddenly she wanted to cry, but for a second time she pulled herself together. Tears would not be in keeping with her important mission.

"I had a feeling when I got up this morning, that this would be the day. You're going for the doctor too?" Kathryne was reaching for her wraps as she spoke. Annie nodded, still trying to catch her breath.

"There is no need to fret. These things take time and when you have told Doctor Martens, don't run back home. I'll be there looking after your mother.....just take your time." Her aunt added a quick hug to her reassuring words as they parted at the gate.

Annie's heart felt lighter as she forced herself into a more leisurely pace. Dr. Martens's house was at the other end of the street in the Kleine Gemeinde part of the village—an area she wasn't familiar with but she did know which was the doctor's house. She had had a previous experience with him which made her dread talking to him again. He had come to their house to assist with Abram's birth. He was fat and hard of hearing. Annie's job had been to make a cup of coffee for him while he waited for Abram to make his appearance. They were alone in the kitchen. When she served him his coffee at the table he asked her how old she was. He didn't hear her mumbled reply.

"Come closer my dear. Speak up."

When she reluctantly edged her way closer, he reached out his hairy, pudgy hand, touching her shoulder. "I'm t-t- twel......twelve," she tried to say in a loud voice but her tongue tangled her words. His insistent hand was clumsily sliding down her back. She backed away in horror and fled the room. He picked up his cup and took a delicate sip.

Luckily today the doctor's wife came to the door first. Annie delivered her message and backed away as she saw the doctor coming behind his wife.

"Well.....eh....Lena? What did she want?" His throaty words punctuated with his heavy breathing reached Annie as she left the yard with no wish to dawdle there. However, she stopped behind the nearest bush to watch for when he would leave the house. She would take no chance at his passing her on the road and offering her a ride. It was said in the village that he would never get anything done if it wasn't for his thin, nervous wife. He went about his preparations, muttering that there was no rush, as long as he was there to catch the child from the womb or to close the eyes of the dying.

Annie saw Lena Martens rush out to the small stable, lead out the seedy, unbrushed nag, and hitch her to the buggy. After what seemed an interminable time, the doctor came lumbering out of the house. He heaved his enormous bulk up into the buggy and settled into the seat. His huffing and fuming mingled with the sound of the springs settling with resignation into their accustomed place. With that, Lena Martens dealt a sharp resounding slap to the horse's rump, startling her into a burst of speed. A small whirlwind lifted the doctors long white beard and waved it gaily over his shoulder as he disappeared from view. Annie heard him loudly admonishing the horse to slow down to a pace more suitable to the dignity of the driver and the capabilities of the old horse.

"Well, thank goodness, he is on his way," Annie told herself as she reappeared from the bushes arranging her skirts and starting on her own way home.

Aaron had gone that morning with a load of grain to a village farther down the road to trade for some special grain he wanted to seed that spring. He had taken his two oldest sons along. It had been a day's journey there and back. They returned tired and hungry. They could feel the excitement emanating from the house even before they entered. The faces of the younger children shone with happiness. Annie was laying the table for the supper, proud of the important part she had played in the events of the day. Aunt Kathryne, who had thought it best to stay the night, turned from the stove. "You have another son, Aaron," she announced with a broad smile.

Aaron could not speak. He caught his breath as a flood of relief washed over him. He went at once to the bedroom. He stood for a brief moment at the foot of the bed. Mary's eyes were closed. Her hair lay in two braids on her shoulders. The dimly lit room gave her the deceptive look of youth. He dropped to his knees beside the bed and placed his head on the pillow beside hers. She reached over and stroked his hair.

"Mar.....oh, Mary...thank God it's over....you are alright, aren't you, Mary?"

"We have a fine son, Aaron. Don't you want to see him?"

"Yes, yes, but please, tell me that you are alright."

"Yes, Aaron, I'm just tired. It will feel good to sleep."

Aaron stood up. He was reluctant to leave the room but he knew that he should return to the kitchen and see his other children. He looked briefly at his new son, knowing that his interest would grow with time. In the kitchen the other children were sitting quietly but eagerly on the long benches on either side of the table, waiting.

"Oh, Lord.....bless this food set here before us.....," Aaron began.

"Amen......," the hearty chorus rang out around the table before he could continue. He looked up, startled, the words on his lips died and the stern look in his eye melted as his glance circled the table. Well—he shrugged his shoulders; he would overlook their lack of piety on this occasion, especially, he thought dryly, since they were already delving hungrily into their supper without looking up.

There they were.....all of them.

Peter, his firstborn. Tall, slender, broad shouldered. His clear blue eyes were often distant with daydreams. He was a bit of a swaggerer, but he would grow out of that. It had been two months since he and Annie had been baptized. In accordance with Holdeman rules, there was a soft fuzz growing on his chin—scarcely noticeable. He was actually self-conscious about it but he knew that it was a sin for a man to shave the hair from his face. Aaron sensed that his son's decision to join the church may not have been an easy one.

Annie, the oldest girl, was quiet, sensitive, forced prematurely into womanhood. Now that she was a member of the church too, she wore the required small black shawl at all times. Aaron had detected no visible signs of soul-searching in her decision.

Then there was Isaac, a stocky, well-built lad. He was more like his father but Aaron was pleased to see that he would be taller. Aaron's own small stature had always been a sore point with him.

And Katie, she was a strong, large boned girl. She had a practical nature, though her stubbornness and sometimes acid tongue could be irritating to those around her.

Next in line was Gertrude. She asked the most questions and seemed more complex than the others. She would need guidance but she was most like her mother which gave her an edge in his secret heart. She was delicately turned out, evoking in him a protective tenderness.

Joseph whose birth came very close after Gertrude's, was a small, tenderhearted little boy. He was content to be Gertrude's shadow at this stage. They were inseparable playmates.

Jennie was the youngest girl in the family. Her large, hazel eyes looked soberly at the world around her. She preferred to play by herself most of the time, with a slightly disturbing tendency to secretiveness.

Abram, until now, the youngest, was pampered by the older children and as such had not yet fully claimed his individuality. Now that would change.

Aaron was truly proud of his offspring. Soon his new son would be taking his place within the group. Then the picture would be complete.

Mary did not rally after the birth of her ninth baby. Child-bed fever took her, pitilessly, in its firm grip. As the days slowly past, her cheeks became more flushed with the rising fever. Her eyes were bright and sunken. The people around her despaired. Dr. Martens was summoned but he gave Aaron little hope and less comfort.

"It's God's will whatever happens," he sighed and shrugged his huge shoulders. "Usually after the third day the fever begins to go down." The third day had come and gone so there was little solace in the doctor's words. Aaron looked at him. His eyes were clouded over with weariness. Then, suddenly, they cleared and narrowed as he looked at the doctor with undisguised hostility and accusation.

"You are the doctor. You should do something..... why don't you do something? Your words are good for nothing," his face contorted with rage as he pounded his fists on the table.

The doctor looked at him in astonishment, then hastily made a clumsy retreat to the door, muttering, "It's God's will......it's God's will." The vibrations of the slammed door merged into the echo of that meaningless phrase—the phrase which was shouted from the pulpit to explain the obscure; the farmer used it when his crop lay in ruins; the bereaved murmured it when they lost a loved one; the doctor uttered it when he could not prolong life.

Aaron began to wonder if he was being punished for the smug contentment he had felt in the evening after the new baby had been born. They were taught that hardship was punishment for misdeeds but surely he did not deserve this cruelty.

With the passing hours, Aaron looked searchingly for signs of a change for the better in Mary's condition. He could only see her hold on life weakening.

Aaron did not leave Mary's side through the long, lonely night. In the morning, half asleep, he heard the quiet, distant hum of life in another part of the house as though it were another world. Then he heard a small voice calling him and he struggled to remove the great pressure from his chest and force his eyes open. With a jolt, he straightened in his chair. Mary's eyes were bright and piercing.

"Mary......did you call me? "

"Aaron," she said again as though he had not spoken. "Aaron, I want to see my children."

"Yes, yes, of course, Mary. As soon as you are a little stronger." He reached for the cloth in the pan of water beside the bed. He squeezed out the cool water and gently wiped her brow. With lightning speed she caught his hand and held it in a vicelike grip.

"No, it can't wait. I must see them now, Aaron. I must see them.....just once more." He had to bend closer to catch her words.

"Oh, no, Mary, please don't talk like that......there'll be many times."

"No, Aaron, there is very little time.....so little time." Her voice was barely audible but she would not let go of his hand and her eyes were pleading.

"Alright....." The lump in his throat stopped him from saying more. He loosened her fingers gently one by one and kissed them tenderly—if only he could give her strength. He placed her hand under the covers and knew that he must let her go—he had no right to make it more difficult for her. Her eyes thanked him for freeing her. Slowly he left the room. His feet moved him through the empty, abandoned kitchen. He saw his children in the yard. They stood about, listless, forlorn. Abram's attempts at getting attention were being ignored but they all looked up when they heard the door close behind their father.

"How is Mama?" Annie was the first to speak.

"She has asked to see all of you."

Annie's face brightened. Mama must be feeling better if she wants to see us but when she looked closer into her father's face, she knew it wasn't so.

Silently, they followed their father. They filed into the darkened bedroom. Mary's eyes opened and a faint smile crossed her pale lips as she saw her children. Each, in turn, knelt beside her and received a kiss, a whispered word, a fleeting caress. Mary bade farewell to the children she had brought into the world and sent them from the room back into the cold sunshine.

As evening's twilight fell, Mary closed her eyes forever.

In his memory of the following days, there was a blurry haze which Aaron could not bring into clear focus. And he was thankful. Only one clear picture stood out. It was when the box which held his Mary was lowered into the ground. At that moment he said his final goodbye to the woman he loved. The children were pressed closely around him. Gertrude pushed her little hand into his and curled her fingers around his. She looked up into his face and saw two big, round tears making their way slowly through the deep crevices of his weatherbeaten cheeks and disappearing into his golden beard.

The summer was difficult. Aaron had let Kathryne take the baby, despite the vehement protests of the other children. But the baby had not long survived the separation from his mother and unable to thrive, followed her to a small unmarked grave beside her.

* * * * *

Aaron's memories faded as he drifted back into a few more minutes of fitful sleep. Then he forced himself awake. He rose with the morning sun. He roused the sleeping household making sure that Gertrude came downstairs to watch Abram and that Annie and Katie were getting the kitchen ready for their breakfast. Then he left the house to go to the barn. As he walked across the yard, he knew he would have to make a decision in the next few weeks. The thought of trying to survive a Manitoba winter without his wife Mary seemed impossible. But maybe he would not be alone after all. He wondered how the children would take to having their mother replaced. The church elders had already approached him. He was startled into remembering that this process was not new to him. His first marriage had been a short, happy, poignant interlude—all but forgotten—lost in the contentment of his life with Mary. Now he must make the decision again. His pace slowed with each step. He had discarded the idea of bringing in the widow with children of her own—but Elizabeth Froeze—she was strong and healthy—not too old to bear him more children. The anticipation stirred a feeling of excitement but it was quickly squelched by remorse which rushed upon him. He placated himself. Mary would understand—but—would she? Would the children? It annoyed him that his thoughts again turned to the children. When he had broached the subject with them the other morning at breakfast, he had sensed their hostility. His steps again quickened. Angrily he kicked at a stone in his path spraying mud and water in all directions. Recalling last night's storm momentarily increased his anxiety. In an attempt to explain his mood to himself, he decided to blame the storm, however, he knew he could not manage the burden of being alone much longer.

He opened the barn door for the cows who were waiting outside. As they passed him on the way to their stalls, he gave them each a friendly slap and called them by name. He fed them and returned to the house, his boots gathering the heavy mud. He glanced up as a cloud passed over the sun. The storm was not over, he thought. He scraped some of the mud off his boots and picked up the milk pails which Annie had set just inside the door. The cloud had become dark and threatening. Aaron turned his head and hesitated as though someone had called him. In that brief moment, a vicious flash of lightning made its way from the top of the chimney, through the house, and out the open door where he stood. Aaron stiffened—a look of surprise and disbelief covered his face. Then he fell heavily. The sound of his fall was lost amidst the deafening crash of thunder.

For a few seconds stunned silence filled the house. Gertrude's hand froze on the cradle. Her breath stopped. Then with a scream, she jumped up and ran wildly out of the bedroom. She saw her father lying in the open doorway. His face was ashen—a thin stream of blood was trickling from his ear and down the side of his cheek. The milk pails were still rocking in the far corners of the kitchen where they had been hurled. Peter and Annie were already kneeling beside Papa, crying his name and begging him to answer. Gertrude flung herself across his chest. Their pleas were in vain. The uncaring drops of rain fell and mingled with their tears.

Chapter Two

Gertrude was a light sleeper at the best of times, but because of her underlying excitement, she woke even earlier than usual, before there was any stirring elsewhere in the house. It was Sunday! She lay very still, jealously guarding the spot under the heavy wool quilt which her body warmth made bearable in the icy room. Her sister Jennie lay very close to her, still sleeping.

It was mid winter—only about half a year since Papa died. During the short time since her father's sudden death she had succeeded in putting to rest the doubts she had had about him. Now, she was convinced that he would never have married Elizabeth Froese. He would not have betrayed them and Mama in that way. Gertrude remembered seeing Elizabeth crying unabashedly and noisily at the funeral and thinking that she had no right to carry on so. Later she felt guilty realizing that all of the women had been crying. Papa had returned to his revered spot in her memory—after all, when people died, they were beyond criticism, weren't they? The thought comforted her.

Though Mama had died only three months before Papa, it seemed much longer than that. It was Mama that she missed most. She did not mean to be disloyal but Mama had always been there. She missed the stories that Mama had loved to tell them about their people. Gertrude had never tired of listening and asking questions.

* * * * *

Sitting at her mother's knee, Gertrude learned that her parents, Aaron and Mary Penner, had come to Canada in about 1875. They came from Russia. "But Mama, does that mean that we are Russians?" Gertrude wanted to know, a dubious frown crossing her face.

"No, no, child, " Mary assured her. "Our people have lived in many countries. First of all, many years ago, they lived in Holland. They have also lived in Germany. I guess that's why we read the German Bible. But your father and I came from Russia—in fact, we were born there. But we are not Russians."

Gertrude was relieved, for the very word Russian conjured demon-like creatures in her fertile, young imagination. "But what are we called then?"

"Wherever we go, we are called Mennonites."

"But what does that mean? "Gertrude persisted.

"It's our religion, that is all. You do ask a lot of questions but I guess you have a right to know," Mary sighed. She was well aware that it was Gertrude, of all her children, who had the most inquiring mind. Sometimes Mary felt a vague uneasiness in the face of Gertrude's many questions. Asking about Mennonite history was one thing but when she wanted to know more about what was going on outside of of their own cloistered world—well, that was something else.

Mary often thought sadly about her younger brother Johann. He had been her favourite brother. He too had stood out from his peers because of his far ranging curiosity about the world around him. He had reluctantly joined the Holdemans at the same time as Mary and Aaron. But shortly thereafter, he started spending more and more time in Winnipeg and even got a job there but Mary wasn't sure what exactly he did.

Necessity dictated that the church elders traveled to Winnipeg on behalf of the rest of the community a couple of times a year to do the business aspects of farming that could not be handled locally. On one of these visits they ran into Johann on the street. He had long sideburns and a carefully manicured moustache that curved upward ever so slightly at the ends and it was obvious that he had shaved off the rest of his facial hair. He was wearing a necktie. He had a flashy ring glinting on one of his fingers. From the look of him there was no telling what else he was up to. They immediately insisted that he return to Blumenort and repent his sins in front of the congregation. He refused which resulted quickly in his excommunication. Excommunication was a powerful tool used to bring errant members back into line and it usually worked.

Johann didn't respond in the expected way. Instead of coming home, confessing his sins, asking for forgiveness and pleading to be reinstated as a church member, he stayed away from Blumenort. Then, a year or so after the excommunication he decided to make a visit home with Penelope his new bride. She was a young woman of English extraction. His plan was to stay three days and see if he could repair some of the bad feelings that existed between him and his family. He wasn't too optimistic about his brother Klaas or his sister Kathryne but he had high hopes that Mary would be pleased to see him and eager to become friends again. He was right about Klaas and Kathryne, wrong about Mary.

The visit proved to be unbearably awkward for everyone. At the sight of him, Mary's first impulse was to rush to him and take him in her arms. Aaron, sensing that this was what Mary might do, resolutely placed his left hand on her shoulder to warn her to stay put. Mary's arms hung limply at her sides and Aaron carefully positioned his right hand behind his back. Johann hesitated and then falteringly introduced Penelope at which time Aaron made a big show of shaking Penelope's hand and Mary followed suit. The children stood around with wide eyes saying nothing. They had never seen people who looked like Johann and Penelope. Penelope's clothes alone were enough to render them speechless.

Penelope joined them at the table for meals but Johann sat alone by the kitchen stove balancing his plate on his lap.

Mary cried a lot. Penelope was confused and embarrassed and Johann became increasingly angry. Johann's hope for at least a partial reconciliation was shattered. After one day, Johann and Penelope returned to Winnipeg. Several months later, he sent word that he and Penelope had moved to Toronto. Johann was the first in their family to cast aside the Holdeman belief system but he would not be the last.

"I wonder why we have moved so much?" Gertrude persisted, bringing Mary back to the present.

"It has been mostly because of our religion. You see.... you see....we don't believe it is right to have wars—our men do not want to go and fight. They won't kill, so before they can be forced into service we flee to another place. So it was that we finally came to Canada, to Manitoba."

Mary often told stories of the long trip which brought them, at last, to where they were now living. Here they had established the village which they named Blumenort. They experienced many hardships on the long sea voyage and when they reached Canada, they still had a long way to go from Nova Scotia to Manitoba. They traveled by wagon and on foot and crossed the Great Lakes on flatboat.

"Now, I think we will stay here," Mary said, as much to herself as to the children, expressing the hope that lay deep within her that now, at last, they had found a place where they could stay and not be uprooted again.

"But won't there be wars here too, Mama? "

"Oh, my child, God forbid! But even if there are, our men will not have to go into the army." Mary did not understand it too well but she explained as best she could that the Canadian government had promised them that they would not be conscripted into Canada's fighting forces and they would not need to take part in political affairs.

They had taken up homesteads and built the churches which were the nuclei of their lives. They did not mix with people outside their communities and held tenaciously to their traditional religious beliefs, their unique dress and their dialect which was a mixture of Dutch and Low German. It was not a written language so it had many idioms suited to the daily vicissitudes of their lives. For the written word in their church services and in their first schools, they relied on

High German. Over the centuries there were many branches formed out of the original teachings of Menno Simons. These sects differed in many respects but basically they all stuck to the core tenets of Simons's original Protestant ideas. Inevitably some of the sects became more worldly while others sank deeper into themselves, thickening their protective shell.

In the years to come, as Gertrude became more acquainted with the non Holdeman world, she felt a growing sense of shame in knowing that her people played no part in creating great paintings, great musical works, magnificent architectural structures—nothing. She was forced to acknowledge that they had made no contribution to the cultural enrichment of the world around her. Sadly, she could only stand by and watch as the talents of her people were being left to wither like unfertilized seeds, lying dormant in the rich earth around them.

* * * * *

"Children!" The quiet dawn was shattered by Gertrude's Uncle Klaas. The door at the bottom of the staircase shut quickly punctuating the brittle command, sending it soaring upstairs. It hung on the heavy, cold air above the heads of the sleeping children. There was no means of escape.

"Jennie," Gertrude whispered urgently, shaking her sister. "Wake up. You know Uncle Klaas will be calling again in a minute. If we hurry, we can go down before the others. Then we can get behind the stove, where it is warmest." She reached for their dresses and drew them under the covers. In the winter, they kept their underskirts and under-drawers on for the night—sometimes even their woollen stockings. Gertrude avoided that if possible. She disliked the way they got twisted and turned. Sometimes they came off completely and got lost in the bedding.

"Come on, Jennie." Jennie groaned and burrowed deeper in the bed. "I'll help you with your dress, then we'll take our shoes down to put on. Uncle Klaas will call.....," she repeated just as she heard the door opening again.

"Oh Gertrude, you're letting in all the cold," Jennie complained.

"Do you know what day this is?" Gertrude kept on.

"No." Jennie's utter disinterest was maddening.

"Well," Gertrude paused significantly. "It's Sunday!"

That, of course, brought about Jennie's complete cooperation. There was always a great hustle and bustle before they were ready to go to church and with Aunt Liza's lack of system, the confusion was at times unnerving. Gertrude was expected to do more than her share in the preparations but she did it willingly because this was the only day in the week when she would see her brothers and sisters.

* * * * *

After their father's funeral, the Penner children had gone back to their lonely house in the vain hope that they could manage on their own. They did their chores in the barn and prepared some food which none of them ate. Annie did her best to supervise bed time, making sure that Abram was kept warm, snuggled between her and Jenny. By morning, following a sleepless night, she realized that staying together on their parents' farm was not going to work. She and Peter talked briefly. They didn't know what was going to become of them but haltingly tried to prepare the younger children for an unknown future.

They didn't have long to wait. Their aunts and uncles arrived. The children, their eyes wide with a mixture of hope and fear drew slowly together, their movements stiff and jerky like puppets ready to receive the final blow to their shattered lives. And like puppets, they were divided and parcelled out as their kin saw fit.

It was a good thing the children were ignorant of what had taken place the night before. First of all, the burden of more mouths to feed and bodies to clothe had been paramount in the discussion. Then they were concerned with how much help each child would be to them and the discussion grew heated. Pandemonium reigned until one perceptive gentleman remarked that it might best be left to the church council to decide. That cooled the temper of the meeting enough that they made their decisions quickly.

So it was that Annie and Abram had gone to live with Mary's sister Katheryne and her husband John Loewen. Gertrude and Jennie moved in with Mary's brother Klass Toews and his wife Liza and Katie and Joseph went with Aaron's sister Anna and her husband Henry Friesen. The two older boys, they decided, could work out, as they put it, wherever they were needed.

* * * * *

"Gertrude, will we see Annie?" asked Jennie.

"Yes."

"Will we see Peter and Isaac too?" Jennie persisted.

"Yes, yes, and Katie and Abram and Joseph," Gertrude finished the list. They went through the same procedure every Sunday but Gertrude didn't mind. She left Joseph's name to the last because next to Annie, she missed Joseph the most. "I hope Aunt Kathryne will ask us for dinner," she said. Invitations were always left until after church.

After breakfast and morning chores were done, the girls dressed hurriedly in their Sunday best dresses. They were made of a soft, grey flannel. Gertrude loved to caress the thick fluffiness of them. Next winter they would wear them for every day. By then they would be hard from many rough washings, and Aunt Liza would be complaining about having to let down the hems because the tops of their shoes would be showing again. Today's dress was Gertrude's first to button down the front. It made her feel very grown up. She longed for the summer when they could wear their percales in a dark blue print. They were long and plain too but Gertrude felt prettier when she was wearing her best summer dress. She had to button Jennie's down the back. She would have to do that for a few years yet, she reminded herself.

After the last button was fastened and they were wrapped in their large, warm winter shawls, they returned downstairs and stood patiently at the door until they heard Klaas drive to the house with the horses and sleigh. That was the children's signal to file out into the sharp, cold air. The horses were stamping the snow under their big feet—straining at their bits, eager to go after their long night of confinement. The air around them was thick with white steam rising from their warm bodies and curling out of their flaring nostrils. Klaas gave a boost to each child and they tumbled over the side of the sleigh, scrambling for their places in the depth of the big wooden box. There were five of them, Gertrude was thinking, not counting the baby—she and Jennie made seven. Gertrude hung back to be the last, so she could be the first one out.

"You can put your head in my lap, if you want to, Jennie," Gertrude offered as Klaas brought out the large stone that had been warming in the oven, placed it in the bottom of the sleigh among the children's feet and threw the big fur robe made of horsehide over them. They could hear Liza coming out of the house, her heavy tread crunching the crisp snow. Klaas helped her onto the low seat in the front of the sleigh while the baby whimpered from the confines of his heavy wrappings. Then with a slap of the reins and a loud 'giddap', they were off. The jerk of the sleigh and whine of the runners on the hard snow as the horses fell into their pace, put a sudden end to the children's noisy chatter. The wriggling mound of humanity sank into a solid mass of breathing contentment.

Liza Toews settled herself as comfortably as she could, jiggling the baby to quiet him. She placed her feet gratefully on the bundle of warmed sad irons Klaas had hastily grabbed from the back of the stove and wrapped in rags before Liza came out. Now Klaas, towering above her, became very preoccupied with managing the horses, hoping to escape the reach of Liza's all too often acid tongue.

Liza had found it difficult to reconcile herself to having Mary's two children in her home. Even now, she felt her resentment rising as she recalled how Kathryne laid claim to Annie who would, of course, be the most help. In a high-handed manner, she first offered to take Abram, who obviously needed the most attention knowing then that the others could scarcely object to her taking Annie. She reminded Klaas frequently that he, at least, could have stood up to them—they were, after all, his side of the family.

"You'll have to admit, Liza, that Gertrude isn't so bad," Klaas would often remind her.

"Well, for all her puny appearance, she is quite a help to me," Liza would grudgingly concede, "more so than our Mary. And Mary is a few months older. Oh well, it still isn't fair."

Liza had had her own children in quick secession. The birth of each child took its share of her once comely, voluptuous figure. With the years, her body grew shapeless and heavy. She still, however, felt a thrill of pleasure when she remembered how Klaas had succumbed to her subtle flirtation. Her eye had been on him long before he was even aware of her. Her physical attractions brought her other offers of marriage but she was determined to wait for Klaas. The day came when she was sure she was winning but then Liza's father discovered them on the sunny side of the haystack, clasped in each other's arms. Klaas was avidly exploring Liza's soft curves while Liza was pretending to protest. Klaas was forced to confess his indiscretion to the minister and both were called before the Brotherhood Council (all who had joined the church were on the council) and were severely chastised. Liza was stripped of her dignity and Klaas, seeing her discomfiture, was flooded with guilt. The sharp taste of the pleasure he had experienced, coupled with his remorse, led him to ask for her hand in marriage. It was agreed by all that it was the only solution in the wake of such unheard of conduct. The wagging tongues were stilled.

Liza's spirit had been revived but she found that the pleasures of marriage were fleeting and enjoyed mostly by her husband. When she looked at his still lithe, slim handsomeness, she felt it was she who had made all the sacrifices. In retaliation, she had become querulous and unhappy. She made little attempt to hide her discontent.

Gertrude heard Klaas reining in the horses and she caught the faint strains of singing coming from inside the church. Would these people never get to church in time for the first hymn? Every Sunday, she had to deal with her exasperation and endure her embarrassment at being late. When the horses came to a stop, Gertrude lost no time in jumping out of the sleigh and with Jennie in tow, she scurried across the snow. Inside, she noted that they were just beginning the third verse—she knew all the songs by heart. It would give them time to find their seats. Gertrude scanned the sea of black shawls on the women's side of the church until she spied her sisters. She pulled Jennie unceremoniously down the centre aisle and then past several pairs of unyielding knees. The older girls knew that Gertrude and Jennie would be late, so with the silent collusion of the women around them, they sat well apart with wide-spread skirts so the smaller girls could squeeze in quite comfortably between them.

The singing stopped as abruptly as it had begun and it was time for the first long prayer.

'Let us pray' was the preamble to much commotion and rustling. The women turned to kneel with their elbows on the seat. The younger ones slid easily into place while the older ones, with their rheumatic joints, had to search for the most comfortable position. Across the aisle the men fell forward to their knees. It was in this interval that many a furtive glance was exchanged. Many hopes were born and many were shattered across those wooden benches. A scattering of discreet but pointed coughs quieted the congregation at last.

While the prayer droned on, Gertrude peeked up from between her fingers and across the many bowed heads, searching for Joseph. He looked up just as she spied him. Their eyes met in a moment of pleasure.

Gertrude did not like the sermons. She wished she could just shut her ears and not hear. They filled her with fear and awe. The damnation and hell-fire which flowed so easily from the pulpit pounded in Gertrude's eardrums with an almost physical pain. It was beyond her comprehension but her vivid imagination built it into a formidable picture. She could dismiss it all in the daytime but very often at bedtime, she would cringe under the covers she pulled over her head, fearful of what dire fate lay in wait for her. She felt the beads of sweat all over her body until sheer exhaustion sent her to sleep. Sometimes, Liza would find her so and was unwittingly filled with compassion for the little motherless girl as she gently uncovered Gertrude's head. Somewhere in her subconscious, Gertrude caught a fleeting glimpse of the love thus offered her and her face lost some of its anguish as Liza tucked the covers under her chin.

At long last, the service was over. Gertrude was only too relieved to get onto her all but forgotten feet. Her back ached from sitting so long on the hard, backless bench.

As they moved slowly along with the others to the back of the church, Annie smiled fondly at her sisters. She scrutinized them carefully with a maternal eye. She could not have borne it if they had been neglected. On the surface, at least, they passed her assessment. She looked to the other side of the church and saw Peter and Isaac. They threw friendly glances her way but were quickly otherwise occupied. She was saddened to think that the older boys were already drifting away from the rest of them. Then, seeing Joseph, looking so forlorn, Annie's maternal instincts again rose to the surface.

"Do you think we might come to your place?" Gertrude asked Annie.

"Well, I wouldn't wonder—Aunt Kathryne mentioned that she would ask Aunt Liza and Aunt Anna too."

Gertrude, with Jennie, sidled up to Liza and stood quietly watching for an indication of her plans. "Ah, there you are, Gertrude," Liza looked up from wrapping the baby. "Take these baby things and you girls get out to the sleigh. Tell Uncle Klaas I'll be right out." Seeing Gertrude's hesitation and her questioning face, she added impatiently, "Yes, yes, we're going to the Loewens' for dinner. Aunt Kathryne asked us. Now hurry on." Liza was not one to refuse a dinner invitation.

Gertrude swept the baby things into her arms and ran happily to the sleigh. Soon they would have some time together. Shortly, they were on their way.

Gertrude liked to dwell on what they might have for dinner—maybe ham—well, more likely smoked sausage at this time of the year. The ham was apt to be saved for the spring. It would keep into the summer. In all the years to come, the nostalgic memories of springs past were laced with the delicious aroma of frying ham. The week's baking, buns and bread, was done on Saturdays, so while the stove was heated for the baking, they would boil a pot of potatoes to set aside for frying later. They might also cook dried plums and raisins in milk thickened with flour and seasoned with cinnamon and nutmeg. Ah, yes, it was all an integral part of Sundays.

Gertrude was not alone in preferring to go to the Loewens', though her motives were guileless. The day to day life in the community was notably unpretentious but they did have their social ladder and all the rungs were occupied, the Loewens being well at the top. Whoever had the most company, from near or far, was carefully observed and marked with envy or triumph, depending on which rung you yourself happened to occupy.

It was regrettable that after so much loving care in the preparation, the meal was so hurriedly consumed, for talk was at a minimum at the table. It was only after, when the men went into the 'big room' which was their way of referring to the parlour, that the women gathered together in the kitchen and the young folks went upstairs. Even among the young folk the boys went to one room and the girls into another. It was only after this ritual of segregation was completed that the conversations began to flow. Despite the closeness of the family and church groups, the gaps between the sexes and the generations were wide. Their customs, heavily flavoured with religious taboos, were such that the girls and boys had little opportunity to interact socially so they grew up in painful ignorance of what they would encounter in the adult world as women and men. Sex was never discussed but dismissed as an animal instinct. That would take care of itself in the marriage bed. The inevitable secret explorations and experiments driven by biology and curiosity in the dark conners of their youth, only led to a heavy burden of self-incrimination.

Gertrude stood by waiting for the older girls to finish the dishes—her offer of help had been brushed aside. She saw the men coming in from the barn, where for some reason they always went after eating. She watched the great clouds of cold, white air roll in from the opened door and it sent shivers up her spine. On their way into the big room the men wore expressions of the contented male whose physical wants had been satisfied.

"Come." Gertrude was startled at Annie's touch on her shoulder. She followed Annie up the stairs.

They all sat on the edges of the beds, close together—there were no chairs in the room. The only source of heat was the stove pipe which came up through the floor and passed through the wall.

Gertrude trembled. Annie pulled her closer to her saying, "It will soon be a little warmer in here," but she knew it was more than the cold which made her shiver.

As usual, the constraint with which these gatherings began, started to ease and the chattering gained momentum. The Penner sisters too, felt more at ease with each other and started to visit quietly among themselves. "I had so many things to tell," Gertrude began, "but now..." She brushed her sleeve across her face and caught the tear which had not quite fallen.

"I know...I know...," Annie said as she looked searchingly at her sisters. "What have you been doing? Do you help your aunts and mind them like you should?"

"Yes...well, I do, anyway," Katie answered without hesitation. Her terse manner of speech was apt to give the impression of belligerence. "I even help with the milking!"

"Milking?" Gertrude could scarcely contain her envy.

"Uncle Klaas says I can milk soon too." Annie frowned. Even if she couldn't detect outward signs of neglect, she had begun to sense that her sisters were being taken advantage of—especially Gertrude who was so small, somewhat frail and under the thumb of Aunt Liza.

"Hah! That I'd like to see. You don't even know how to do it," Katie grinned. So, once again Katie succeeded in ruffling Gertrude's calm.

"Aunt Kathryne said I could come to Aunt Liza's this spring and help with the sewing," Annie told them. "I can sew your dresses—and, no doubt, do some of Aunt Liza's too. Katie will have to come too so she can fit hers—she can help, I dare say. Anyway, it will give us a good excuse to be together."

"Oh, goody, goody," Gertrude bounced up and down on the bed. It would certainly give her something to look forward to. She looked around to see what Jennie had to say, but to her amazement, she saw that she had fallen asleep with little Abram curled close beside her.

"Did you ever go to school, Annie?"

"No, there was none to go to. Why do you ask, Gertrude?"

"Well, Uncle Klaas promised me I could go next winter. I wanted to go this winter. Cousins Pete and Jake went, but he said not till next year for me. It's not right that we all can't go to school. Even Papa could read and write some German."

" Ha, ha, he's just putting you off." Katie just couldn't resist her little jibe.

"He is not!" Gertrude was becoming quite provoked. "You went to German school last year, didn't you?"

"Well, yes, but I'm not going anymore. Besides, Uncle Henry says it's not necessary for girls to go to school," Katie added smugly.

"I don't care! I want to go, and I am going to go! I'll learn English too someday."

"English?" Katie was overcome with laughter.

"Now, now, girls," Annie gently cautioned them.

Gertrude went on, "Our Peter went to English school and he can read English books. He can even write." She threw back her shoulders with pride for her older brother. "And that's what I'm going to do."

"That's good, Gertrude. Uncle John has been teaching me some German. He says that, at least, a girl should be able to read the Bible," Annie said. That met entirely with Gertrude's approval.

"Well, as far as I'm concerned, it's a lot of foolishness." Katie put in her last word and for all she cared, that was the end of that. Gertrude could not dismiss the matter so lightly but feeling the warning pressure of Annie's hand on her arm, she said no more.

The sisters turned their attention to the other girls in the room. Soon Gertrude's heart grew heavy as she saw that the light at the window was greying. She hadn't even had a chance to talk with Joseph. Maybe they could steal a few moments together just before fastbah—that was what they called their late lunch on Sunday afternoons. The sounds from below reminded them that it was time to go down. Fastbah consisted of buns and coffee—maybe some jam or syrup—then it would be time to leave again. Always they must separate. They could do nothing about it. Gertrude felt helpless. It was all so hopeless.

Sunday was over.

Chapter Three

Gertrude idly swished the dishcloth over the pots and pans. The dishwater was heavy with grease—the water in the pan for rinsing was cold and totally useless. Even though she was anxious to get into the fresh air, her hands seemed detached and incapable of moving faster. The fire had died out in the cook stove but the oppressive heat hung thickly in the room, filling it from corner to corner. Gertrude felt a drop of sweat making its way down from her forehead to the tip of her nose. She swiped at it angrily with the back of her hand, sending drops of water flying through the air. Her fair hair, pulled tightly back from her face, was damp; a few wisps which had escaped, clung limply to her cheeks. The braid, hanging down her back burned through her clothing. To add to the discomfort, the buzzing of the flies grew louder and more insistent. Every summer, they invaded the house. The sticky flypaper hanging from the ceiling was covered with helpless victims but it made little difference.

Gertrude could not keep her eyes from the small kitchen window. She watched, enviously, the younger children playing in the yard. Today they would be allowed to stay up later because the low-ceilinged bedrooms would be steaming with heat. How she longed to be running too, throwing off her shoes and stockings with complete abandon, her hair loose, flying in the breeze, her skirts billowing as she ran to just nowhere. She grieved for the childhood that had stopped so suddenly when Mama and Papa had died. She scarcely remembered it.

It was five years since she had come to the Toewses'. Her body was still immature but she felt old beyond her years. Uncle Klass had been true to his word and allowed Gertrude to attend German school during her second winter with the Toewses. She managed to squeeze out four winters of education. But this last spring, Uncle Klass had said that was enough. She had been told she was now needed at home full time to help her aunt. Her schooling had been cut short. Her life was filled with hard work—no chance of English school now. The occasional displays of affection that were offered felt to her, more often than not, like token gestures. The day to day drudgery of constant physical labour in the house, the barn and the fields was beginning to have a numbing effect on her spirit. She remembered with self pity the times she had fallen asleep milking, her head resting in the soft hollow beside the cow's bulging belly until the restless movements of the cow reawakened her with a start.

Shortly after her uncle's announcement she resolved to leave, go out on her own—to hire out. She had confided this to no one. She hoped such a move would help her to gain some sense of independence and control over her own life—something which she felt she desperately needed if she were to survive. I can't imagine doing this much longer, she thought. Annie has already hired out. They will say I'm too young but I don't care. I want to have money of my own. I won't get much pay but it will be better than nothing.

Summertime was the best because the girls were pressed into service in the fields along with the boys. They helped with the haying in the early summer. Gertrude learned to set a haystack with the best of them, then in the harvest season they stooked and stacked. Oh, the freedom of being out in the open air! Then at threshing time, they were back in the kitchen full time cooking to feed the hungry men.

Since Gertrude had joined their household, Liza had borne two more babies, with another one on the way. She left more and more of her responsibilities to the others as her preoccupation with the wretched state of her health had grown and her nagging and complaining increased. Gertrude and Mary were fond of each other in an on again-off again sort of way. At times they enjoyed an intimate companionship but more often they regarded each other with only a semblance of tolerance. When it suited Mary, she was not beyond letting Gertrude know in a most subtle way, that Gertrude, after all, was not really one of the family. Following her mother's example, she could easily plead a headache or some other inconvenience, leaving Gertrude to cope alone.

So what was there to keep Gertrude from leaving? Jennie had been taken to the Friesen's several years ago. Liza and Klaas were glad to be relieved of the extra burden that Jennie posed to their parental responsibilities and Anna Friesen, who had remained childless was only too happy to add Jennie to her made-to-order family. Then, when the John Loewens had moved to another village, they left Abram with them. Katie, Joseph, Jennie and Abram—the Friesen family was complete.

Even Sundays were not what they used to be. She still looked forward to them but more because they were a break in the long endless weeks. She was always glad to see any of her brothers and sisters but over time, the anticipation had lost its sheen.

It was just last Sunday that Gertrude had sat in church and heard the announcement of her sister Annie's forthcoming marriage to Jacob Unger. She had been warned of the impending announcement but it had, nevertheless, been a distinct shock to actually hear out loud the final confirmation of it before all the church people. She still wasn't used to the idea. It had been her foolish hope that somehow it might just not be true. Two weeks earlier it had been decided upon in the brotherhood council—that was the way of the sect. As with all such announcements, it was to be a closely guarded secret until officially proclaimed in church. However, in reality, pending wedding plans usually became the subject of conjecture and gossip long before a public announcement was made. The marriage negotiations were generally overseen by the preachers and some of the unions thus planned held so little of romance, that they defied anything but complete incredulity upon their disclosure.

* * * * *

The day of the brotherhood council meeting, Gertrude had returned home after the morning's service with the rest of the family. The Loewens came for dinner but returned, along with the Toewses to the church immediately after. This meeting was for church members only so it included the older children who had been baptized into the church. After dishes had been done, Gertrude slipped away from the others to walk by herself among the trees. Shortly, she heard the chinking of the harness rings and the sounds of the horses hooves heralding the return of the travellers. She surmised that they must have had little to discuss at the meeting. She watched disinterestedly as they alighted from their buggies and saw the other girls emerging from the house to greet them. All were immediately engaged in animated conversation. She saw one of the girls nodding and motioning in her direction as Kathryne detached herself from the group and started walking uncertainly towards her.

"Gertrude," she called. Then she caught sight of her. "Oh, there you are."

"Yes, I'm here," she answered as her aunt came with a more resolute step in her direction.

"Why are you here all by yourself? You should be with the other girls—enjoying yourself. It's such a nice day, too." Gertrude said nothing but reached into her pocket for a handkerchief and wiped her aunt's brow whose breathing was laboured from exertion and the heat.

"My it's hot today. But then I don't suppose you mind it so much—you're so thin. I envy you. It was a good thing they didn't draw out the council meeting today. Sometimes they know no bounds. Isn't there some place to sit down?"

"Oh, I'm sorry. Here." Gertrude pointed out a board laid across two tree stumps. "It's not much but ….."

"As long as it will hold me." With a grin, Kathryne

sank gratefully onto the proffered seat. The board bent precariously under the weight of her body which had grown heavy with the years. She fluttered her hand in a futile effort to stir up a little breeze to cool herself.

"Come," she patted the place beside her, "I think it will hold you too."

Gertrude looked dubious but sat down gingerly over the other stump at the far end of the board.

"You look peaked," Kathryne remarked. "Do you feel well?"

"I'm fine." She often felt she was singled out to be asked about her health as though people couldn't think of anything else to say to her. It irritated her. She knew, however, that Kathryne's solicitude was genuine so she didn't mind.

"My but you have grown! When I look at you now…and think of when you were first here, I find it hard to believe that the time has gone so fast but then it's been ….," she looked searchingly at her niece, "how long has it been?"

"It will be five years in another six weeks."

"My, my, to think that it's really been that long." For a moment she was lost in her own thoughts. "And now Annie's ready to get married."

"Married?" Gertrude's head jerked back in surprise. Then she understood. Her aunt was merely making conversation. "Oh, yes, I guess she's almost old enough to get married. There for a minute, I thought ….."

"But Gertrude," Kathryne interrupted. "Haven't you wondered why the meeting was called today?"

Slowly it began to penetrate Gertrude's mind that this was no idle chatter. "I hadn't thought much about it ….," she replied with mounting apprehension.

"My goodness. You would have thought Annie...after all she is your sister. Hmm.....well.....I'm so glad we are having this discussion because otherwise you might not have known about it before you heard it in church or some busybody took it upon themselves to tell you. The announcement will be in two weeks and then in another two weeks she'll have the wedding."

The mere thought of Annie's marriage filled Gertrude with mixed emotions. Marriage was such a vague, future sort of thing. Of course, every girl dreams of babies in her life and she knew that that required a man but—oh gracious! She couldn't even picture it, reminding herself that Annie was still only 18. She leapt from her seat, first looking away and then back at her aunt. "Who ...who...?" was all she could manage to say.

Kathryne reached out her hand to Gertrude, "Here, here, come sit down. I had no idea the whole thing would be such a complete surprise to you. Didn't you have even a small hint of what was going on?"

"I.....I've seen so little of Annie this summer," Gertrude said lamely. She herself had made no more effort than Annie.

She asked again, "Who ...?"

"Oh, I keep forgetting that you don't know. Well the man's name is Jacob Unger."

"Jacob Unger?" At this incredulous disclosure, Gertrude did sit down not even noticing how the improvised bench swayed precariously. "Why...he's...he's so....so old!"

"Oh come now, he's not that old," Kathryne clucked her tongue. "There may be a few years...."

"At least ten!" Gertrude interrupted.

"It won't be so bad," Kathryne offerd her solace. "He will be better able to take care of her. Since he is a little older, he is more settled than some. No..... no," she repeated. "I don't think it will be so bad for Annie." She wondered what more she could say, then with feigned gusto, she declared, "My goodness, you know, it won't be long before you'll be joining the church and then before you know it, you'll be the one that's getting married!" She prattled on trying to quiet Gertrude's agitation.

Gertrude had always considered Jacob to be part of the older generation, so she had not deemed it necessary to decide whether she liked him or not. Now it struck her. "Why, I don't even like him," she blurted out before she thought.

"Oh dear me Gertrude, you shouldn't say such things. Anyway, when you know him better, you'll feel different."

"He isn't even nice looking." She thought of him as tall, skinny, stooped shouldered and besides his scraggly beard hung down too long. Again, before thinking, "I shall never marry a man with a beard!"

"Oh, Gertrude, Gertrude," and Kathryne broke into a hearty laugh. "What else can you do? Where will you ever find a man without a beard?" The two of them locked eyes, a smile creeping on to Gertrude's face. Then she too began to laugh. Their laughter increased while they vainly tried to regain their composure. They made the mistake of looking at each other again which brought on even more gales of helpless laughter.

Finally, they were spent. Kathryne suggested they be getting back to the house. "Lunch will be ready soon and we must start for home. It will be a long hot ride. I sometimes wish we still lived here in the old village but....." She shrugged her shoulders and rose from her seat with a deep sigh. About three years ago they had moved to the next village of Steinbach. John, who deplored farming, the traditional occupation of his people, had started a small German newspaper there.

"We are going to pick up Annie," Kathryne was saying. "She will be staying with us until the wedding." Annie was working out and had not been with the Loewens for some time now. "I want you to come and spend some time with us too while she is there. And please, don't worry. I assure you everything will work out for the best. Annie is more mature than many girls her age." It was the irrefutable price of being orphaned Gertrude thought as she nodded. "An older boy is probably much more suited to her needs. I'm sure she will be happy," her aunt added. Gertrude smiled uncertainly to which Kathryne immediately responded as they walked arm in arm to the house.

The Sunday of the announcement two weeks later, turned out to be one of those most perfect summer days of which Manitoba is capable. The sun shone, the breeze was soft and the temperature just right. After the service, Gertrude had spoken to all her brothers and sisters except Annie. The others had expressed varying degrees of excitement over the marriage. Gertrude had not spoken to Annie because she was surrounded by a group of chattering women. Gertrude held back, feeling somehow that by joining the group she would be intruding. So now she walked slowly across the church yard to their buggy, deep in thought. She did not hear the quick footsteps behind her.

"Gertrude...wait, Gertrude....wait," she heard. She turned to see Annie hurrying after her. Annie was wearing the blue dress—the dress which had caused such a flurry of admiration among the girls and considerable clucking among the women. Gertrude had thought it beautiful beyond words. The skirt hung in gores from the fitted waist, to a flaring fullness which swirled around her feet when she walked. Annie had dashingly added a wide strip of black velvet around the hem of the skirt and narrower ones to trim the wrists. The blue deepened the colour of her eyes and gave them an added lustre. But now, Gertrude noted with consternation, the velvet strip had been carefully removed and any vestige of its ever having been there had been skilfully ironed out. Gertrude had a feeling that something else had also disappeared along with the velvet but she couldn't put words to it. She told herself that she would think about that later. As they stood there, all she knew was the church had ordered the velvet removed.

"Yes, Annie, what is it?"

"Do you have to hurry so? I thought you might be coming along with me to the Loewens' today."

"Not today," Gertrude answered without elaboration.

"But why not today?" Annie insisted. "Katie is…and next week Jennie will come too."

"Well…," Gertrude paused significantly.

"Were you surprised at the news of my wedding, Gertrude?"

"Yes, I certainly was. At first I could hardly believe my ears and then I thought, why am I hearing this first from Aunt Kathryne? If she hadn't told me…." The veiled accusation was not lost on Annie.

"I'm glad she did but I know it should have been me. I meant to but I just never seemed to get to see you, though it's really a poor excuse." Annie knew her explanation was inadequate and she was crestfallen. They walked a few more steps. Impulsively, Annie reached for Gertrude's hand and said unhappily, "Aren't you happy for me?"

Gertrude was momentarily take aback and at a loss for words. When she looked into Annie's pleading eyes, a wave of remorse washed over her. How selfish she had been, nursing her own injured feelings. Quickly, she threw her arms around Annie.

"Of course, Annie, I'm happy for you." She kissed Annie's wet cheeks. "I'm very happy for you. And I will come to the Loewens....next Sunday, I'll come," she promised. "So don't cry." She fumbled in her pocket for her handkerchief. "Here...here," she murmured as she wiped the tears from Annie's eyes. She had to hurry to the waiting buggy and as she was about to round the corner she looked back to see Annie still standing there laughing and waiving Gertrude's forgotten handkerchief.

That same afternoon, Gertrude had taken a long walk to her own family's homestead. She had not seen it for a long time and knew this would be the last time. She had heard talk of its being cleared away soon to make room for more crop land. Mary had turned away sulkily as Gertrude brushed aside her offer to accompany her. She did not wish to be subjected to Mary's empty prattle and restless urging to hurry on. Gertrude wanted to take her own time and savour this last visit alone.

She walked along leisurely, delighting in the quiet, broken by only the almost imperceptible murmurings of nature. The countryside which had once been covered with trees and scrubby bush, now had many clearings for crops and pastures. The grain fields were starting their transition from green to the golden yellow that would signal the start of the first stage of harvest season. Grasshoppers jumped about as Gertrude disturbed the grass along her path. She passed a small herd of cows, chewing their cuds without interruption as they looked with mild curiosity at her. Then a meadow lark, sitting on a fence post sent its full throated song soaring. For a second it seemed suspended in mid air as nature gently cupped it in her hands.

Gertrude could scarcely see the house for the trees, the underbrush, and the weeds which had run riot. When she came upon it, the house looked small and forlorn. No one lived there now. In the first years after they had left, a few itinerant families had stayed there and then journeyed on. None had seen fit to remain. The plaster which had been so carefully applied, had mostly fallen off, revealing the logs with which the original structure had been built. There was only a trace of whitewash under the eaves where the weather could not reach it. The wild winters had torn at the defenseless house. With no life to give it warmth from within, it had been unable to withstand the onslaught. The summer, too, had been unkind, driving its rain and heat through the widening cracks. Gertrude slowly opened the door and stepped carefully over the sill. Her eyes took a moment to adjust to the light. The kitchen looked pathetically small with bits of broken furniture scattered about. The door to her parents' bedroom stood ajar but she drew back from its pain-filled memories. She looked at the stairway. It looked unsafe. Her glance fell to the chimney and she saw the uneven crack down its length. It was the path left by the lightning which had struck down her father. No one had ever repaired it; mute evidence of the careless apathy of those who had passed this way.

Gertrude turned away and stumbled blindly out the door. She drew it shut firmly behind her.

She went to the barn. She did not go in. She stooped to peer through a crack in the door. It was dark and filled with the strong musty odour of hay left to rot. She straightened, not knowing where next to turn. The ruin around her was the picture of broken dreams, including the one she had held on to for so long, that one day they might come back here and all live together again. She thought she had let it go, but now realized it was only after hearing the news of Annie's marriage that she finally, really, understood that the dream was over. She felt the utter futility of it all. Was she right in thinking that the others didn't care as much as she did? She didn't know.

Sight of the little house her father had built over the spring brought her back to her surroundings. She ran to it. The spring.....oh dear God.....the spring! Was it still running? She tugged frantically at the door until she wrenched it open. To her joy, she heard a small gurgle. At last—something that was unchanged. She put her hand into the water and let it play over her fingers. She bent and took a long drink of the cool, sweet water. She knew that as long as she lived she would never find water that would taste so good.

"Aaron.....Aaron," —she could hear her mother calling— "Come here....." She imagined them walking around their homestead, wondering where to build their house. "Look, here is a spring, Aaron...here we will build...we'll never be without water as long as we live..."

Now she heard her father's voice. "Mary, how good it is......" Then their voices faded away —evaporating into the past along with Gertrude's dream.

Sadly, she started for home. She looked back only once. She waved good-bye. As she did so she saw her mother and father standing beside the spring house. They waved in return and they were smiling.

* * * * *

Gertrude finished the last pot and emptied the water into the slop pail. In the morning someone would take it out to the pigs. As she hung the pan on its nail on the wall, she saw Liza coming into the room. She had the dress over her arm. She had been working on it sporadically for the last few days.

"It's late, you shouldn't still be working on my dress, Aunt Liza."

"There's only the hem left to do. See?" She held it up for Gertrude to see. Gertrude's eyes lit up when she saw that Liza had added a belt and a collar.

"Oh, it's beautiful!" Gertrude burst out. "Thank you so much." Impulsively, she gave her aunt a big hug.

"Oh,...it's nothing..." Liza looked away embarrassed. She had risen to the task but it had been a taxing effort. The intense heat and the imminent birth of her baby had sapped her flagging energy but in her desire to contribute at least something to the wedding preparations, she had said she would give Gertrude a new dress. With a flurry of aroused excitement, she rummaged into the depths of her chest and came up with a few yards of material she had laid away some time ago. She had thought it might make a dress for herself after the baby was born, however, decided there wasn't enough cloth—instead she would use it to make a dress for Gertrude.

"Let's go outside for a while. It must be cooling off a bit by now. I'll take a chair out for you," Gertrude offered.

Liza stepped clumsily off the step at the door and lowered her unwieldy bulk into the chair. "Ah, that's better," she sighed. Gertrude sank down on to the stoop beside her. She watched the clouds forming in the western sky. Soft flashes of heat lightning danced among them. She squelched the painful anxiety that lightning now inevitably gave her and forced herself to dwell on how good it was going to be to have a short reunion with her sisters at the Loewens' next week.

Chapter Four

It was mid June. Gertrude was sitting at the sewing machine, her feet swiftly pumping the treadle. She had come here to the Fehr's to help with the sewing that would outfit the family for the coming fall and winter. Since leaving the Toewses some four years ago, she had worked at many different places in the community and had become a proficient seamstress in that time. She was always happy to come to the Fehr's. She and Margret had become good friends since Margret had married William Fehr. William was Liza's younger brother and he had brought his bride to live with the Toews' for a few months when Gertrude was thirteen. Margret was not one of their people. She felt lost and out of place. She and Gertrude had gravitated to one another and found comfort in each others company.

Gertrude had known of Margret's family, the Harrisons, but that was all. They had come from England some years after Gertrude's people. They had arrived in Manitoba, just the one family, and made their choice of a homestead mainly because the land and location appealed to them.

As they became aware that their neighbours belonged to a sect that was foreign to their experience, they pulled back, not quite knowing how, if at all, they should engage with them. They viewed the Holdemans as peculiar. The Holdemans, in their turn, regarded the Harrisons with some degree of suspicion, not knowing if their presence in the community would somehow exercise a disruptive influence on the Holdeman way of life. The Harrisons were a quiet family who preferred to mind their own business and the Holdemans did seem harmless enough so they slipped into a kind of uninvolved friendliness. This put the Holdemans more at ease so, over time, a status quo was established that was reasonably comfortable for everyone. Contact was limited and confined to the activities required by the conventions of good neighbourliness.

This superficial coexistence continued until William Fehr went to work for the Harrisons. He fell in love with Margret, the youngest of the family, She returned his love but when they wished to be married, they were confronted with a very real problem. If William were to marry outside of the church, he would be excommunicated and subjected to the indignities of being punished by the congregation. Margret had two brothers and two sisters, the elder Harrisons having departed this life some time earlier. So, among themselves, the Harrisons all decided to join the Holdeman church together—it would take care of many problems. There was no church of their own nearby. Maybe joining the Holdeman church would fill a void. After all they told themselves, we do read the same bible and follow much of the same teachings so why not? They felt willing to make the adjustments that would be needed to make this work and set the stage for Margret and William's marriage.

So, they were married. As for the other Harrisons, after the first excitement of belonging to a congregation again had passed, they gradually attended less and less. There was also the language barrier, so they quietly withdrew and lived much as before, only making an appearance on special occasions.

"Come," Gertrude felt Margret's light touch on her shoulder. "I've brewed a pot of tea....you need a rest by now." Margret had not abandoned the traditional cup of tea enjoyed by her people. Though it had been strange to Gertrude at first, she now quite liked it.

Gertrude had always admired Margret. Though she wore the black shawl and plain clothing as required, she carried them with aplomb and stateliness. Gertrude thought she had changed very little since they had first begun their warm, unique friendship—unique in that they communicated, each in their own tongue and had little difficulty in understanding each other. But that was changing. Gertrude, seeing how effortlessly Margret's children spoke English, was making her first halting attempts at speaking the new language too.

"Your month here with us is almost over," Margret spoke as she poured the tea. "And I can't persuade you to stay longer?"

"I would like to stay," Gertrude answered, "but I just have to go to Annie's. She has begged me to come for so long....I can't put it off any longer. Much as I'd like to...."

"I can see you don't look forward to going there. Do you think the work will be too hard?"

"No, it's not that—I know I'll have to work hard but she

wants me for the whole year and I just don't know how I'll stand it that long."

"That's a long time but she's your sister. It might be more like home," Margret suggested.

"That's what worries me. Annie has changed so. She is never satisfied with me. I make my dresses too pretty—I'm too unsettled—I'm not paying enough attention to finding a husband. Before I joined the church that too was a constant topic of disagreement." Gertrude laughed shortly. "Of course, I blame Jacob. He is very strict with her and the children. It's made Annie a nervous wreck and she is constantly next to tears."

"I see. But it might be different now, She may have a different attitude now that you have joined the church. But tell me Gertrude, are you happy that you did it?"

"Well," Gertrude hesitated, "I don't know—I suppose, in a way but....," she spread her hands in a helpless gesture. "But, what else is there?" She paused to think as she sipped her tea. "If there is something else, I don't know what it could be. I had hoped for something special to happen—that it would be an enlightening thing, but I don't feel any different. I still have the same doubts." Gertrude had asked herself many times whether it had been mainly a futile gesture on her part, done only to please other people. She wondered if anyone else felt the same way.

"Now that you belong to the church, do you go to the Brotherhood Council when they have one?"

"Yes, I do—usually, but I don't remember ever seeing you there."

"No, I never go anymore. I used to, but when I got to understand the language better, I just couldn't go anymore.

I… .I just don't belong there. I guess there are some things that you have to be born to….."

"Even then…..it….," Gertrude didn't finish her thought.

"Have you ever gone when they put someone out of church?" Margret shook her head. "I did," Gertrude continued. "That was when Agnes Friesen was put out. I knew it was a meeting about Agnes but I wasn't prepared for what they did. Anyway, she was one of our bunch. We were often together. We had heard the rumours that she was going to have a baby. We didn't believe it so we all went to the meeting to show her our support. I wish I'd never gone. It was true. She was expecting a baby. After they questioned her, she had to confess. It was awful to see. Then we had to vote to put her out. Everyone in turn had to say 'yes'. You couldn't do anything else. She had sinned but…"

"Poor Agnes, why didn't they make the father marry her?"

"They couldn't. He was a stranger—a man they had hired for a while and he was long gone. No one knew about it until the baby began to show. Even Agnes didn't know what was happening to her."

"How sad."

"The girls were all so shocked and said they would never again have anything to do with her." Margret had only heard about this event second hand and hadn't known all the details but she had been told that Gertrude went to Agnes after the meeting and put her arms around her in a long hug.

"I've heard about the hug," Margaret said with a small smile.

Gertrude blushed. "Ah yes… the hug. I got a lot of criticism for that."

"You did the right thing."

They had long since finished their tea but they lingered on.

"What do you suppose you'll do after you have been at Annie's for a while?"

"That seems a long while ahead but you know, I would just love to go and work in Winnipeg for a while. I'm sure I could get a job in one of the rich people's houses as a housemaid. In the mean time I will have to work on my English."

Margret was surprised. "That would be something different and interesting. But what would your people say? Do you think they would let you go?"

Gertrude shrugged her shoulders, "I'm sure they wouldn't like it but who is there to stop me?"

"Then you've been to Winnipeg?"

"Oh yes. I've been there twice— once when I was about twelve with Uncle John Loewen and his daughter, Bertha. We went by horse and buggy, then last year Bertha and I went again, this time by train."

* * * * *

The first trip to Winnipeg was a grand and wonderful experience. Gertrude had never been away from her native community. After leaving the familiarity of the bush country, they had travelled across many miles of prairie emptiness. At sundown, they had gone about two-thirds of the way so they stopped at a wayside farm. John told the girls that with an early start in the morning, they could finish all their business in Winnipeg and get back to the same farm again tomorrow night. John had stopped at the McDuff's many times before and was greeted as an old friend. The girls stood shyly by as the men took care of the horses. They listened wide-eyed to them talking volubly in English. That McDuff talked with a thick burr and John with a heavy germanic accent was lost on them for they didn't understand a word. In the house, they ate a hasty supper set for them at one end of a long table. Every time they ventured to glance up they saw a different youngster of a different size peering back at them. They were all red-headed but of various shades of red and their faces were sprinkled with freckles. Gertrude and Bertha were shown to their room by one of the older girls who carried a bucket of water which she poured into a flowered pitcher on the washstand. She turned down the bed and left without a word.

"Oh," the two chuckled gleefully. They touched the pitcher and the basin. They had never seen such a lovely set with flowers and everything painted on it. "And look Gertrude, here's the pot!" Bertha exclaimed. It too was of porcelain, with a lid and decorated with the same flowers.

"Do you suppose anyone ever uses it?" Gertrude wondered, imagining how carefully you would have to put the lid back on so no one would know that you had. Thankfully, they had gone to the outhouse before they came up. They could not bear to blow out the lamp and darken the room just yet, so they fell into the soft feather bed and from its luxurious depths, they looked and marvelled at every detail—the striped wallpaper, the lacy curtains, the hand-hooked rug—there was even a picture on the wall. It was of a round-cheeked little girl with golden curls. She held a basket of wild flowers in her chubby arms and a kitten sat at her feet.

"The Englanders sure have everything nice. I wonder why we can't have things like this?" Gertrude questioned naively. "I never saw anything like it before," she added as she got up to blow out the lamp.

The next day, filled with the sight, the smell, the sounds, the mere physical being of Winnipeg, the girls waited around not knowing where to look next. John had tethered his horse and gone off to take care of his business so they ventured along the sidewalk and peered into the shop windows being careful never to lose sight of their rig. Then they sat down on a bench and watched the people walk by. Two girls about their age ambled toward them. Gertrude and Bertha avidly took in all the details of their attire—the ruffled dresses, much shorter than theirs—the ribbons in their hair which hung down in curls just like the little girl in the picture last night. To their surprise, they stopped and said hello to them. They spoke some more but Gertrude and Bertha, not being able to understand them, merely nodded and smiled in return.

"My but aren't the Englanders friendly?" Gertrude watched wistfully as the young girls continued so unconcernedly down the street.

Later when John had left the horse to be fed and watered, he took the girls for a walk down Main Street. The street was wide and dusty but they were unaware of the discomfort. He took them to see the city hall. They stood, awe-struck before its grandeur. They felt small and unimportant standing in its shadow. Walking around to the back of the city hall, John led them into a long building through a fancy, curved arch. He told them that this was the market. Their first impression was of the loud, raised voices echoing throughout the space. John explained to them that the shouting men were bargaining over the prices of their wares. They looked at the stalls filled with farm produce, eggs, poultry (some dressed, some live), freshly churned butter. There were meats of all kinds (some dressed, some live). The aisles were teeming with humanity but to Gertrude it seem a hopeless confusion and she was relieved when John led them out of it.

Soon after that, they left Winnipeg. The girls looked back at the receding city for as long as they could until it disappeared beyond the horizon. They left with some regret, wishing they could have stayed longer but at the same time feeling somewhat relieved. Their first taste of another world was potent and heady.

* * * * *

"That first trip to Winnipeg must have been wonderful for you," Margret said. "You know, Gertrude, you have such an open mindedness about everything. I envy that in you."

"Ha," Gertrude laughed. "I think I have enjoyed that trip much more in retrospect than I did at the time. It was a bit much to take in all at once. Our second trip was different. We were older and on our own. We went to look at some of the houses. It was then that I made up my mind to go back there to work someday. But now, I guess I'd better get back to work right here, eh?"

She returned to her sewing with renewed energy. She felt full of life. Visiting with Margret was just the best thing!

As she worked she made up her mind to go to Annie's just as soon as she left here at the end of the month. She could not shirk the issue any longer.

Chapter Five

Gertrude stood at the upstairs window of the bedroom she had occupied the last year. She was waiting for her cousin Pete to fetch her to her Aunt Liza's. She had long since finished her packing but on the pretext of some last minute touches, she had fled Annie's doleful presence. Since first thing in the morning, Annie had been building up toward an emotional blow out. Gertrude was determined to keep the goodbye as short as possible. For weeks now, Annie had been looking for valid excuses to force Gertrude to stay on. Gertrude could only repeat that she had other plans. To Annie's reminders that their home was Gertrude's home, she could only utter her thanks with difficulty. Her mouth felt dry and bitter.

As soon as Pete turned onto the yard, Gertrude gathered her bags and boxes and carried them downstairs. Annie stood at the door and watched silently, the tears welling up in her eyes, while Pete and Gertrude loaded the baggage. When they were ready to go, Gertrude made her approach to Annie who rushed forward throwing her arms around

Gertrude, clutching her tightly and sobbing convulsively. Gertrude patted her reassuringly with what little sympathy she could muster but it wasn't until the crying of her little daughter came from inside the house and penetrated her grief, that Annie relinquish her hold and let Gertrude go.

"Well, at least my baby still needs me," Annie managed to say. "Even if you don't anymore...." Then much to Gertrude's surprise, Annie produced a rare whimsical smile, waved and went into the house.

Hmm, thought Gertrude, maybe I won't be missed that much after all.

There was no sign of Jacob. She had not seen him since he grudgingly paid her off early in the morning. It was painful for him to part with money. As they left the yard, Gertrude looked back and saw him standing inside the barn door. Was that a sneer? This time it was Gertrude's turn to smile and wave light heartedly. He immediately disappeared into the bowels of the barn.

Gertrude felt her body relax into the buggy seat. She was leaving behind what she considered to be a lost year. She had gone to Annie's telling herself she had no illusions but despite that, the cold reality of life on the Unger farm was worse than she had expected. The change in Annie from the kind, loving, happy girl she once knew into a quavering, deeply unhappy woman, was most appalling. In Jacob's presence, she cringed with fear lest she bring on his disapproval. The children, she alternately nagged and spoiled outrageously. Gertrude, too, was often the target of Annie's unhappiness. Gertrude attempted to cope by maintaining a cool reserve, trying not to be pulled into Annie's vortex of anxiety and frustration. Annie interpreted this as a rebuff, feeling that Gertrude didn't love her anymore. Gertrude was afraid that she was contributing to Annie's feelings of inadequacy and resentment but she didn't know how else to keep her head above water.

* * * * *

When Gertrude first realized that she was expected to do a great deal of the outside work, she protested to Annie that it was she, Annie, who needed the help. Where upon Annie immediately dissolved into tears and muttered that it was Jacob who was paying her. It was not long before Gertrude was relieved when she could get out of the house no matter what the task.

Every night after supper, Jacob reached for his bible which he kept on a high shelf out of the children's reach. He sat down at the table and without further ado, he opened it at the place where he had left off reading the previous night. He drew the lamp up close, the better to see, his huge shadow growing on the wall behind him, dancing eerily to the flickering, sputtering flame from the charred, untrimmed wick. The light added a steely glint to his small eyes, peering out beneath the long, scanty, tangled hair of his brow. As his glance circled the room, all sound ended in a sudden death. There was a pause, while Jacob, not looking directly at anyone in particular, stared past the light into the dim room. Then he startled everyone with the loud clearing of his throat as he bent to his book. Verse after verse poured from his lips as the chair seats grew harder and harder.

When at last, Jacob bade them to kneel in prayer, one part of the anatomy was eased only to be replaced by suffering in another. Jacob's prayers were never short. The shock of silence at the end jerked most of the group out of semi-consciousness into a confusion of activity. The harsh scraping of chairs, along the bare, crude, wooden planks of the floor, as they were being pushed back into place, rang in Gertrude's ears long after she made her groping way to bed. It echoed far into the future and whenever she heard that sound again, she sensed a fleeting touch of futility and loneliness.

One night after Gertrude had been there only a few weeks, and not yet fully appreciative of the full extent of Jacob's domain, she tried to make her escape through the stairway door—the natural sequence to a long, tiring day's work. "Gertrude!" She stopped short with her hand on the knob. "What do you think you are doing?"

"Why....why....I was just going...."

"Sit down!" Jacob ordered.

"But, I'm very tired," Gertrude began.

"In this house," Jacob spoke as though she had said nothing, "no one goes to bed before the reading of the word." His eyes did not waver from her direction but they looked straight through and beyond her, taking away any satisfaction Gertrude might have had in meeting his eyes in an open challenge. His strategy left her defiance hanging limply in the air between them. Gertrude looked helplessly toward Annie and saw that she was sniffing quietly into her handkerchief. So, with a shrug and keeping her eyes riveted on Jacob she took the nearest chair feeling the sting of reproach from all around the room. Jacob's gaze swung coldly to his snivelling wife rendering her instantly silent.

And, the evening ritual began.

The days rolled on despite their grinding tedium. They came to a Sunday in August. Church was never missed. Everyone climbed into the buggy. It was a two seater which Jacob had bought in the spring. It had been the first in the community and eyebrows had been raised and tongues wagged. When something new was introduced, it was generally viewed with suspicion. The thought was that if we've been getting along so far without this new innovation, then indeed, it must be an unneeded luxury. But, failing an initial clampdown from the church elders, the novelty item would slowly became more common-place. Neighbours would talk themselves into believing that what they once thought to be unnecessary was indeed a much needed item. In this way, luxury was ground through the mill of pragmatism until it came out as necessity. There were now several more such buggies. Some even had retractable tops which Jacob had declared to be entirely unnecessary. Jacob and Annie, holding their youngest, John, sat in the front seat while Gertrude and the hired man, Abe Klassen, sat in the back with the other two children, Aaron and Martin, crowded between them. This is certainly an improvement over the wagon Gertrude thought to herself.

She stole a glance at Abe. He looked clean and scrubbed, his hair and beard combed which was more than she could say for him during the week. Though she had known him all her life, she had nothing to say to him. Abe was well aware that Gertrude had noticed him. He was very conscious of the fact that Gertrude had grown from a thin rather plain child, into a very comely maiden. Her fair hair had darkened to a golden brown and her skin was smooth and unblemished. Her grey eyes, usually sombre, did sometimes flash a little sparkle and when accompanied by a slight grin, caused in him a vague uneasiness—what was he missing? She was slender, her back straight and recently, he had been noticing more than ever how her shape was delicately rounded in all the right places. Abe had never dared corner her in some dark recess of the barn. She was not like some of the girls on other farms where he had worked, he thought wryly.

How fast the countryside was changing, Gertrude thought, as they bounced and jiggled on toward the church. Most of the bush and trees were now cleared. The old log cabins were being replaced by frame houses and summer kitchens were being built, attached or separate to keep the heat and flies of summer living out of the rest of the house. They were a great convenience, though they did add many more steps to the already overworked women of the households, Gertrude thought ruefully.

When they neared the church, Gertrude turned her attention from the changing countryside to the populace converging on the church yard. The bright sunshine merely served to emphasize the colourless, drab, grey aspect of the picture. The Sunday, going to church faces, were impassive, humourless masks, leaving the imagination to conjure what their every-day faces might be.

Very few would be absent today for the word had spread that there was to be a guest preacher. He was John Enns from Rosenort where there was another Holdeman settlement. It was some fifty miles to the west on 'yonder side', meaning that they had to cross the Red River to get there. Peculiarly, each settlement merely referred to the other as 'yonder side'. John Enns was a widower which, in itself, gave rise to inevitable speculation. He was also known to have a large family. As Gertrude, making a cursory glance around the congregation, took her seat beside Katie and Jennie, she noticed a young man whom she had never seen before. He could be none but a son of John Enns. He bore so striking a resemblance to the older man. In a quick, whispered conversation, Katie, who had visited Rosenort, confirmed Gertrude's conjecture as to his identity and added that his name was David. David….. she turned the sound of it over in her mind. It suited him. He stood out above the crowd in stature and Gertrude saw immediately how his fine, handsome, intelligent face also set him apart.

After the service, Katie, mentioning that the Enns men were expected to be at the Friesen farm for dinner, asked Gertrude if she would like to come too. "Well," Gertrude hesitated. "I haven't made any special plans for today," which had certainly been true up until that very moment, "but…..yes, Katie, I think I will." They started for the Friesen buggy, but Gertrude laid a detaining hand on Katie's arm. "Let's walk, it's such a beautiful day."

"Oh, let's!" Katie agreed. Seeing Jennie's imploring look, she called hastily, "We'll see you at home Jennie." When they were out of ear-shot she said, "We so seldom see each other alone…."

"That's true. I can't remember when…..," her voice trailed off as they slowed to a more leisurely pace, waving on the passing friends who offered them a ride. Gertrude looked back. How quickly the church was deserted. The yard, bereft of its recent activity, left the church looking deflated and shrunken. Each Sunday, it was like a little death. Was that why it looked so lonely and forlorn when you passed by during the week? It's all so predictable she thought. She knew exactly how the rest of the afternoon would go. The boys, to their parent's dismay, would gulp their food, then hurriedly leave the house to meet with each other in the yard to cruise about aimlessly, exchanging quips and silly jokes—some on their latest and most envied possession—the bicycle. The luxury verses necessity jury was still out on that one. Before the girls could steal a few minutes of quiet visiting, they would be left to do the cleanup chores while wondering what it would be like to enjoy some of the same freedoms that the boys had. "I've heard that the Ennses were at your place a few days ago, " Gertrude mentioned casually, as she stooped to pick a few wild flowers along the roadside feigning disinterest in what Katie's answer might be.

"Yes, they came over Friday afternoon—stayed for super too," Katie answered. "By the way, what do you think of George?" Katie asked. He was another of John Enns's sons who had made the trip. "Don't you think he's nice?"

"Yes, I guess so," Gertrude said offhandedly, but thinking that he didn't compare with David. She glanced at Katie and noticed the heightened colour in her cheeks.

"What would you think.....?" Katie floundered while Gertrude's curiosity grew. "What would you think if I went to Rosenort to live?"

"Oh, Katie, why ever.....?" She stopped in her tracks and threw up her hands, her eyes widening, the forgotten wild flowers scattering in the wind. "Oh, Katie.....why Katie—that's it! Your thinking of getting married to George. I should have guessed. So that's why they're here. Did you have any notion of it before.....that....that this might happen?"

"Yes," Katie's eyes dropped in sudden embarrassment. "I wasn't sure, of course. I did hope."

"Oh for goodness sake. When will it be? How did he ask?"

"You know how it is, Gertrude, like they do. Mr. Enns asked Uncle Henry, then they called me in to ask me and said I should think about it. After they left, we all talked and agreed to it. Mr. Enns and George stopped by this morning before church and Uncle Henry told them how we felt. It was decided to make the announcement in the Brotherhood Council next Sunday and so you know the rest."

"That's wonderful, Katie! It's just such a surprise." But how else could it be? It sounded so simple, but was it? Gertrude wondered how she would feel about marrying a man who was more or less a complete stranger. There was no courtship, no opportunity to get to know one another, even superficially, before others made the decision on behalf of the young couple to be. Gertrude had a pretty good idea about the intimate goings on between a married man and woman but to think of starting that part of your life with someone you hardly knew….?

The girls walked on slowly but their thoughts were far from calm. Katie dreaming of her future, with excitement but not without misgivings. Gertrude wondering what kind of a wife Katie would make, Katie with her blunt, irritating ways. No doubt she would never let herself be broken to any man's will like Annie had done.

"But, Katie, It will be months and months until we see each other again. It's so far away…"

"Yes, I know. That's one reason that makes me wonder. One minute I want to get married and the next, I don't. Then I remind myself that it really isn't so far away—not like Kansas where Peter has gone or even Alberta where Bertha went."

"No, I guess it's not *that* far. Poor Peter. Have you heard anything from or about him lately?" But Katie could only shake her head sadly. It was as though Peter had vanished from their lives.

* * * * *

It was scarcely two years since Peter had lost his young wife and their unborn child. She had left him with two small children, a boy and a girl. He had gone into such deep shock that he was unaware of his children and incapable of making decisions. The people around him felt it necessary to intervene so with the best of intentions, arranged a marriage for him. Before Susie was a full three months in her grave, his new bride to be arrived from Kansas. She had been persuaded that it was a charitable act. Peter needed a wife and the children needed a mother. Her father, however, had made one stipulation before giving his consent—that her new husband and she would come to live in Kansas in the event that things did not go well for her in Manitoba. Tina Wiens came with great hopes and determination. After the first flurry of her arrival and their subsequent marriage, life was expected to return to normal. Peter did not rise to the occasion as anticipated. He went through the marriage ceremony in a daze. In the following weeks, he remained unapproachable and preoccupied.

Tina started to flounder and lose track of her determination. Friends and family began to blame her for the lack of progress and were not able to completely mask their growing disappointment in her. The children saved Tina from despair. They were too young to grasp the complexity of the situation, so, willingly, accepted Tina's kindness. She in turn, reached out for the warmth they offered her. In growing to know and love them, she was naturally curious about their mother. What had she been like? What did she look like?

"Peter," she began one day. "Peter, what was she like? What was Susie like?" She was greeted with stoney silence. She persisted. "She must have been a lovely person to have borne such fine children...," but there still was no response. After Tina made several more futile attempts to open the subject, Peter, his face distorted and ugly with pain, rose to leave the room.

"Never, never, mention her name to me again—not for as long as I live!" he shouted as he slammed the door behind him. He avoided her for days afterwards. The right to grieve had been cruelly snatched from him by his hasty marriage but in forbidding any further mention of his first wife, he drove his torment even deeper. Tina was now as deeply wounded as he.

A few weeks later, Tina hoped that by telling him she was carrying his child, things would change. They didn't. How could Tina know that in their most intimate moments, Peter had thought only of Susie? Now there was to be a child and it was not Susie's Had he actually committed adultery, it would not have been as painful.

A few days later, as Tina watched Peter staring sightlessly out of the window in utter dejection, she knew that she could not bear it any longer. "Peter," she said, his indifference infuriating her. She walked determinedly over to him and grasping him roughly by the shoulders, shook him violently.

"Peter, listen to me!" Her knees began to give way and she sat down, with a thud beside him. "Do you remember my father made us promise that we would come to Kansas if things—if we didn't"—she didn't know how to finish the sentence. She had felt for days that if only they could get away from here where everything reminded him of his sorrow, they might have a chance.

"Yes....," Peter said slowly.

"But have you not thought that maybe that's what we should do?"

"No I haven't," he said simply. For a second, she thought she saw signs of surprise and then relief cross his face. It was the first change of expression that she had seen in him for a long time.

"You know," Tina felt she must go on talking so as not to lose what she hoped she had gained. "When Papa asked it of us, I thought, how foolish. It was impossible for things to come to such a state that we would ever think of returning to Kansas."

Peter looked at her. Really looked at her. Then after a long silence, he uttered a low moan. A sound the like of which Tina had never heard, coming from somewhere deep inside of him. He tried to speak, his rigid jaw barely allowing him to form words. Finally, haltingly, words came. "Maybe.....maybe.....we could start over again," but the anguish had not left his face. She reached over and cradled his head against her breast like she would sooth a hurt child.

"It's alright. It's alright," she murmured over and over again. As she rocked him, his arms moved to encircle her. Ever so slowly, the strength of his hold on her increased until it was as though he would never let her go.

In that moment, their decision was made. They moved quickly to sell their farm. They said their goodbyes and set out for Kansas in the hope of finding a new and better life together but Susie's name was never mentioned between them again.

* * * * *

"Gertrude!" Katie brought Gertrude back to the present. "What on earth were you thinking about? You look so sad."

"I'm sorry. I was just thinking about Peter. I hope things are really going better for him there. It's not the sort of thing you write about in letters. I worked at Tina's quite a lot at the time and I could see how things were going but this is not the time to be worrying about Peter. This is the time to be thinking about you isn't it?"

When they reached their destination Gertrude waved to Joseph and Abram who were leaning lazily against the side of the barn. Abram's face broke into a wide smile—her baby brother. He reminded her of an overgrown, friendly puppy—his big hands and feet clumsily getting in his way, waiting for the rest of him to catch up. Joseph remained sober. He was short and fine-boned, more reserved, almost delicate in nature.

Joseph had joined the church six months ago. The slow growth of his scanty beard caused him much anxiety but he wore it with somber acceptance. When he first revealed his intention to join, he had told her about his feelings openly and elatedly, taking it for granted that because he had made his decision, she too had surely done the same. Gertrude responded by saying she wasn't ready, that she still had a lot to think about. In her turn, Gertrude had assumed that Joseph would be going through the same questioning as she, so his announcement surprised her. Gertrude then added that she thought Joseph was too young to make such a decision but as soon as she said it she knew that she was sounding more critical than she intended. She immediately realized that their mistake had been in not sharing their thoughts much sooner, before Joseph had made up his mind. Joseph felt somehow betrayed and hurt. He had revealed himself to the one person he trusted most and who he thought would automatically share his joy. Instead she turned out to be a sceptic. Throwing his young age at him made it even worse. Nothing had been the same between them since. To the dismay of them both, it was as though the closeness of their childhood had been damaged beyond repair.

* * * * *

Katie's marriage took place and they were off to Rosenort to set up their life on George's farm.

Summer had turned to fall and then to winter. Christmas brought the excitement of Katie's first visit back to Blumenort. She carried with her the miraculous secret of her impending motherhood. She begged Gertrude to cut her year with Annie short so she could be with her for the birth but Gertrude would stick to her plan and come later—as soon as she could.

The dubious season which was neither winter nor spring arrived. It was the season of waiting. The tasks of winter were done and they were marking time. It was during this time that Annie, surprisingly consented to go with Gertrude to visit their Aunt Liza who had been in poor health most of the winter. They filled a basket with items of food to tantalize Liza's flagging appetite and they were amply rewarded for their efforts. Before they were ready to return home some of the pallor had left Liza's cheeks and her lethargy had begun to lift. Liza prevailed upon Annie to allow Gertrude to remain with them for a week or so. Annie, hesitated only for a second as she thought about what Jacob would say. Then, in a rare moment of lighthearted defiance, brought on by the welcome change in her aunt, Annie agreed. She was willing to take the consequences. What did it matter? Living with his constant displeasure had become a way of life for her. She wasn't unaware of how she had changed as a result. By giving her consent, she felt, just for a moment, like her old self.

Gertrude's relationship with Liza and Mary had shifted after Gertrude left to go out on her own. A more congenial intimacy had grown out of their shared past. The Toewses were the closest thing she had to a family of her own and the old annoyances and resentments had finally lost their edge. Gertrude was now able to sympathize with Liza's aches and pains and be more relaxed in the easy atmosphere of Mary's nonchalant, at times slovenly, approach to housekeeping.

During this pleasant interlude, Gertrude and Mary decided to make the short trip to Steinbach to visit their Aunt Kathryne and Uncle John. They chose the buggy and hitched the horses. It was that time of year when neither buggy nor sleigh was fully up to meeting the demands made by the soft slushy roads. They set off. Soon, they slackened their hold on the reins, letting the team go along at its own pace. Patches of snow still lay about and the earth gulped greedily at their precious gift of water. They welcomed the slow ride which gave them an opportunity to catch up on times spent apart. When the village came into sight, they straightened up from their relaxed condition, brushed back their hair, re-tied their shawls, buttoned their coats. Then they reined in their horses firmly and proceeded primly down the main street of the village. They became increasingly self-conscious. It was necessary to travel the length of the street as the Loewens lived at the far end. The folks who were on the street made no attempt at hiding their curiosity, pausing to stare at the strangers. Curtains were hastily pulled back so peering eyes could get a better look.

Most of the early villages were disappearing one by one but Steinbach, unlike the others, was growing. It was becoming the trading centre for the widening Mennonite community. The names of the former villages were retained to designate the geographical vicinities in which the villages had once stood. Curiosity about strangers was often expressed by the blunt question, 'Which village did you come from?' The answer instantly tagged and catalogued the individual as to family affiliations.

When Gertrude and Mary pulled up at the Loewens, they heard the hollow echo of quick footsteps on the board walk behind them. They watched with pleasure as the portly figure of their uncle swayed toward them in a spritely manner. He reached out to envelope the hands of both girls at the same time.

"Welcome,welcome," shouted Kathryne as she came bounding out of the house and threw her arms around them in a great, crushing hug. "We haven't seen you for so long."

Her voice shook with emotion and her eyes were filling with tears. "Oh John, you're here." With a quick glance at the girls, "He must have smelled my cooking," Kathryne laughed in a vain attempt to cover her emotional outburst.

"Well, I just came to see the girls," he pointed out.

"Good. So now you can take care of the horses." He climbed into the buggy to take it to the public stables. "Mind, you come right back. We'll be having dinner soon."

"Yes, yes," John mumbled. He had long resigned himself to being dominated by women. He and Kathryne had never been blessed with a son of their own so Abram's move to the Friesens some years back had left him the only man in the household.

"You can see how happy he is to see you," Kathryne said fondly with a contented look on her face.

They entered the little gate in the white picket fence which led to the cozy, white house with green shutters. The white picket fence and green shutters were Kathryne's departure from the usual austere outward appearance of Holdeman houses. Because she lived in a mainly Kleine Gemeinde village they had caused little comment. The shutters were open and the windows, refugees from a recent spurt of spring cleaning, sparkled in the sunlight revealing the crisp curtains within. In the heat of summer, the shutters would be closed keeping the front room, which doubled as the sitting room and the parental bedroom, dim and cool. There, Kathryne or John often sought refuge from the activity of the rest of the house. They followed Kathryne with her wide skirts billowing, along the board walk around to the side of the house where another gate led them into the back yard which was enclosed in a high wooden fence. It was too early, but soon the yard would be a profusion of green shrubs and flowers. Gertrude saw that the garden swing, a great canopied frame from which was suspended two seats facing each other on a slatted floor, had been newly painted. It stood ready, waiting for the leisurely hours which somehow were always available in Kathryne's household. The few drops of oil which John would occasionally dribble into its joints could never long dull the unforgettable, indolent lament which rose and fell as the swing, gently coaxed by the occupants' feet, moved to and fro, to and fro.

There were many bits of news and items of gossip to exchange. They reminisced about Bertha's wedding. She was the cousin to whom Gertrude felt closest. She had been married at the early age of seventeen and the couple had moved to Alberta right after the wedding. She was already a mother of a baby girl. "Bertha was much too young," Kathryne confided. "She should have waited a while. But there was little else to do but let her go. She was always seeing Peter. She thought we didn't know, but we did. It wasn't right. It would be so easy to get into trouble....."

"Bertha is a good girl," Gertrude comforted her aunt, but at the same time was thinking, maybe this is leading up to a lecture in favour of quickly arranged marriages as opposed to any kind of courtship period. She looked at Mary who didn't seem to be getting the same point.

"The older two never gave us any worries," Katheryne continued, "their marriages were both arranged by us and the other parents just as things should be." Aha, thought Gertrude. "I wonder about our younger girls. We live here among Kleine Gemeinde—a few other kinds of Mennonites too, but mostly Kleene Gemeinde. What are they going to do? It pains me to think of it. I often wonder how the Holdemans and Kleine Gemeinde came to be so different when once we were all one people."

"I guess you notice it more living right here among them," Mary observed.

"Yes, Kleine Gemeinde are the ones who run all the businesses here. We are really the only non farming Holdemans around. I, even yet, don't feel at home. They don't accept us, really. I find it quite lonely at times," Kathryne sighed wistfully.

"I can certainly see that you would," Gertrude agreed. "Why did it come to be so—between the sects, I mean. I've never heard too much about that. I guess my mother would have told me eventually. She usually answered my questions but most people seem so reluctant to talk about it."

"Well, yes. It doesn't seem to be discussed very much. You see, girls, when some of us pulled away from the Kleine Gemeinde to follow John Holdeman's teachings, the Kleine Gemeinde began to feel as though they were not good enough for the ones who went to the Holdemans. That's why the Kleine Gemeinde were the first to show their resentment. I can see now that it was only natural and when you look at it from their point of view, they were right in thinking so. The Holdemans wanted to remain friends at first but when the Kleine Gemeinde rebuffed them, they too began to feel angry. That's how we drew apart and we never got back to our old closeness. It seems foolish but that's the way people are. The older I get, the more bewildered I am by what we will do in the name of religion."

It really does seem a waste, Gertrude and Mary agreed.

"I really don't know any Kleine Gemeinde well. Many of them are related to us too," Gertrude said.

Kathryne continued, "Yes, I remember, at the time one of your father's brothers told him that if he did join the Holdemans, he would never talk to him again, not as long as he lived. It hurt your father very much but his brother kept his word. Then when Aaron died he refused to go to the funeral."

"Oh, how cruel!" Gertrude exclaimed, aghast.

"Yes, I guess it was, in a way, but even that I can see differently now...."

"But," Gertrude interrupted her astonishment growing. "How can you justify that, even now?"

"We heard afterwards, that his brother, at home, paced the floor wringing his hands in anguish, while the funeral was going on. I know now that he was afraid of breaking down at the service. He didn't want anyone to see his grief." Kathryne paused, the memories still painful. "Your father's death was so sudden. There had been no time to make amends. And then, they were both very stubborn men. They may have forgiven each other in time but who knows?"

Gertrude sat pensively. Mulling over what she had just heard, trying to benefit from her aunt's wisdom. "You know, speaking of my father's brother, it was a long time before I even knew that he had a full brother. I knew he had a number of half brothers. Imagine! My grandfather, whom I never knew, was, I understand, married several times."

"Your grandfather was not just married several times. In fact he was married five times! His last wife managed to out-live him or who knows how many more he would have had. He was only in his late sixties when he died."

"Oh my goodness. He must have been a very vigorous man!"

"He certainly must have been. Of course, most of this happened in the old country and one hasn't heard all the details. I have heard it told that one of his old friends asked him in his later years, which of his wives he loved the most and he answered without hesitation, that he had always loved the one he was married to at the time the best." Kathryne broke into laughter and Mary and Gertrude joined in. "Sounds to me like a pretty glib answer. The men on your father's side, Gertrude, haven't taken well to living without a woman. Being a woman, I find it hard to sympathize with them at times."

There was no one with whom Gertrude could find greater affinity than her Aunt Kathryne. Not even any of the girls her own age. Gertrude and Mary left Steinbach the next day. Gertrude dreaded more than ever her return to the Ungers but she would stay out her year.

* * * * *

Now, at last, it was July again and the year was over and she was on her way to the Toewses. She could almost smell the aroma of the coffee she knew would be waiting on the back of Liza's stove.

Chapter Six

The Toewses welcomed Gertrude with open arms—a much needed balm to a tired soul.

"Now you can take a long rest," Liza declare decisively. "You can sleep late and do whatever you like."

"Just to be back is enough for me now," Gertrude answered with a small tremor in her voice.

From force of habit, Gertrude did not sleep late but she lay in bed tasting, savouring the luxury of it—listening to the stir of morning like she had as a small child. Her first Sunday there, she stayed away from church, exercising a choice, which she had not been able to do for so long. When the others returned, they brought word that a Brotherhood Council had been called for the afternoon, so she decided to attend.

The meeting was very routine. A few seemingly unimportant items were discussed but the congregation was not yet dismissed. Old John Wiebe and the younger preacher, Albert Bartel, were engaged in a whispered conference while everyone else was waiting restlessly. It was Batrel who came forward to the podium. He looked around rather uncertainly. As his uneasiness grew more apparent, an expectant hush fell over the room. He used all the well known ruses to play for time. He reset his stance, rocked on his heels, cleared his throat. He drew his handkerchief out of his back pocket—looking at it, he paused , and then giving his wife Sarah a beleaguered look loudly blew his nose. Sara cast her eyes down quickly, her face reddening because she had forgotten to replace his everyday blue calico square with a fresh white linen one. Obviously, the trials of being a minister's wife were legion.

"It....it has been brought to my attention that....," he swayed several more times, holding to the podium with whitened knuckles, "that certain of our sisters—the younger sisters.....," he qualified hastily, "that.....that their dresses fit much too well.....much too smooth over....." He was having difficulty in establishing his elusive point and was hoping that he need not say more. The questioning incredulity written on the faces before him, forced him to continue. "It is not right for the sisters of our church to.....uh.....to reveal so much of the shape. I have been told that they, the younger sisters, have been buying these new.....uh....." He plunged headlong to the crux of the matter. "Under garments!"

The silence was heavy. A few whispered glances were exchanged; several eyes fell on Gertrude. Gertrude's cheeks grew hot with indignation. It was becoming increasingly evident at whom the criticism was being directed. Suddenly the silence was broken with a loud angry snort from the back of the church. As one, all eyes turned to see Kathryne Loewen leaping to her feet with a dexterity she had not shown in years.

"Well! That.....that.....," she began, blustering. "That you can stand up there and talk about so personal a matter, oh, it's just too much! And in church, too. And I must say that I'm very surprised at you Albert." She emphasized her words by waggling her finger at him. "That you should be noticing the figures of our younger sisters.....tut..... tut.....and as for these.....uh.....under-garments, as you call them.....what could you know about them? As it happens, they may make the dresses fit better but what is wrong with that? They are a good support for the body. It would be good if more of our older sisters, too, would wear them. It might keep their backs from bending with all the hard work we do, making us old before our time! For shame.....for shame. And to think, I helped bring you into the world." Albert, who had visibly shrunken at this outburst, was now reduced to the status of a shame faced little boy. Kathryne sank to her seat, spent.

"That is all then," Albert managed to mumble, collapsing into his chair. His legs could no longer support him. John rose quickly concocting an on the spot closing prayer which no one heard. The church and the church yard emptied with unusual speed. The babble which generally rose over the noises of the departing rigs, was held in check until each party was out of earshot of the other. Liza was the first to brake the silence in their group.

"Well, I never.....," she burst out when she could no longer contain herself. "Right in front of everybody! I wonder who put him up to it? I doubt if Albert would even have the brains to....."

"I happened to look at his wife," Mary offered. "And she....."

"Oh," Liza interrupted. "That must be it! Who else? Who else, when everyone can see that her fig....."

"Now, Liza," Klaas cautioned as he indicated the others with a small jerk of his head.

"But, Klaas, I don't care.....," Liza persisted but with the commotion which resulted from a loud command to his horses, Klaas managed to drown out the rest of her sentence. Pete and Jake, who were smirking into their shirt collars, stole quick glances at each other but did not dare look at Gertrude or Mary.

"And the way Kathryne stood her ground!" Liza exclaimed. "It did my heart good. You know how pushy she can be—but today—ah, it was good to see."

Gertrude and Mary had difficulty suppressing the mirth which was welling up inside them. Margret Fehr had not been in church. Gertrude could hardly wait to tell her. In spite of her husband's objections, Margret received the Eaton's catalogue regularly and often shared it with Gertrude. The catalogue was Margret's and Gertrude's little window to the world beyond. It was Margret who helped Gertrude order the corset.

"You know," Liza went on, "I agree with Kathryne, I think it would be a very good idea if I bought myself a core....."

"Liza!" Klaas almost shouted with alarm growing in his voice.

The horses mistook Klaas' shout to be directed at them and their second burst of speed drew everyone's attention. Their eyes became glued with intense interest on the rippling muscles under the shiny curried coats and the swishing tails.

Gertrude knew she was letting too many days slip indolently by—that she should go to Katie. No opportunity to go had presented itself and she drew back from making her first trip to Rosenort alone which would involve a train trip to Winnipeg and then a transfer to the train serving the station near Rosenort. On several occasions, Liza had lent her a sympathetic ear. Then one day she reached over and patted Gertrude's hand reassuringly. "Don't worry, Gertrude, I have a plan. I think it will work."

From time to time, she had mentioned to Klaas that they should go to Rosenort but he had never risen to the bait. It was time they made themselves better known. They had several children of marriageable age and the local prospects were becoming appallingly barren. What harm could there be in gathering a few pertinent bits of information in that area and at the same time dropping some discreet hints as to the sterling qualities of their own children? Of course, she dare not use that argument with Klaas. Men were quick enough to jump to the altar themselves but when it came to their children, well humph.....

"Klaas," Liza began that night at the supper table. "Don't you think it would be nice if we went to Rosenort?"

"Why?" Klaas asked shortly, not looking up from his eating.

"Why?" Liza's voice rose mockingly. "Why to visit your niece, Katie, for one thing. Poor Katie, so alone there..... with no one....."

"Pshaw!" Klaas was not touched. "Alone? She has a husband and all those in-laws and now a new daughter."

"Oh Klaas, for goodness sakes, she has a son!"

"Well, she has a son then, whatever difference that makes," he grunted. "I'm sure she's not lonely." Liza knew how to ignore that kind of a Klaas remark.

"She has none of her family there. Anyway, Gertrude wants to go so I thought if we'd take her, we could see what the country is like and visit some of the people who have been here to Blumenort." She paused, looking hopefully at Klaas whose interest was still not rising above his dinner plate. She must try another tack. She became petulant. "After all, everybody has been to Rosenort, everybody except us. When people start talking about Rosenort, I'm ashamed. I know nothing….."

"Ah," Klaas looked up for the first time, his eyes crinkling to hide the glint of gathering amusement. This, at last, was his Liza talking. He rose from the table, saying no more, but as he passed her, he lovingly patted her soft shoulder.

In a few days all was in readiness for the trip. Pete and Mary were left in charge of the family which had grown to eight. Liza turned back and waved tearfully, as long as she could see them. She had never left them for longer than a day before.

There were many Mennonite villages and farms on the way to the first Holdeman village where they would spend the night. To Gertrude's annoyance, Liza and Klaas found it necessary to stop at most of them to satisfy their insatiable curiosity. Rapport was easily established within the Mennonite brotherhood.

The next day was very different. The trees became sparser and there were no more Mennonite settlements. They felt the loneliness of the open spaces and the thinly scattered habitation. When, in the distance, they saw a line of trees, they wondered if they were coming to the Red River but found it to be only a small river for which they knew no name. They crossed a narrow bridge and stopped under the trees to rest. There were settlers on each side of the river and when they had eaten their lunch, Klass wandered around and came upon a small group of men. He approached them and they returned his greeting, smiling and nodding but when he asked the name of their village, he was met with elaborate shrugs and gestures, indicating that they did not understand him. The travellers went on with little regret at leaving the strange community.

When, for the second time, they saw trees, they knew it had to be the Red. The trees were larger with thick trunks—dense, providing shelter to a small village nestled in their midst. It had the quaint look of having been there always. The largest building was white and had a tall structure rising about 3 stories above the front door finishing with a cross at the top. Openings near the top revealed a hanging bell. The church, Gertrude thought. I saw similar bell towers during my visit to Winnipeg with Bertha. There were groups of children playing about but they stopped to stare, wide-eyed as the buggy with the odd looking people passed. Gertrude was enchanted by the picture they made. The children, like the village itself, appeared to be at one with their surroundings. They must be French. Were they perchance the real natives of this country? They did not have the look of being recently transplanted, unlike her people whose roots were still shallow in their new country.

Neither Liza nor Klaas showed any inclination to stop. They felt the strangeness about them. Here, they were the aliens. Rather than test their reception and possibly be rebuked, they went on through, staring straight ahead without tarrying. Suddenly, they came to a sharp turn and a steep drop in the road. In his surprise, Klaas pulled frantically on the reins, bringing the horses to a short stop. Gertrude felt her heart pulsing wildly in her throat. There before their astonished eyes lay the Red River. There was no bridge, just a few boards laid cross-wise where the road met the water. Of course, she knew there had to be a ferry but it hadn't occurred to her that it would not be there to meet them.

Liza clung to Klaas's arm until he laughingly disengaged himself. Having regained his composure, Klass now jumped nonchalantly down from the buggy to reassure the horses. Reaching for their bridles, he stroked their noses and murmured into their ears soothing their ruffled feelings. "See there," Klaas said pointing. "If you look across to the other side, you can see the ferry coming toward us. Why don't the two of you get down and see for yourselves?" The put-put-put of the little engine powering the water wheel on the side of the ferry could now be heard. The ferry swayed somewhat because of the river's current but the rope, anchored to poles on each side of the river, kept it on course. "The ferry man sees us. Already he's waiving. Walk down and wait for him while I hold the horses."

Gertrude and Liza agreed that getting down to walk was certainly a better option than staying in the buggy and run the risk of going straight into the water. So they made their way, gingerly down, Liza leaning heavily on Gertrude's arm. With growing concern, they watched the ferry move slowly toward them.

"I'm not sure I care to go on that thing," Liza said.

"It looks as though it could just as well go on down the stream as not," Gertrude whispered doubtfully. "That rope holding it looks mighty flimsy to me. But it must be safe. We're not the first people to ride this contraption." Gertrude was trying to convince herself as well as Liza. Then realizing how childish she sounded, added, "Anyway, we're here now, and we can't go back."

Gertrude and Liza raised their skirts carefully and stepped onto the docked float. Not until they reached the side rail, holding on tightly to steady themselves, did they dare look up at Klaas who was having considerable difficulty in coaxing the skittish horses down. When the ramp was lifted and fastened in place by the chains, they uttered a tentative sigh of relief as they began to move forward.

With the gentle roll of movement, everybody, including the horses, became more at ease. Gertrude started to look at her surroundings. There were the trees standing careful guard over the wide river. There was the gentle current flowing endlessly on with no hint of the massive power driving the lower depths of the river. There was the light, moist, cool air which seemed to rise out of the water, making breathing almost effortless.

Once they left the ferry and passed through the Red's forest on the other side, they rode into the awesome wide open spaces. They could see for miles around and they felt small and unprotected.

"How can anyone live here?" Liza wondered. "Think of the winter. Snow blowing all around, nothing to stop it. I couldn't stand it!"

"Well, it's not that bad," Klaas explained. "They do build their own wind-breaks. They plant several rows of trees on the north and west sides of their farms. And just think of the many acres they can have. It will be a great grain-farming country. Myself, I think I would like it ."

"Oh Klaas," Liza shook her head, wonderingly.

"I wonder how Katie likes it by now....?" Gertrude mused without expecting an answer.

"I've been told that she lives by a little, winding river," Klaas told her, "so it won't look like this. But they can't all crowd to the rivers. If they want big farms, they have to spread out."

"Oh dear, I just would never have thought it was like this." Liza smiled at Gertrude, "I guess the men discuss things like that. Even the ground looks different," she added.

"Yes it is, too." Klaas stopped the horses and jumped down and scooped a handful of the rich, black earth. He let it dribble slowly through his fingers. "It's beautiful," he breathed. He looked up and away hiding the far-away look in his eyes, reflecting on his dream of owning fields of tall, thick, golden grain waving gently in the summer wind.

"Oh, come on Klaas, come back in the buggy. We have to get on," Liza reminded him. "And besides I heard that when it rains, the mud gets so heavy and sticky that even the horses can hardly move in it." Klaas sighed and resumed his seat. At his giddap and a light slap of the reins, the horses started forward.

"At least with horses," Klaas began quietly......

"What?" Liza asked loudly.

"Oh, nothing." he said.

"Is it much further?" Gertrude asked.

"From the river, it's about ten miles. After we pass the railroad station the first settlement we come to is Rosenort. I'll ask at the store for the way to George's farm," Klaas explained.

They needn't have worried that it was the right farm. When they turned into the yard, the screen door burst open and Katie came running out to meet them. Gertrude jumped off the rig and was the first to receive Katie's strong embrace.

"At last. I've waited for weeks!" Every day I said to George, today.....today she must come but you didn't, but now you are here." Katie then threw her arms around Liza. "This I hadn't expected—to see you too." To his surprise and pleasure, Klaas, too, was hugged and kissed. He looked at Liza with some embarrassment and she threw him a look which clearly said, see, I was right.

"But look at me, just standing here. Come in. I was just making supper. George is out behind the barn somewhere doing chores. Why don't you go around back and find him, Uncle Klass? He'll help you look after the horses."

As she held the door open for them, the women heard a baby's cry. Katie's eyes shone. "Howard wants his supper too," and she led the way to the bedroom.

"Howard?" Gertrude asked and when she saw Liza's eyebrows rising, she added quickly, before Liza could speak, "why Katie, what a nice name."

"Howard?" Liza echoed. "Hm.....hum.....," and shook her head.

"You see," Katie felt her aunt's silent reproof, "we thought it was about time to give new names. We're not the first. Every family has the same old names—Peter, John Henry, Isaac. Soon we won't know who anyone is talking about," she added somewhat defensively.

"Yes, and you're right," Gertrude agreed but Liza's dubious look lingered 'til she saw the baby. Then names didn't matter anymore. There he was, a beautiful creation, lying in the cradle, screaming and wriggling, his fists flailing wildly. Then Katie majestically swooped him up into her arms and miraculously the wailing ceased.

"Ah," Liza cooed, "he just wanted to be picked up. Here....." She reached out her arms. Katie proudly relinquished him. "He has a well shaped head. That's always a good sign.....and see how he can hold it.....and his back is straight and strong." It was everything that Katie wanted to hear.

Gertrude agreed and marvelled, to herself, at the bloom that motherhood had brought to Katie's plain, strong face.

After supper, Liza, aware of the small house, suggested casually that they could go somewhere else to spend the night. Katie would not hear of it. They had an upstairs, unfinished though it twas, with an extra bed. They would let the older folks have their bedroom. Liza promptly vetoed that suggestion. They should not move the baby. With an extra mattress, there was room for everyone. Klaas insisted that Liza and Gertrude share the bed and he would occupy the straw mattress. With an old blanket hung over a rope strung across the room serving as a partition, the women had a small measure of privacy.

Gertrude lay awake far into the night. Not until she had fallen in bed did she fully realize the extent of her fatigue. Every bone and muscle made itself known to her. The sensation of riding, jostling, swaying, the horses hooves beating rhythmically in her ears, would not leave her. She knew from the sounds of Liza's breathing and Klaas' occasional snores that her aunt and uncle had gone to sleep almost at once. Her undisciplined thoughts flitted aimlessly about, the places and people they had seen along their journey, Katie's new life, and ah yes, David Enns.

She had only seen him the once about a year ago, but now she was close to where he lived. She knew she would be seeing him.....but.....when at last she drifted into a fitful sleep, her thoughts turned into disjointed images becoming more and more bizarre as they danced in and out of the chambers and corridors of her dreams.

Chapter Seven

Liza, with her little bag of tricks, ready to drop the tiny seeds where ever she saw fit, hoping they would bear fruit and Klaas, benignly, blissfully unaware at her side, left Gertrude with Katie to embark on their visiting rounds. The girls, who had been impatient to see them go, waved them happily on their way. They looked at each other and a shyness overcame them as they thought of all the intimacies they were to exchange. They giggled nervously, then impulsively locked arms. Equilibrium restored, they returned to the house.

"Oh, Gertrude, I do hope you aren't going back with Uncle Klaas when they leave, are you?"

"Well, I can stay longer if you need me."

"We would like to hire you for a while. Would you consider that? You can see by the condition of my house and garden that I do need some help. We just haven't been able to find anyone. I have had no help since I had the baby."

"George has several sisters. Didn't they come and help out?"

"No they just won't come. I think the younger girls would, in fact I think they would enjoy it, but it's that Agnes."

"Agnes?"

"She's the oldest girl at home. Wait 'til you meet her! She thinks she is the boss. When her married sister, Katherine needs help, Agnes can't get one of the younger girls to her fast enough."

"That's awful! Yes, I'll stay, at least through the summer months," Gertrude promised.

"Oh, I'm so relieved. Thank you so much. We'll show that Agnes."

Gertrude's first project was the garden. It was over-run with weeds. As she weeded and hoed, she marvelled at the luscious growth of the vegetable rows that she was uncovering and at the rich, black loam she turned over with each stroke of the hoe the like of which she had never seen. She paused to gaze at the wide expanse of country. It was so strange to see the vastness of it as far as the eye could see. She felt sad for the prairie grasses and flowers that were being sacrificed to give way to the grain fields. The prairie kingdom was toppling in the wake of man's compulsion to force nature into subservience. The grain grew strong and bore abundantly, however, tillage had established a battle ground between the planted crops and the 'weeds'. What belonged had become the invader but the indigenous growth never gave up trying to reclaim its land. July had been humid with a relentless heat and frequent rain showers which had brought the grain to a thick, heavy growth. But now that August was here, the air had dried and the hot winds blew across the fields ripening them and hastening the harvest. Everything was pointing to a bumper crop.

When the garden was done, Katie came out to admire her beautiful patch of vegetables. "How wonderful! George won't believe it. By the way, he isn't home so I thought we might go out under the trees by the brook and eat our lunch."

They made a bed in a box for Howard and loaded him and their food onto a little wagon. Katie pointed out that David had made the wagon for them as a gift at the time of Howard's birth. With his belly round and full from his recent lunch, Howard fell promptly to sleep. Katie covered the box with a square piece of cotton to keep the flies and mosquitoes from disturbing him. They settled to their improvised picnic.

"How do you like your new home Katie?" Katie looked pensively down at her food. "Do you like.....I mean, *really* like it?"

"Of course, I do. I like being married to George and I like being a mother and having my own house but the rest, I have to get used to it. I haven't been here through the busiest season yet and it scares me a little. George says we do 'big' farming. We have to have all this hired help to get through harvesting and there's so much extra cooking. I'm certainly glad you'll be here. In fact, that's why George isn't here. He, Father Enns, and I think one of the boys, went to town to look for some extra help."

"Where is your town? We didn't pass one on the way here."

"No, you wouldn't. It's on up the river from where you crossed. It's about fourteen miles from here, a small town, English speaking. There are no Mennonites there at all. They have several stores and shops, a doctor too. We had him out when I had the baby. It was strange. We couldn't speak each other's language. The town is called Morris."

"Have you been there yourself?"

"Yes, I have but I didn't like it very much. We went into the stores but George had to do all the talking. They aren't very friendly—look at you as though there is something wrong with you. But, they have more to pick from, like dress goods and such, than the village store."

"You see Katie? Aren't you beginning to realize that we must all learn English?" Gertrude prompted.

"Ugh.....no. I have as much right to my language as they."

Gertrude did not wish to argue. She was as adamant in her opinion as Katie was in hers. Gertrude and Katie belonged to the first generation to be born in Canada and as far as Gertrude was concerned, it was their responsibility to conform to the language and ways of their country. In fact, although writing and reading were still almost impossible for her, she had made great strides in speaking English. Margret Fehr and her children had been her main teachers and Gertrude took every opportunity to practice when with them. Her goal was to someday speak with as little a trace of a foreign accent as possible. The children especially, had no qualms about correcting her mercilessly when needed, resulting in much shared laughter. "Gertrude, it's not 'wary' good, it's *very* good—it's not the 'vint' is blowing, it's the *wind* is blowing," and so it went. Gertrude was something of a natural mimic which also helped her to get her tongue around the Canadian accent.

When they had finished eating and felt relaxed and lazy, Katie opened up another subject. "One of these days, we'll have to go over to George's home and you can meet the rest of the family. It's less than a mile from here."

"Oh, I would like that, " Gertrude agreed quickly. "I'm very anxious to get to know the family you married into.

Do you get on with them—well everybody, that is, except Agnes? Have they been good to you?"

"Well.....well.....," after her hesitation, she jumped quickly into what she was sure of. "Father Enns has been and is very good to me. He makes me feel just like..... well.....just like as if he is my father. He always comes in when he is on the yard and asks how I am and makes a fuss over the baby."

A sharp pang of envy shot through Gertrude's body. Would she ever find a man who she would be willing to call 'father'? She didn't think so. The memory of her beloved Papa was still too real. Katie seemed to have slipped into it easily enough.

"I guess it would have been easier if George's mother had still been alive when I had the baby, at least I like to think so. But then you never know. It might be her mother that Agnes takes after. She certainly doesn't take after her father, that's for sure. I do like the younger girls but you can't get close to them. You can always feel Agnes's presence between them and you, even if she isn't there."

"Oh, poor Katie, it must be hard for you."

"Yes, it has been. But I'm learning to accept it and to get around Agnes even though I still feel hurt many times." She had reached out her hand to them with eager anticipation but it was not warmly grasped by the Enns women.

"Well, that takes care of the girls. How about George's brothers?"

"The men are a different story. There are two boys still at home, David and Peter. They are very nice. They often come over to give George a hand, so I actually know them better than the girls but you know boys, you can't get far with them in any case. There are two married ones, too."

"Oh, say, I remember there was Margaret Plett from our neighbourhood who married Henry Enns from here. Is he one of them?" Gertrude wondered.

"Yes, that's right. They live here but they are moving back to her parent's farm on the other side. Henry is the second oldest. They have no children. Margaret has not been happy here so everybody thinks it will be for the best all around. I'll miss her. We do have a lot in common—an enemy perhaps?" Katie laughed.

"Then there's one more?" Gertrude prompted.

"Yes, John. He lives close by too. He married a girl from around here, Mary Isaac. They have five children already. Oh, I hear George coming home so we'd best get to the house. I'll tell you more about John when we have more time. He should prove interesting to you I dare say." They gathered up their things and hurried to the yard. "And oh yes, the young girls are Martha, Maria and Sara," she hastened to add.

George was just turning on to the yard. His father was still with him and a stranger who no doubt was the new hired hand. Father Enns jumped lightly off the buggy and bounded toward the picnickers with great strides as was his wont—he never seemed to simply walk. After a quick look at his grandson, he took hold of the wagon's handle and walked them to the house. When they had unloaded, he took Gertrude's hand and grasped it firmly, warmly in his, welcoming her to Rosenort.

"So you're Gertrude. I can't tell you how good it is to have you here. Katie has needed someone from her family here very much." How very perceptive for a man Gertrude thought. "I can see it already has done Katie a world of good. She hasn't looked so well in a long time. You're the best medicine she could have had, Gertrude. We didn't see you two in church on Sunday. I'm sure every one was disappointed at not getting a look at Katie's pretty sister. I hope you'll be coming next Sunday."

"We'll be there," Katie said and Gertrude agreed with a nod.

Father Enns left and Katie went to the bedroom to perform the little miracles which babies require to make them comfortable. Gertrude laid the fire in the cook stove for the late afternoon coffee. As she bustled about the kitchen she glanced out the window and saw George and the new man come toward the house. The stranger was a tall rangy looking fellow, slim and broad shouldered. He was blond, very blond. She was used to blond. It was a characteristic of her nationality but he was much more blond than anyone she had ever seen before.

"Gertrude," George announced as they came in the door. "This is Sven." Gertrude nodded and when Katie appeared, George added, "My wife,Katie." Katie too, merely nodded shyly.

The men drank their coffee quickly and Sven left the house but George drew back at the door. He sidled up to Katie and gave her a surreptitious hug and a quick peck on the cheek.

"Oh George....." Katie pulled away and threw an embarrassed glance at Gertrude who was making out as if she had not seen.

"We'll be in for a late supper. Have some bedding ready so I can fix Sven's bed." To Katie's further discomfiture, he stole another kiss. Katie was grateful for Gertrude's impassivity and launched into an overly elaborate explanation of the room they had fixed up in the barn for the hired man.

The following day, Katie and Gertrude hitched one of the idle horses to the buggy and they went to the country store for supplies. Gertrude expressed surprise at her discovery that the tradesmen here were KIleine Gemeinde just like at Blumenort. On the way home, Katie mentioned that there was a good sized community of them just to the south. "What a coincidence!" Gertrude exclaimed.

As Katie further described the situation it was difficult to believe that here in Rosenort, as in Blumenort, the same situation existed and persisted despite the fact that it had now been many years since the schism in their original church. There was little social intercourse between the two sects and inter-marriage was an almost unheard of occurrence. Although there were many blood relatives between them their aloofness toward each other was like a public denial of kinship. The churches had never really forgiven each other. The bitterness festered between them. There were inherent physical characteristics which were similar and could not be denied but there were many superficial differences like the Kleine Gemeinde men being allowed to shave their facial hair and wear neckties. And the women were allowed to wear plain hats when going out in public but not in church. Neither Katie nor Gertrude had any idea what the more important theological differences were or if, in fact, there were any. Through the years more everyday differences grew out of the lack of influence each sect had upon the other.

Soon after the young ladies had returned home, Gertrude found herself alone in the kitchen when she heard a timid knock at the door. She opened it to find two young girls standing hand in hand, looking at her, their eyes squinting in the bright sunlight. Their faces were filled with unmasked curiosity.

"Hello. Is Katie home?" the older one asked.

"Why yes, she is, but come on in out of the heat. You must be Katie's little sisters."

"Oh, no, we're George's sisters," the smaller girl corrected her just as Katie came into the kitchen. The remark, though innocent, was not lost to Katie.

"Hello, girls," Katie greeted them, then indicating each one in turn, "this is Maria and this is Sara. Sara is the youngest in the family. My, how nice that you came to visit us."

"Father told us we had better go and see Katie's sister, or she might not come see us either," Sara started in immediately and without taking a breath continued. "Agnes said we had best stay home to take lunch out to the field but father said, no,we should come here. Actually, he told Agnes she could take the lunch out herself. He said it might do her good. So we hurried away before father left the house or….." Sara obviously had more to divulge but stopped, looking around uncertainly when she felt Maria's sharp tug at her sleeve.

Katie gave Gertrude a knowing look and Gertrude set about putting their visitors at ease and making friends with them. Gertrude was beginning to look forward to her stay in this new community.

* * * * *

Gertrude opened the lid of her trunk. She often referred to it lightly as her 'home'. She need merely to shut it and she was on her way. She eyed the contents listlessly.

The thunder storm of last night had sapped her energy. Since the storm, which had buried its sword into the heart of her family so long ago, the Penner children would, without fail, stop what they were doing or, if asleep would rouse at the first hint of a storm and sit watching with rigid, pale faces until it passed. When circumstances allowed they would gather and sit it out together. When separated from the others, which for Gertrude had been since Jennie went to live with Uncle Henry and Aunt Anna, each would keep their sad vigil alone. The situation never changed. Without a word, Katie and Gertrude had awakened and gone downstairs to sit. George, who understandably did not quite see the need of it, accompanied them. He was still willing to humour his young wife.

Gertrude went to the window—she breathed deeply—how quickly the world revived! The sky looked blue and innocent of last night's angry black force. How contrary that the earth should look cleansed and so beautifully rejuvenated when she felt so depleted.

Gertrude returned to the trunk. She must choose carefully what to wear for her first visit to the Rosenort church. She wanted to look her best. She pulled out her blue skirt. She held it up against her. Yes, she would wear it. It fitted so well. Daringly, she had gathered it at the back to simulate the bustle and made it to fit smoothly over the hips. It fell to a semi-fullness at the hem. It was wrinkled and she would have to put the iron to it when she went downstairs. She threw aside the ecru coloured, eyelet cotton blouse and chose the blue one. The sleeves were gathered at the top to hint at the mutton sleeve. She knew that she was skilled enough to create perfect replicas of the stylish clothes she had studied in the Eaton's catalogue. She sighed, rueing the fact that she and the other girls could only hint at the styles of the day but even these little hints elicited criticism from the older women. The chastisements which they received for these and other minor rebellions, such as not wearing their shawls around the house, were tempered by the hope that the girls would magically fall into line as soon as they married. Gertrude added a leather belt at the waist and a neat, little black tie at the neck—the finishing touch. She knew she looked good. As she went down the stairs, she laughed to herself. If only Albert Bartel could see me now!

As soon as their rig turned onto the church yard, Gertrude's eyes were drawn to a young woman; a rather handsome one as far as she could make out at that distance, standing near the church door. Her hair was black and thick, atop which was jauntily perched a modish straw sailor hat. That alone would draw anyone's attention midst the sea of black shawls around her.

Gertrude had been holding Howard during the ride so Katie scrambled down from the buggy first so Gertrude could hand him to her. George went to park the buggy and the sisters moved toward the church. Nodding in the direction of the straw hat, Katie said with raised eyebrows, "That's our Agnes!" A wealth of sarcasm spiced the spontaneous, private introduction.

"Oh," Gertrude answered lamely, "oh, of course—I should have guessed that, but then I hadn't quite pictured her like that. I had in mind a colourless, plain individual." They smiled at each other in mutual understanding. As they reached the door of the church, Agnes stepped forward and planted her feet firmly, directly in their path. Gertrude sensed Katie stiffen as they stopped.

"Well, Katie," Agnes began brusquely, without preamble, "you have certainly managed to hide your sister from us. Why haven't you brought her over to our place?" It seemed more like an accusation than an invitation.

"Well, we've been meaning to come—but we just haven't found the time. We....." Gertrude looked at Katie in surprise, missing the sharp retort which she half expected to hear from her lips.

"Pshaw," Agnes dismissed Katie's lame excuse with a wave of her hand. "You, I suppose, are Gertrude," she said, turning to Gertrude.

"Yes, this is my sister, Gertrude." Katie interjected.

Agnes reached out her hand and offered Gertrude a firm, strong handshake, but it lacked warmth and Gertrude felt chilled. As she slightly inclined her head to the left—a pose which, Gertrude learned later, Agnes had perfected by studying herself in the mirror—her dark, piercing eyes had an almost physical impact on Gertrude. A cool reserve involuntarily rose up in Gertrude—a reserve which Agnes, over the years, never succeeded in breaking down. In the right situations it could infuriate Agnes—Agnes the master of control.

"I hope you won't feel too out of place here in Rosenort after living in Blumenort all your life," Agnes stated.

"Oh, no," Gertrude answered cooly, "I like it here already."

They were attempting to move around Agnes, when another voice halted them. "Hello, Katie."

"Oh.....Peter....., Gertrude, this is George's brother, Peter."

Gertrude deftly turned her back on Agnes and saw the warm friendly smile on Peter's face. The rigid atmosphere around her melted away. She liked him at once and after a few words between them, Peter said to a young man standing quietly behind him, "David, come and meet Gertrude." Gertrude had to look up into his face and her heart beat faster as she realized that her first impression of him was only strengthened on seeing him again.

"Yes she said shyly, we met last year in Blumenort." David extended his hand to her giving her the second warm Enns smile of the morning.

"It's so nice to see you again." The four exchanged a few more words and then filed into church with the others.

On the way home, Gertrude maneuvered the conversation to the Ennses. Her curiosity had been thoroughly whetted.

"I was very surprised to see Agnes wearing a hat to church," Gertrude observed casually.

"Yes, well! she hasn't ever joined the church," Katie informed her with her old spirit restored.

"That's odd—isn't it?"

"Not for her, it isn't. I doubt if she ever will. George says she's too stubborn. He says when he was still at home, she often said it was the last thing she would ever do—right in front of her father, too, and him being a preacher and all. Now that George has left home, we don't hear too much about it. He and Agnes never did get along too good, so she isn't apt to run over and confide in him. Oh, but she dotes on David. I pity the girl who is ever going to marry him. As it is, she thinks none of her brothers wives are good enough for them."

"But," Gertrude persisted, "why won't she join the church?"

"Oh, don't ask me—George knows more about it than I."

"For one thing," George took up the ball Katie had tossed him, "she says she'll never stoop to going around and asking every one to forgive her." It was one of the requirements for preparing to enter the church—to cleanse one's soul of any sins they may have committed against anyone. Gertrude remembered her painful experiences of having to ask for this forgiveness and the equally embarrassing situations when she was the one being asked to do the forgiving. What had most of them done that would require such action? She knew that some were driven to invent wrongs, just so they could fulfil the penance. For the timid, it was pure torture; for the proud, it was degrading.

George laughed heartily. "What's the matter?" Katie asked.

"I was just thinking, if anyone has reason to ask for forgiveness it's Agnes, but she thinks she can do no wrong," he answered. "That aside, she actually tells the men in the family what she thinks is wrong with the church and argues points of religion with them!"

This Gertrude found very intriguing. In her experience, criticizing the church was unheard of. No matter what one thought, you never talked about it. If anyone did have doubts about church doctrine they kept them tightly to themselves so no one knew. This created the impression that there were no questioning souls among the Holdemans.

"How about David?" Gertrude, having her own concerns about some of the Holdeman teachings, was eager to learn where he stood on church issues. Did he think like Agnes? Although there was something that she admired about Agnes's honesty, she was having difficulty condoning such bold aggressiveness. "Does he belong to the church, I noticed that he isn't wearing a beard?"

"Oh, yes, he does, but he has a naturally sparse beard, so he trims what there is with scissors. His father gave him permission—as long as he doesn't shave."

Gertrude was relieved, but found it quite amusing at the same time, for she remembered the time when her sister Annie got married and she vowed to her Aunt Kathryne that she would never marry a man with a beard. She coloured at the memory and asked no more questions.

Neither Peter nor Katie volunteered any information about John during this discussion. It was later in her stay that Gertrude learned from Katie about John's disagreements with the church.

The weeks sped quickly by and the farm work became increasingly hectic. Sven remained with them while other hands came and went. Gertrude had never said more than 'hello' to him. He assumed that she, like Katie, spoke no English, so he directed all his remarks to George when in her presence. Gertrude began to feel guilty as she saw the loneliness growing in his eyes, but she did not know how to approach him.

The opportune moment came quite unexpectedly when Gertrude had gone to the barn for some chicken feed. She hurried out of the door just as Sven came rushing around the corner and they collided with enough force, that Gertrude landed on her seat, the chicken feed scattering all around her. She looked up at Sven and his astonished face sent her into peals of laughter. Seeing that she was not hurt, he too, began to laugh. In taking her hand to help her up, he let go of a gaping hole in his overall leg.

"Oh!" Gertrude burst out sympathetically, "you've torn your overalls!"

Sven forgot his embarrassment and looked at her with surprise, "Why, you *do* speak English."

"Just a little.....it is not very good. "

"Oh, but it is." he marvelled. "But you are shy..... "

"I will mend it for you, " Gertrude offered, pointing at the rip.

"If you just give me a needle and thread, " he began, "I....."

"No, no—after supper you bring them to the house. I will do them," she said firmly. She picked up what she could salvage of her chicken feed and hurried to the hen house.

They both knew that Sven would be leaving as soon as the fall work was done so now that they were talking, they made the most of what opportunity they had left to get to know one another better and practice their English. Sven, too, was new to the language. Gertrude learned about his homeland Sweden, and she explained the things about her people which he had not understood. After Sven left, Gertrude began thinking about going home. She broached the subject with Katie, who begged her to stay just a little longer. She wanted some work done on the house and with the extra help they would require, she would need her. So Gertrude promised to stay until the work was finished.

One morning, shortly after, George was sitting in the kitchen, his chair tipped back against the wall, his thumbs hooked around his overall straps, enjoying doing just nothing. It was a luxury which he had not been able to indulge in for a long time.

"George!" Katie broke into his complacency. Her imperious tone brought his chair down on all its four legs, his mouth fell open and he gasped at her speechlessly as she went on. "I will not go through another summer without a summer kitchen. Oh, what I went through with the flies and the heat—and the upstairs—it has to be made into rooms. We can't even ask anyone to spend the night here."

"But, your Uncle and Aunt stayed.....we had no....."

"Oh, George, you don't know how embarrassing it was."

"But.....but.....the work is too much for you. You are not yourself yet, since the baby."

"My health is just fine, thank you." George was inclined to agree with her. "And Gertrude is staying on."

"But how can I.....," George began lamely.

"You know, George, your brothers will help you. Don't they always?" She had subtly touched a sensitive nerve and he acquiesced.

Katie had learned that George was clumsy with tools. She herself, often did her own handiwork. Katie found that George was in the habit of asking his brothers for help when any project was beyond him. She had also noticed that he accepted compliments on the work done, as though they were his own efforts. Katie willingly participated in this little harmless ruse. By directing her praise at George she salved her conscience for using this mild form of blackmail when she wanted something done.

The work was duly begun. Gertrude was pleased at the opportunity of getting to know David and Peter better and their father, too, who often came to lend a hand. Gertrude was impressed with David's talent with tools. She admired his long, slender hands. Because of her secret admiration of him, she was self-conscious and shy in his presence. David, aware of her reticence, maintained a respectful reserve towards her. With Peter, however, she formed a free and easy relationship. She was reminded of her brother Joseph before he had become so sober and pious.

As the work was nearing completion, Gertrude's need to return to Blumenort became stronger. It would soon be Christmas, and she felt she had been away from home for an eon. She wanted some time to put into motion her plan to move to Winnipeg. The day of 'goodbyes' came too soon for Katie but Gertrude was not to be shaken again from her purpose.

George took Gertrude to the little station house which Gertrude had passed when she first came here with Klaas and Liza. They watched the cloud of black smoke approaching from the South and Gertrude's apprehension mounted. She had never traveled this route before, and wished for a companion to share it with her. She was to make a brief stop-over in Winnipeg. They checked her trunk to go in the baggage car and she hoped she would see it again. She almost fell into the first seat she came too for her arms were laden with her other various pieces of luggage, and her knees were weak. As she waved at George though the murky, grey film on the window, the train started with a jerk which almost threw her off her seat. She grasped the arms of her seat and held on until the train was well under way.

When she began to relax, she took a tentative look around and noted that there were only a few men here and there, sharing the car with her. They were, no doubt, transient workers just like she was, returning home, somewhere, for Christmas. She turned away from the noncommittal faces of the men and the depressing interior of the car which at one time must have been beautiful, luxurious and even gay looking, but now was only drab and dull from the dust and grime that had been gathered along the way. She turned her thoughts inward. She thought of Katie—how her marriage was so different from Annie's. Katie had found a man whom she could manipulate even though it all seemed to be accomplished in a congenial and happy atmosphere. But, Annie—had she too found what was best for her—maybe what she actually needed? She had never thought about it that way before. Could it be that her pity for Annie had been misplaced? Fate must, after all, be playing a part in drawing together people who needed each other. She looked candidly at herself. Neither of these partnerships appealed to her. Her ideal was an equality between two beings—would that be too difficult to find? She feared she would not be satisfied with less. She began to think of George's brother John. They had little more than met but he had made a deep impression on her. He was a handsome man with a remote, far-away look in his grave eyes.

It had been quite some time before Katie had gotten around to discussing him with Gertrude and her curiosity had mounted. It seemed to her that Katie drew back from the subject. But the day did come when Katie finally opened up to Gertrude's questions.

* * * * *

"Well, it's not pleasant to hear, but if John doesn't change, he is going to find himself put right out of the church!"

"Katie!" Gertrude was shocked. "What are you saying? Whatever could he be doing to deserve that?"

"It's.....it's not that he has done anything....," Katie stopped.

"For heaven's sake, Katie, what then? Don't just sit there!" Gertrude almost exploded, "What could it be?"

"Well, it's not that he has sinned exactly.....you know, actually sinned the way we usually think of it.....it's so hard to explain.....I don't even like to talk about it." She dropped her voice to a mere whisper and looked furtively around even though she knew they were alone in the house. "He has been reading books on another religion!"

"Oh, is that all?" Gertrude sank back in relief and slowly exhaled the breath she had been holding.

"Is that *all*?" It was Katie's turn to explode. "Is that all you can say? I can tell you it has everybody worried—that is everyone in the family—I don't think it has gone any further. But you never know. In these small communities you can't breathe without it getting around. So, please don't mention it to anyone."

"Oh, I won't," Gertrude promised. "But how did this all get started—I mean, his reading the books?"

"He and David used to teach school in communities south of here," Katie made a vague, wide sweep of her hand, "amongst Mennonites, too, but not our kind. Some of them had already left their particular Mennonite church and gone over to this new religion. John showed some interest I guess, and they gave him these books. They were written centuries ago by some man called Swedenhoff - or - Swedenborg or something. Imagine! Books on religion. Ha! Isn't that stupid, when everyone knows that all we need is the bible?"

"How does Mary feel about it?" Gertrude wondered.

"She doesn't say much to anyone, but I'm sure she tries to get him to stop it. There's one thing I'm pretty sure of and that's that Agnes must be reading them, too. That's likely where she gets so many of her outlandish ideas."

"I don't think you should feel so strongly about it, Katie. How could that lead to being put out of church?"

"Oh, Gertrude, you just don't understand. But then I knew you wouldn't. That's why I didn't like to tell you but you mark my words, there's going to be trouble." For now, Gertrude decided to let the matter drop.

* * * * *

Gertrude leaned back and closed her eyes. As she thought about John, her interest was thoroughly aroused. What exactly was John finding in these books? She wished she knew. He must be finding some answers to his questions. She couldn't even begin to think about answers until she had untangled her thoughts enough to know what her questions were. She wished John luck, for, somehow, her sympathies were with him.

Gertrude's quest for something more than what was at hand, lay deep and mostly unspoken within her, shrouded painfully by the veil of her heritage.

Chapter Eight

Gertrude stepped down from the train in Winnipeg and went into the station. Knowing that she would have a wait before her next train was to leave for the country, she selected a seat with a good view of the waiting room. She placed her bags and boxes in a neat pile at her feet. She tugged and patted her somewhat rumpled clothes into a semblance of neatness, took a disciplining swipe at a stray lock of hair, then settled herself decorously into her seat. Her lively interest wound effortlessly among the varied assortment of travellers. Their dress spoke of many nationalities which Gertrude, in her ignorance, could not place. Many were alone—most of them men—but here and there were family groups. The one thing most of them had in common was the look on their faces—immobilized expressions of patient weariness due to long waits and slowness of travelling. Gertrude was the only woman sitting alone.

Her eyes were drawn to a family at the door to the street. They were obviously waiting for a carriage. The father, mother and three children were all dressed in the height of fashion. There appeared to be a wide difference in the age of the children. The youngest child was romping and running about in a carefree display of innocent amusement. He was not restrained or chided by the others who looked on indulgently. What a contrast to the family sitting a few benches away from Gertrude. They, too, were father, mother and three children. It was a much younger family, the children, close in age. They sat pressed together, surrounded with bulging bags, bundles and boxes bound with heavy twine. Their clothes were thick and serviceable, nothing more. The children sat still with wide unblinking eyes, although Gertrude detected their occasional slight wriggles which drew their parents instant, scowling disapproval. The second family reminded her uncomfortably of her own people, but it was watching the first family that strengthened her resolved to return to Winnipeg to find work in one of the fine houses she and Bertha had so admired when they went to Winnipeg that second time, which now seemed so long ago. Today, Gertrude was unaware that circumstances would conspire to keep her from fulfilling her dream for more than another year.

After her three hour layover in Winnipeg, Gertrude boarded the train again and arrive at Steinbach Station, the little siding that served as the sole train stop for the village of Steinbach, several miles to the south, and the other Mennonite communities to the west, including Blumenort. Because of their need to remain as isolated from outside influence as possible, the Mennonite settlers did not allow the rail line to pass directly through any of their villages.

She was picked up by Jake and taken to Klaas and Liza's where she was to stay for the next little while until she decided what to do next. In mid January, she succumbed to Annie's pleas and agreed to go to her place for one week to help with a backlog in the family sewing which Annie had let pile up. Near the end of the week, Annie and Gertrude were having afternoon coffee and Annie took the opportunity to put the final pressure on Gertrude to stay longer.

"Gertrude, you know what a hard time I have keeping up with the work around here and it's getting more and more difficult to find girls who will work for us. It would be such a help if you would stay for the rest of the winter." As Annie spoke, Gertrude was reliving some of the details of her year as Jacob's employee. After all, as Annie had pointed out, it was Jacob who employed her . He ruled with a heavy hand, dictating Gertrude's every move. Because this week focused on sewing she had had little to do with Jacob but even so there was no escape from evening bible reading and prayers. Just thinking about having to attend those nightly rituals for the rest of the winter made Gertrude cringe.

"Gertrude, please reconsider."

"I haven't decided what I'm going to do so I can't make any commitments." Gertrude certainly wasn't about to share with Annie any of her thoughts on moving to Winnipeg to work.

"That doesn't make any sense. You have to work somewhere so why can't it be for me?"

Gertrude felt as though she were being backed into a corner. How could she tell Annie that she would never again agree to be part of Jacob's household? Then, she thought of a response that she knew Annie would not be able to accept. "Last time I worked for you I ended up doing mostly outdoor work. I won't do outdoor work anymore unless I get paid a man's wages to do it."

"Gertrude! That's outrageous! Jacob would never pay you as much as he pays the hired men." Annie paused, her eyes narrowing, a look of suspicion creeping into her face. "You know, Gertrude, it seems like there is something different about you lately. You're not the same as you used to be and I don't like it."

Gertrude could feel her anger mounting and she knew that it was just about time for Annie to burst into tears. Ignoring Annie's last comment she said, "Annie, you cannot change my mind about this." Gertrude's tone of voice made it clear that the discussion was over.

Annie burst into tears.

Gertrude got up from her chair. "I'm going back to my sewing." She left the room.

In February, Klaas, Liza, Pete and his new bride (who came from Rosenort, much to Liza's satisfaction) travelled to Alberta, leaving Mary, Gertrude and Jake in charge of the farm. For the last year, in spite of Liza's objections, Klaas had been quietly looking for a buyer to purchase their farm and now he had closed a deal which would involve transfer of title in June. Liza had put up a good fight to stop the move but in the end had had to give in to the men in her family. The new owner would take over the planting of the crop for this coming spring and the Toewses would have the time to finalize their affairs and organize their move. Klaas had been corresponding with several people in Alberta and he had lined up two available farms which he was certain would meet with his requirements.

Three weeks later, they returned, the proud owners of a 'big farm' just about 50 miles north west of Calgary. Even

Liza seemed enthusiastic.

Gertrude's work was cut out for her during the next few months helping the Toews family put closure to life on their Blumenort homestead. The day of their departure was a sad one for Gertrude. They said their goodbyes at Steinbach Station. One by one she shook hands with each of them but when it came to Aunt Liza, they embraced, clinging to each other in a hug that neither of them wanted to end. She watched the train leave. The people who were the closest thing she had to family since mama and papa died were waving to her from the open train windows. They were leaving and she had no idea when, if ever, she would see them again. She waved both hands vigorously but as the train disappeared from view, she felt the strength in her arms disappearing too. Her wave dwindled as her arms slowly lost their momentum and became still at her sides.

Gertrude had moved her trunk to the Fehr's two days ago. She thought she would stay with them for about two weeks and then she would leave for Rosenort to help Katie with her second baby. While with the Fehrs she was going to pay one more visit to Aunt Kathryne before leaving for Rosenort. Her Aunt had been in fragile health but recently seemed to be rallying, closer to her old self.

Margaret was still the only person that Gertrude had confided in about her plan to work in Winnipeg. They were going to study the latest Eaton's catalogue to pick out a dress they would recreate for Gertrude to wear when she went job hunting. So now she climbed into the Fehr's buggy and drove herself back to their farm.

"We need to make something that is a combination of plain enough to be suitable for a country girl looking for a job as a housemaid but at the same time has a slightly stylish flare to it so that it will set you apart. A country look with a bit of big city." Margaret was rising to the task with relish.

Gertrude thought she understood exactly what Margaret was saying. As they flipped through the pages, Gertrude stopped. She was looking at a page of shirtwaist dresses. "How about something liker this?"

"Yes, I think so but we would have to make the pleats in the skirt less flared to get the effect we are looking for." Then they went to the dress goods section and picked out a fabric described as dark blue grey.

"Now, what about a hat? I definitely can't wear my Holdeman black shawl." They went to the ladies' hat section. "Oh my, these all look too fancy."

Margaret agreed but then pointed one out. It was small, made of black felt and shaped something like the popular small summer straw hats with a little cluster of flower-like shapes on the brim that looked like they were made of the same felt as the hat but probably a bit lighter in colour.

"If we order this one, remove the flowers, and replace them with a band of plain, black ribbon we will have what we want."

They enjoyed the leisure time they had together while waiting for their Eatons order to arrive after which it only took three more days to sew the dress and modify the hat. They spoke only English and to everyone's satisfaction, Gertrude's vocabulary and accent showed steady improvement. Even the children were impressed. The outfit was finished. Filled with hope for her future, Gertrude was ready to leave for Rosenort.

It was a busy time on George and Katie's farm. With a new baby in the household, Howard demanding his share of attention and harvest season almost upon them, Gertrude was kept busy. She stayed through to the end of October. There was little time for socializing accept Sundays after church. She took these opportunities to exchange a few pleasantries with the Enns men while keeping her contact with Agnes to a minimum which was not all that difficult because Agnes was attending church less and less. When the men made their appearances at George's farm to help George out, there was little time for visiting. Father John Enns did take time to sit for a few minutes here and there and share a cup of coffee with Katie and Gertrude when he could. It was after one of these times with Father Enns that Katie chose to finally say something more about John's 'folly'. He had refused to give up his Swedenborg books. Quite the contrary, he insisted on arguing theology with the church elders. It took several stormy sessions of the Brotherhood Council. They eventually agreed. They had no choice. He was excommunicated.

"Can you imagine?" Katie expostulated. "He is actually saying that the bible should not be taken literally! He has a word that I can't remember but I think it means that the bible says one thing but means another."

"Does that mean that John has to completely relearn the bible?" Gertrude asked somewhat incredulously.

"I don't know and I don't want to know. I find the whole thing horrifying."

"Did they put Mary out of the church too?" Gertrude wondered.

"No, they didn't and Mary is staying in."

"I wonder why. It seems to me that if I were she I'd....."

"Well, it isn't you," Katie interrupted testily.

"But what could be their reason for keeping her in?"

"George told me—in the strictest confidence, mind you—that they expected she would not share the table with him."

"In their own home? Surely not!"

"Oh yes, but that's not all. It was even suggested that she should not share his bed....." Now it was Gertrude's turn to be horrified as she started to understand how this tactic was meant to force John back into the church.

"I know that she doesn't approve of what John does, but she is standing by him. She pays no attention to what they are telling her to do. But it is very hard for her. And Agnes, of course, is trying to stir up the pot. She even accused Mary of trying to force John to return to the church and it infuriated Mary. Agnes would just have loved to have been at the council meetings in the midst of the fighting, but since she isn't a church member she couldn't go. Good thing, too, I would say." Katie closed her mouth, her lips pressed closely together. She had said enough.

Gertrude was badly shaken. Hearing about her people's apparent cruelty toward John and Mary was a distasteful revelation to her. It was well that she could not foresee the future. So far, she had no idea that she too, was to become embroiled in the same cause which John Enns had started.

Chapter Nine

There, before her eyes, was the house! It was just like she had pictured it, with the fancy trim, the big porch all across the front and along the sides and the large front windows with little panes of coloured glass in sections along the top. It was a tall house, three stories, or more aptly described as two and a half. In an uncharacteristically bemused state, her good sense having deserted her, she was certain that she would have turned back had it not been exactly as she had pictured it. She stepped down off the rig that had brought her here with her new employer, and stood still, gazing, lost in thought.

* * * * *

Gertrude had reached the city the day before and had been directed by a kindly caretaker at the station, to the 'Girl's Home of Welcome', a hostel for women. There she could spend the night and they would direct her as to how to find employment. At the hostel, she was given a bed and for an extra, small sum, she was also offered supper. She was told that she was bound to obtain work almost immediately for there was great and constant demand for domestic help. The wages, too, were good, they said—ten or fifteen dollars a month. Gertrude thought of the thirty dollars she had earned for the entire year at her sister Annie's. She was tired and went to her bed as soon as she had eaten but found it difficult to fall asleep—what would face her tomorrow? When, at last, she did sleep, she was awakened countless times by the unfamiliar sounds of the restless, sleepless city outside her window.

In the morning, wearing her new hat and her new dress underneath her coat, Gertrude found her way to the employment office where, upon entering, she was directed by an unsmiling, austere individual, to a door which was lettered with the terse words, 'Women's Dept.' She opened the door and saw that there were already several women sitting stoically on the benches placed along the bare, cold walls. She chose a seat beside a middle-aged woman who had a kindly, motherly look about her. She noted that the surroundings were simple but adequate for their function. Behind a wooden fence with a swinging gate, were several women who were busily engaged at their work, never giving her as much as a glance. She was wondering if she should go over and speak to them, when she was nudged by the woman beside her.

"Have you been here before?" she asked in a whisper.

"No," Gertrude whispered back.

"I thought so." The woman shook her head sympathetically. Gertrude was somewhat chagrined at being so easily labeled. "You have to go up to the desk and give your name," the woman explained.

Gertrude rose determinedly and walked briskly to the fence. After some time and when her spirits had begun, visibly, to sag, the lady at the nearest desk looked up brightly from her work and chirped, "Yes, what can I do for you?"

Gertrude was startled but lest she be further ignored, she spoke rapidly, "I've come to work.....to find work."

"Ah—yes," she looked at her, her eyes squinting speculatively, tapping her teeth with her pencil. Abruptly she seemed to have come to a conclusion and motioned Gertrude to come through the gate. "Come here and sit down beside me and we will fill out the form."

'The form' had a formidable ring to it, She waited for what would follow.

"Name?"

"Gertrude....." The lady wrote it down and with poised pencil, looked up expectantly.

"Uh.....Gertrude.....Gertrude Penner." Why was she giving the impression that she couldn't remember her own name? She took a deep breath. Why should she be so nervous? These people are merely working for a living, just like she.

"Address?"

"I came from Blumenort."

"In Manitoba?"

"Yes."

"Age?"

"I am twenty five," she answered wondering why all this should matter.

"Now then, what kind of work do you do?"

"House work.....any kind of work in the house."

"Domestic servant," the lady murmured, writing on her paper.

"Have you any references?" At Gertrude's questioning look, she clarified, "Where did you work before?"

"I have not worked in the city before.....only on the farm.....all kinds of work....." She was hesitant and becoming somewhat disheartened. Maybe working on the farm would not qualify her for work in the city.

"Oh.....I see.....well," her feigned doubt was for effect. She well knew there was a high demand for girls from the country. They were generally known to be hard working. Then, rising with an air of dismissal, she said, "Now if you'll just take a seat, we will see what we can do."

Gertrude returned to her former seat, relieved and more at ease. "Do you just sit here and wait?" she asked her neighbour.

"That's best. You get on much quicker.....sooner, that way. When someone comes in for a maid, they pick from what's here first—it's simpler than to get in touch with you if you leave." So Gertrude settled back to wait as the others were doing. "You usually get hired the first day," she assured Gertrude.

Gertrude regarded the girls behind the fence with some awe. They were so zealously intent on what they were doing. Clad in plain, white shirtwaists and black skirts, they wore their hair alike—swept high into severe pompadours into which they repeatedly thrust their pencils without disturbing a hair.

In the course of the morning, more women and girls came until the benches were filled. A number were hired but by noon, Gertrude had not been considered. Her bench companion asked her to go out with her for lunch. Seeing Gertrude's reluctance to leave, she assured her that no one was apt to come in at noon—they would hurry back.

While at lunch, she told Gertrude not to feel bad at her lack of success so far. She explained that most of those who had come in to hire were 'regulars'. She intimated that you were best off not to get hired by regulars because they were the ones who were hard to work for—that's why they came in so often looking for girls. She added that many of the girls were also 'regulars'. (The women in the office were well aware of the situation and they operated on the assumption that the two deserved each other and skilfully steered them together. Alas, it was a never-ending circle, but then, it was not their worry.) Gertrude was wondering if her companion was a regular, when the woman confessed that she, herself, was forced to come quite often—not for the usual reasons, of course. Most of the others were lazy good for nothings—a slovenly lot. *She* only left a job under unavoidable circumstances, such as an 'act of God'. Gertrude was not familiar with the expression and she had never before heard God mentioned in such a flippant manner either.

It was early in the afternoon when Harry Stanton walked in. Gertrude liked the look of him at once and found herself hoping that he would choose her. He was young and handsome. He had dark hair and eyes and he wore a dashingly, trim moustache. His brow, furrowed in evident annoyance at his errand did not hide the undeniable friendliness in his eyes. After a short consultation, the girl who had taken Gertrude's application looked around the room, her eyes sweeping expertly, unwaveringly over the varied assortment of job seekers. Then, without a flicker of an eyelash, they returned to rest on her, Gertrude. She rifled quickly through the papers she held and then, shattering the pregnant silence, called out clearly, "Gertrude Penner!" Gertrude rose proudly to meet the man who subsequently hired her and now she was about to enter his house.

The house faced the sun. Aunt Kathryne always said that a house should face the sun. That gave it a look of welcome, even before the door was opened. It penetrated the walls and warmed the hearts of the people within. Even though it was still January, its warm rays had melted a little bit of the snow from around the base of the house. She was already realizing that city snow behaved differently than country snow. She felt an eternity away from the countryside which she had left only yesterday. There the snow lay thick and heavy over the fields, the mountainous drifts around the farm yards giving no indication of yielding their imposing positions. Until she would see her home again, Gertrude would have the feeling that she had stepped from winter into spring.

Gertrude suddenly became aware that her feet were cold. The hem of her skirt was damp. She looked at Mr. Stanton, who was smiling at her with some amusement. "Well, this is it," he said as though he had read the disbelief on her face. He picked up her bags and motioned for her to follow him to the back of the house.

"Ellie!" he shouted, as Gertrude held open the door for him, then followed him into the kitchen.

"Ye-es, coming.....oh, Harry, I see you found someone. Thank goodness. I was almost beside myself.....no, don't put the things down. Take them right up to her room."

"Alright, Ellie, but, first, this is Gertrude..... Gertrude.....?" he faltered.

"Penner." Gertrude finished for him.

"Good afternoon, Gertrude. I'm certainly happy to see you!" The worried expression with which she had swept into the room disappeared into a broad smile which transformed her rather plain face into near beauty. Gertrude saw that her new mistress was tall, slim and, she thought, carried herself in a manner befitting the lady of so fine a house.

Mr. Stanton relinquished part of his load to Gertrude, upon her insistence, and they followed Mrs. Stanton who lightly preceded them up the stairs which led from the kitchen, past the second floor and on up to the garret at the top. Mrs. Stanton opened the door leading to a small room which was to be Gertrude's for the duration of her service here.

"You may remove your wraps and put your things away and when you come down, I'll explain your duties and show you the house. Don't hurry—you might take a little rest before coming down," she added for she could see the weariness in Gertrude's pale, drawn face. "I'm glad you came, Gertrude," Mrs. Stanton said with a smile. "I do hope you will like it here," and with that the door closed gently behind her new employers.

Gertrude was grateful for the little time to herself. She threw off her hat and coat and stretched out full length on the bed. She felt the tension which had been mounting gradually in the last few days, slowly drain out of her body. She closed her eyes and a tear slipped out of one corner and made its way down her temple. The relief of easy tears was not hers. She often envied the more indulgent of her sex the luxury of theirs. So ignoring the uninvited tear, she opened her eyes wide, folded her arms beneath her head and took stock of the room. She liked the low sloping ceiling in which was tucked a small, recessed window. It was dressed in a white, ruffled curtain. The window looked out upon the street and beneath it was a built in seat. Later, she discovered that a lid opened and revealed it to be a chest. From the centre of the ceiling, hung a twisted wire with a bare, glass globe at the end. She would have her own electrical light! What a miracle, to pull the chain and flood the room with light! There would be no lamp chimneys, blackened with soot, to clean. How she had always detested that chore. The walls were papered in a gay floral design. In the corner, stood a small wardrobe; beside it, a wash stand with a white basin and pitcher. The only other furniture was a straight backed chair.

After some time, Gertrude put away her things and then went slowly down the stairs. She was in the kitchen again, but now, in the middle of the floor, stood a dainty little creature whom she had not seen before. The bright eyes, in the eager, shining face, were looking out at her with open curiosity.

"Well.....hello," Gertrude said.

"Hello. I've been waiting for you to come down. Mama said you would come down when you were rested. I guess you were very tired. That's why it took you so long." She stopped for breath. "I'm Dodo. I'm four years old."

"Dodo?"

"My name is really Dorothy Anne Stanton but they call me Dodo," she explained.

"That is a very pretty name. Mine is Gertrude." She wondered if there were more like her but she found that Dodo was her only charge. She stood uncertainly, wondering what she should do when Mrs. Stanton came bustling in and pointed out the most important areas of the kitchen. It was, of course, one of the rooms where she would spend a lot of her time. There were many secrets yet to be discovered.

Mrs. Stanton led her into the pantry which separated the kitchen from the dining room. It was a well worn trail with cupboards and drawers at either side and a pair of swinging doors at each end. Gertrude was shown the entire house, all the while being informed of her expected duties. As she tried to remember all the information Mrs. Stanton was giving her, she had to force herself not to feel completely overwhelmed.

The rooms were large and high ceilinged with tall windows, which were hung with lace curtains and heavy, dark drapes. The furniture looked cumbersome, with curved, ornately carved legs and rich plush upholstery. The sliding doors of the dining room and a like pair into the parlour, faced each other across a wide entrance hall from which rose a stair case with an ornate balustrade. In days to come with duster in hand, Gertrude realized that many of the pictures on the walls in the parlour and dining room were actually original paintings. Yet another something she had never seen before. She couldn't resist the temptation to touch the irregular surface made by the artist's brush strokes. In one corner of the dining room there were three pipes painted white rising out of the floor and disappearing through the ceiling to the second floor, announcing to those in the know that the house was equipped with running water and access to the city's sewer system. Another room, which they entered beneath the stair way, was referred to as Mr. Stanton's den but it was clearly much lived in by the rest of the family with news papers, magazines and toys strewn about. It was the only room with a homey atmosphere. Two of the walls were lined with floor to ceiling shelves full of books. Ah what mysteries must be contained between the covers of those books! Gertrude made a mental note to get to work learning to read English. Upstairs were four bedrooms and a bathroom. It was the bathroom which made the biggest impression on her—she had never been in a house with one before. She was to find later, that as part of her employment, she was allowed one bath a week in the grand white tub with the big claw-like feet. A whole tub of water all to herself to leisurely soak in! What a difference from the primitive bathing arrangements on the farm.

In the next weeks, Gertrude began learning the reality of the taxing routine required to keep house in the lavish Stanton establishment. The beautiful furnishings and drapery lost much of their glamour to the hours of dusting and brushing they required. Her admiration for the stylish clothes, dimmed considerably as her feet and back suffered through the long hours at the ironing board while she meticulously pressed the ruffles and laces to meet the demands of her mistress. At times she was tempted to flee in the face of each new day. But she kept telling herself that it was bound to get easier with time. The days, from early morning until late in the evening, demanded all of the energy and time she had to give.

When Gertrude first came to the Stantons, she was told that she would have each Thursday afternoon and one Sunday a month as her time off. For the first few Thursdays, just to retire to her room to rest and relax, was enough. She would mend or do some hand sewing or leaf through the newspapers and magazines which she took up to her room.

By sheer force of will and determination, she was teaching herself to read English by association of events which she had heard discussed and the pictures which were part of the articles. But as the days started to become longer and brighter with the approach of spring, she became restless. The only time when she had been away from the house, was when, weather permitting, she, in the line of her duties, had taken Dodo for short walks down the street or to the little park nearby. She learned that little ladies did not leave the yard unattended and were carefully chaperoned away from home. Gertrude enjoyed these little sallies as much as Dodo. She was seldom irritated by Dodo's incessant prattle. It was an education in itself to listen to the child who was remarkably grown up for so little a person. Dodo's unquestioning acceptance of Gertrude, gave Gertrude new confidence in her mastery of the English language. She was finding, too, that learning to read English was helping her to express her thoughts more clearly.

Mrs. Stanton, who was very anxious to keep Gertrude contented in her place with them, had been wondering what she could suggest to encourage Gertrude to step out of her shell. So one Thursday morning, she decided she would do something about it. "It's such a lovely day, Gertrude, just perfect to go out. Have you decided what you are going to do today?"

"Well, no, I haven't made any plans."

"Have you met the girl who works for the Smith's next door?"

"No," Gertrude shook her head, "but I have seen her in the back yard."

"Well, we'll just have to remedy that." This could be the answer Mrs. Stanton thought as she went on, "I'll go over with you and we'll get acquainted. I don't know her last name, but they call her Tilly. She looks like a very nice, well-mannered girl. The Smith's think very highly of her. She has her Thursday afternoons off, too, and maybe you could do something together.....maybe go downtown or something.....you must have shopping to do....."

It was thus that Gertrude's friendship with Tilly Rempel, began. Upon hearing Tilly's last name, Gertrude knew at once that they would have at least one thing in common, for the name conveyed to her that Tilly, too, was Mennonite. From that first day, Gertrude and Tilly spent most of their days off in each other's company. They made their plans in advance, over the back fence or during the occasional visits they paid each other in the evenings.

They discovered many things about each other. Tilly was, as Gertrude suspected, a Mennonite from a sect located south west of Winnipeg near the American boarder. They shared a common history with the Holdemans and the Kleine Gemeinde dating back to Menno Simons's teachings in Holland and the migrations to Germany, Russia and Canada. They also spoke the same dialect, but as they discovered, with many subtle differences. Gertrude's people referred loosely to them as Bergthallers. They knew little about the Bergthallers but did view them as far too worldly to really be considered part of the Mennonite fold.

Tilly's family had come to Winnipeg several years earlier when Tilly was just a young child. In fact, members of Tilly's sect were among the first of the Manitoba Mennonites to forsake the agricultural life for urban living. Winnipeg absorbed many of them in the years to come.

When together, Gertrude and Tilly spoke mostly English.

Their dialect seemed out of place in the Winnipeg setting. But when they did use their own language they were delighted and amused at the varied twists in pronunciation and phrasing which came to light in their common tongue. These differences, as well as numerous other customs, had become localized through lack of communication and were the distinguishing marks of their separate cultures.

Their routines were briefly interrupted by the prodigious task of the annual spring cleaning. Had that come at the beginning of her employment, it is doubtful that Gertrude would have survived the ordeal. The daily grind was completely dwarfed by the yearly frenzy of the spring ritual. It was an operation which required all the brawn and ingenuity that the women of the day could muster. In this, Mrs. Stanton worked along with Gertrude. Sun, air and lye soap were their greatest allies. The walls, curtains and windows were washed, the floors polished, the rugs, drapes, bedding and winter clothes had to go out to be aired, shaken and beaten. The chorus of slamming screen doors and groaning clothes lines echoed in unison up and down the street. For many days the back yards revealed to the discerning eye, the status of the occupants of each house.

When things returned to normal, Gertrude and Tilly continued to explore the city. They would ride the street cars and get off at random and walk until they were tired and then catch another car. They indulged endlessly in window shopping and browsing in the shops and departments stores. In the evenings, after their Thursdays, Tilly usually went home to her family for supper and Gertrude returned to her room at the Stanton's. Gertrude liked the time to herself. Tilly invariably invited Gertrude to her parent's home and though she went occasionally, she usually declined with the explanation that she did not wish to wear out her welcome. The truth of the matter was that Gertrude's reticence stemmed from the fact that she felt hopelessly out of place with the Rempels.

They were a large family. The children filled the entire gamut of ages from toddler to early twenties. The head of the family was a huge, bear-like man, with a low slung posterior. His bushy, unkept beard did not muffle his rough tongue and loud speech. He worked intermittently at odd jobs, and spent the rest of his time between the saloon and his well worn chair which no one else dared occupy. From his shabby throne, he argued, mostly about politics, with his two grown sons until the fumes of his earlier imbibing anaesthetized his thinking processes and he fell into a fitful, noisy sleep.

The sons seemed no more inclined to work at steady jobs than their father. They were more a clutter than a presence in the room, tilting back their chairs, insolently propping their feet on the table, smoking vile smelling, cheap tobacco. Their motley group of friends hung about at all hours of the day, and, according to Tilly, often into the early hours of the morning, showing no more respect for their surroundings than their hosts. Tilly tried to explain to Gertrude the gist of the men's discussions but she said most of it was entirely over her head. They apparently were against all or most forms of government. She said that they blamed the rich for the fact that they were poor and had to work so hard to scrape together a living. Gertrude made a mental note to herself. I must make a point of learning more about the governments of Manitoba and Canada

Tilly's mother was a thin, emaciated woman whose back was bent and whose face was etched in lines of unhappiness. She had an insatiable compulsion to clean her house. She scrubbed the bare, wooden floors until they were almost white from the strong soap which reddened and roughened her hands. Her stove and her pots were spotless from constant scouring. But she could not cleanse the tainted, polluted air which hovered about the small house. The men never spoke to her except to order her to fulfil their wants.

The girls were sent out to work as soon as they were barely old enough, to whatever menial labour they could find and were expected to bring their wages home without fail. Gertrude became painfully aware of another aspect of the disrespect the men held for the women who came into the house. She was not excluded from the meaningful glances they exchanged and the narrowed eyes with which they looked the women over. It left Gertrude feeling stripped and unclean. It was only when the men left the house, that Gertrude enjoyed her visits there.

One day, Tilly confided her desperate hope that she would not end up in a situation similar to her mother's but she did not know how to avoid it.

"When I see the kind of family life my friends have, I say to myself, that's what I want," Tilly said sadly. Gertrude had visited some of Tilly's friends and their families and she knew what Tilly meant. The atmosphere in those families was so different from what she had seen at the Rempels.

Gertrude tried to reassure her that she would be able to find a way to live a better life but her own lack of experience prevented her from offering any tangible advice. Gertrude wondered what qualifications were needed to find jobs like the women at the employment office. Did they earn enough money to support themselves on their own? Neither of them knew, so their discussions about Tilly's future tended to go nowhere. She told Gertrude that she had managed to finish several years of education before being sent out to work so she did have a working ability in reading and writing English which would be an asset in finding other than domestic work. As they spoke of Tilly's future, Gertrude was also silently thinking about her own. So far Gertrude had managed to support herself without having to depend on a man but her jobs always included a roof over her head and three meals a day. If she continued on her own, did she want to do housework for the rest of her life?

Gertrude had been in Winnipeg about four months when she decided it was time she bought some new clothes. She was tired of looking like the girl from the country on her days off. She and Tilly had window-shopped long enough. Gertrude had saved most of her wages and Tilly confessed to her that she, too, had put some money by. She had not told her family of her last raise in pay but had secreted it in her room at the Smith's.

It was one of those rare days in May. The sun was warm without being too insistent and there was just enough breeze to caress your cheek but not enough to ruffle the hair out of place. From time to time, Manitoba magnanimously offered a perfect day when all of nature fairly preened, rising to the occasion. "We couldn't have had a better day," Gertrude said breathlessly as they fell into their seats. "How lucky it came on one of our Thursdays!" Tilly barely managed a nod. They had both hurried through their last minute chores and after changing to their street clothes had to rush to catch the street car.

"Have you decided what to buy?" Tilly finally asked.

"I think maybe I'll get a suit. I've never had one—you know with the skirt and jacket to match—like we looked at long ago. But I'll see. You know," she mused idly, "I've never even had a dress I didn't make myself. And you?"

"I haven't too much to spend," Tilly said tentatively after a short silence. "But I thought maybe a skirt—maybe a waist." She sounded wistful.

"Why Tilly, what's the matter?"

"Oh, nothing—really—it's just I feel guilty. It's the money. It didn't bother me to hide it away but now that I want to spend it on myself—maybe I shouldn't."

Gertrude reached over and patted her hand, "I don't think you ought to feel that way. You do so much for your family. Surely you have a right to spend something on yourself."

"But what will I say when they ask about my new clothes?"

"We-e-ll—you could say—they were a present from the Smiths," Gertrude suggested.

Tilly's face brightened, "Yes, I could. You're right. I could say they bought them for me. If I said they gave me the money, they would scold me for not bringing it home." After a moment's thought, she gave Gertrude a quick hug and said, fervently, "Thank you, Gertrude."

Gertrude was pleased to see Tilly's change of mood but she felt she did not deserve the thanks. She was starting to lose patience with the way Tilly allowed herself to be used by her grasping family, although it did appear that she had little choice short of cutting herself off from them completely.

They shopped with care, examining every article closely. Knowing they were going to buy gave them added confidence and they refused to be hurried into quick decisions, ignoring the insistence of the sales clerks.

Tilly had just purchased her skirt and waist, when Gertrude's eyes fell on the suit. It was exactly what she had in mind. It was draped on a clothes model in the back of the shop and she hadn't noticed it until the clerk handed Tilly her parcel. When she inquired about it, the clerk suggested she try it on. She agreed and found it fitted as though it had been tailored just for her. The jacket was double breasted and close fitting to the waist where it fell into a flared peplum. The skirt was slim and narrowed to the hem. The colour was dark grey, the jacked trimmed with a black braid.

Gertrude walked to the full length mirror and before she could believe it was her own image coming towards her, she took a stealthy glance over her shoulder to see if there was someone behind her.

"Oh, my, it's beautiful," Tilly breathed. "It just suits you."

Gertrude hesitated, running her hands gently over the soft material, looking again into the mirror, then casting aside her indecision, she said, "I'll take it."

"Would you like to wear it?" the clerk asked.

The idea was new to her, but she said, "Yes!" Then turning to Tilly, "But only if you wear yours, too." The clerk carefully folded their old clothes and put them into two bags for them. As she took her parcel, Gertrude thought, yes, I'll still need this dress for when I go home to visit.

When they walked out of the shop, wearing their new attire, they would not have been recognized as the two plainly dressed young women who had entered the shop a short time earlier. They mingled with the host of pedestrians who had evidently been lured out to take advantage of the lovely day. For the first time since she left the country, Gertrude felt at ease in her new environment. With every step, she felt her self-assurance grow. Now she was a part of the city crowd.

They stopped to look at a display of hats in a milliner's shop window. The ones set out to catch the eye were adorned with a profusion of flowers and feathers. To Gertrude's amazement, some were even garnished with artificial fruit as well. "A hat is one more thing I need," Gertrude said, "but I could never wear one of those."

"Maybe they have something inside—," Tilly offered helpfully.

They went in. There were indeed many plain hats. They were mostly sailor straws with a black ribbon band. Gertrude knew they were the most popular of the day, but, she told Tilly, they were too common. Then she saw the red hat. Though it was plain, it had an elegance which set it apart. It's only trimming was a red pleated ribbon around the crown with a small grey feather emerging from it and pointing gracefully to the back . The lady in the shop set it expertly on Gertrude's head at just the right angle, for her approval. It would put the finishing touch to her costume, Gertrude decided as she studied her reflection carefully. Then with the same carefree mood which had taken hold of her earlier, she counted out her money, popped her old plain black hat into the bag with her dress and they went gayly on their way.

And so it was that Gertrude's first tangible outward rebellion took the form of rejecting the restrictions on what Holdeman women were allowed to wear. When the big step of buying that first suit and hat finally came, it seemed almost like a natural thing for her to do. She had liked the look of stylish clothes ever since she and Margret first studied the Eaton's catalogues. Having accomplished her quest to find work in Winnipeg, it was only a matter of time before she started to imagine herself as looking like the other women around her. Her big questions about what was and what was not important to religious faith were still scattered. They didn't have shape. Without making a conscious decision, her road to emancipation began when she started discarding those parts of the Holdeman way of life which she concluded were *not* important. She had no way of anticipating that the important answers for which she yearned would only come as part of her union with the man who was to become her husband.

But for now, Gertrude knew that she could not wear her new clothes when she went home to visit her people. She would have been proud to show off what she had earned. It saddened her to know that she could not, for it would only invite sharp criticism and censure and would rob her, needlessly, of the pleasure of wearing her modish outfit in the city. Whenever she did return home, she reluctantly put on her shawl and old dress, leaving her suit and red hat hanging forlornly in her room at the Stantons.

Late that evening, the Stantons were enjoying their favourite time of the day—bedtime—lying side by side, propped up on their pillows reading, stopping often to talk about the events of the day. "You should have seen Gertrude when she returned home today. She looked lovely! She was wearing a new, very stylish suit topped off with, of all things, a beautiful red hat! I'm afraid our country girl is just starting to make her mark in the world."

"Glad to hear it. When we met at the employment agency I had a feeling that there was more to her than first met the eye. I wonder how long she will be content with doing domestic work?"

"Yes, she is a good worker. We're lucky to have her for as long as she is willing to stay.

"Tomorrow I must call on your sister and have tea. It's been several weeks......."

As the summer rolled on, Gertrude drank in many more new experiences. Music. Oh the music! Gertrude's knowledge of musical instruments had been limited solely to the mouth organ or perhaps a small accordion, which one or another of the more adventurous young blades brought out from some secret hiding place, into the midst of clandestine gatherings of the young folks who had not yet joined the church. The thin, wailing tunes (though in memory she heard them as cries of anguish) did inspire gaiety and toe tapping; and when they were far enough removed from the danger of discovery, they were not too shy to try their skill—using what little they knew—at square dancing and playing swinging games. But these frivolities vanished as they later knelt at the baptismal font. Now, with the Stantons, Gertrude found that music was an accepted, important part of their lives. They had a piano on which Mrs. Stanton played with remarkable ease. Whenever Gertrude dusted the ivory keys, she could not resist picking out one-fingered tunes. Then there was the gramophone which Gertrude had to learn to play for Dodo. It opened a whole new world for Gertrude. The mechanics of it confounded her to no end but it was the music she treasured. She had never heard anything like the beautiful melodies that floated out of the big horn resting on top of the cabinet.

There were so many things to learn and do. There were so many new things to weigh against past experiences. In this, her biggest experiment to date, she was still having difficulty feeling like a participant. It would take time and persistence before she would feel like more than just an on-looker.

Chapter Ten

It was strange to Gertrude how the seasons seemed to melt so silently together in the city. So far, she had been able to observe only the little signs—the return of the first robin, the budding leaves on trees and bushes, the blossoming of spring and then summer flowers. She feared that summer would slip into fall and then winter before she even knew it had happened. She was missing the things which set the seasons apart from each other, giving them their undeniable place in nature's colourful scheme. Spring had come and gone. Spring was when you held a handful of seeds, each with its tiny germ harbouring so much promise, before you thrust it into the soil to await its ultimate fulfilment. The barns were filled with the sounds of new life—the greedy suckling piglets nudging mercilessly at the soft nipples of the sow, exhausted from giving them life—the bleating new born calves, taken from their mothers who called to them in mournful lowing, for now the freshened cows must again supply the milk which had dwindled from the farmer's table to almost nothing. Spring was the sound of meowing kittens from their warm nest, hidden somewhere deep in the sweet smelling straw while the mother cat went in search of food for herself so she could replenish the flow of nourishment to her babies and from unknown, but undeniable sources, came the high pitched squealing of wee mice demanding their share of the life so liberally doled out. Only then was it spring! Spring gave way to summer during the haying season. The animals and the crops were almost forgotten while haying took all the attention. The grass was cut, dried, gathered and stored . That done, the farmer had scarcely time to wipe the sweat from his brow before harvest was upon him. He hitched the horses to the binder that cut the grain and tied it into sheaves, ready to be stooked and dried before being gathered and taken to the threshing machine—the unmistakeable herald that now the autumn was in full swing. Harvest finished, the fields were tilled in preparation for next spring's planting. The winter was the longest season of them all. Only in rare moments could Gertrude appreciate the physical beauties that winter held. At other times, she could only see bleakness in the drifting snow, hear the cry of loneliness in the howling winds. They filled her with obscure, unfathomable longings. But even the winter had its place in the scheme of things. Besides the butchering, there were the small things—sewing, quilting, knitting, machinery repair, horse tack maintenance—things that had been neglected throughout the rest of the year but which kept hands and minds busy. Farm life had a rhythm that gave vitality to life. That was what Gertrude missed most.

Gertrude looked at the calendar and saw that it was August. She leafed back through the pages of the months since she had been at the Stantons. She counted them quickly and found that it had been seven months. The days and weeks had slipped by in their sameness and the summer was more than half over. With growing alarm, she felt, for the first time, a need, an almost physical need, to go home. She must see that nothing had changed. The last time she had seen the country, it was covered with snow. She must erase that picture from her mind. The Stantons, realizing that one Sunday a month was of little value to Gertrude, for she could not go home and return in a day, willingly gave her several days for her trip. Without any hesitation, she chose to go to Blumenort. It was to her childhood home that she must go!

Gertrude arrived at Steinbach Station. Not having had time to warn Annie and arrange for someone to pick her up, she set out to walk. She stopped to pick up a handful of blueberries that grew by the roadside and noticed that the wild cherries were beginning to ripen on the few trees left standing since the land had been cleared. In the fields the grain was beginning to turn gold. She had told herself that it would be so, but to see it and know that she had had no part in any of it, made her feel small and unimportant. It had all gone on without her! It was a very warm day and when a passing neighbour offered her a ride to Annie's farm, she did not refuse it.

Annie was overjoyed at the sight of her. Gertrude registered the proper disbelief at the phenomenal growth of the children since she had last seen them. They crowded happily around her, vying for her attention. Gertrude saw the unmistakable signs of imminent pregnancy in her sister, another reminder that she had been away too long. She expressed her happiness at Annie's good fortune. Annie's eyes shone with pride, for she was first of all, a mother.

But as the afternoon wore on, the tenor of things began to change. The visit began to deteriorate. Annie, as she was wont to do, began to criticize Gertrude and beg her to leave the city. She iterated that it was time for her to settle down and raise a family—she was not so young anymore. Who would ask her if she was so far away? She pointed out that her citified airs would surely frighten the young men away. Gertrude said very little and Annie, feeling the futility of continuing, let loose her ready tears and wept loudly into her sodden handkerchief. The children who had ceased their play, looked on wide eyed with wonder. Gertrude who had long since disdained to be moved by Annie's tears, managed to hang on to her composure but she knew it was inevitable that in the minds of Annie's children, she was marked as the villainess in the tawdry charade.

Nothing had changed in the Unger household, even to the nightly bible sessions and prayers, which brought back painful memories. From early on, Gertrude had been of the silent opinion that Jacob could have at least dispensed with his crusade on Saturday nights, for Saturday was always the women's busiest day with the extra baking and cleaning in preparation for the Sabbath. He could easily have left it to the preachers at the next morning's service to make an extra effort to salvage the weary souls who, in the interim, were too tired to add to their sins anyway. But she could see that Jacob's fervour had not cooled with the years. Saturday nights were still the acme of his week's vespers.

During the last two or three years, Gertrude had been vaguely aware of inevitable changes occuring in the community that had always been the centre of her life. She had been away twice for extended stays in Rosenort, but her seven months in Winnipeg seemed to emphasis for her, the obvious. Sunday morning at church, she was looking at the congregation with new eyes.

Many of her friends and relatives were missing. Some had moved away. Others had passed from this life. But the prolific growth of the remaining families filled the church to overflowing. There were so many young folks. Some of them, to her chagrin, she could not place. It made her conscious of the flight of years which had borne her along until she was no longer part of the younger generation. She had made a special effort to make sure she looked like she still belonged but she couldn't fool herself. She was starting to feel like a stranger in her old home. It was a chilling thought. The greetings of many friends and acquaintances after the service, did little to dispel her gloom. She felt aloof and wasn't comfortable with the feeling. Did any of them sense what she was feeling?

"How nice to see you back in Blumenort." It was Albert Bartel's wife Sarah. "Are you back to stay?"

"No, I just have a few days off work so I came for a visit."

"What exactly are you doing in Winnipeg?"

"I work for an English family—housework. I also tend to their young daughter."

"You must be ready to come home soon. You should talk to Albert. I'm sure he knows of people here who need help. I've never heard tell of any other Holdemans living in Winnipeg. Its not the kind of place where we can live a Godly life. You've been away for many months. That means you haven't been to church since you left.....," punctuating her unfinished sentence with an unfriendly smile.

Gertrude was thinking, what business is it of yours how often I attend church? She returned the smile in kind. "I read my bible on my own when I can't go to church. And Winnipeg isn't nearly as ungodly as you think it is. I've met some very nice people."

"I find that hard to believe. I hope they aren't just taking advantage of you. We have to be so careful when we are out in the world."

Somehow, Sarah's manner and tone of voice belied her words of concern. Not being able to resist putting too fine a point on it she added, "I hear there are lots of temptations in Winnipeg waiting to catch the careless."

"Lucky thing for me then, that I've never had a problem with being careless."

That seemed to silence Sarah. Not knowing what else to say she waved to someone behind Gertrude and walked away. Gertrude stood lost in thought for a moment. She was trying to fight off an overwhelming sadness. Is this just the beginning of what is in store for me?

Gertrude went home with Jennie from church. Jennie, Joseph and Abram were still at home with their Aunt Anna and her husband Henry Friesen. They asked Gertrude many questions about her job and about Winnipeg, as they ate their meal. She kept her answers as light and impersonal as she could while trying not to give the impression that she was being evasive. Even so, it was apparent that everything she said was merely a confirmation of their preconceived ideas of the wickedness rampant in the city. As they emitted their token 'ohs' and 'ahs' of wonderment, they clearly remained smug in their impeccable morality.

When Gertrude and Jennie were left alone to do the dishes, Jennie continued in the same vein. The feeling that she was being subjected to an inquisition instead of sharing in a friendly visit, had been growing on her and Jennie did nothing to soften the impression. She looked carefully at her youngest sister and what she saw filled her with apprehension. Jennie had grown into a tall, handsome young woman, with an intelligent face but her eyes seldom smiled. Anna Friesen was a quiet, undemonstrative woman who had not fulfilled Jennie's need for affection. Jennie had learned to protect her sensitive nature by developing a crust of cool self sufficiency. Much too often her eyebrows were raised in sarcasm. The lack of warmth was a far cry from the little Jennie who had clung so desperately to Gertrude when she had been taken away from her to go live with the Henry Friesens. Gertrude wondered if she should have done something to try and stop the move. But what could she have done? She was too young herself to have any influence on the adults who were in charge of their lives.

Abram, who had now grown into a large, well built, fine looking lad of seventeen, did not seem to have suffered in the sterile surroundings. He was outgoing and generous in nature and Gertrude doubted that he had ever harboured an active dislike for anyone. It amused her to wonder what he might think if he knew that he still gave her the impression of an over-grown, loveable puppy.

Joseph was still his quiet, reserved self—meticulously obedient to his church. He need not have apologized for his small, wiry stature but the need to prove that he was a match for anyone was ever with him. In addition to helping on his Uncle Henry's farm, he was also working land of his own which he had purchased near by. Jennie mentioned, off-handedly, to Gertrude, that she wouldn't be surprised if he got married in the near future. He had been in correspondence about a girl in Kansas—a sister of Peter's second wife. Gertrude wished that Joseph would confide in her but she knew that he would not. How far they had drifted apart! To think that she would ever feel as though she were prying if she were to ask him about his plans!

After they were finished in the kitchen, Gertrude and Jennie joined the others in the 'guest' room. It was their way of referring to the room in which formal visits were held. Very often, as on a Sunday when there were many visitors, it was only the men who, after returning from their post dinner visit to the barn, would congregate there, leaving the women to the kitchen. Around the room, straight backed, wooden chairs stood austerely against the walls. A table placed squarely in the middle of the room, held only the family bible. A surprising note was the bed dominating one corner of the room. It was stacked high with all the extra quilts and pillows in the house and draped with a snow white heirloom bedspread. The imposing bed was used only for very special guests when it was dismantled to useable proportions.

The room did not lend itself to relaxation at the best of times and today their few stilted attempts at conversation echoed into the ensuing silences and hung about them like large, invisible cobwebs ready to snare the first unguarded remark. Then they heard the sound of an approaching horse and buggy. Relieved to have a diversion, Jennie jumped to the windows and peered intently out between the folds of the curtains.

"Why, it's Bartel—Albert," she informed the others. "And he's alone. I wonder why he didn't bring his wife? I saw her talking to you, Gertrude, after the service. He can't be coming for a visit," she deduced, "or he would have brought her along. It's Sunday so he's not here on farm business. Why is he here?"

"Oh, Jennie." Gertrude chided disapprovingly.

Ignoring Gertrude, she continued. "Well, he isn't coming in. He's just sitting there waiting for someone to come out. He can't be coming for a visit," she repeated needlessly. Henry had already left his chair and was on his way to the back door but Jennie, not taking her eyes off Albert and his rig said, "I think you had better go out, Uncle Henry."

It was painfully clear that Albert Bartel's unexpected appearance was the highlight of Jennie's day. Gertrude felt embarrassed by Jennie's wholesale display of curiosity in the situation. At the same time, she felt embarrassed for being embarrassed. She could not really blame her. She knew all too well, from first hand experience, the narrowness of Jennie's social upbringing. She couldn't imagine this same scene talking place in any of the Winnipeg households she knew. Then she stopped herself—what a shameful thought! Who am I becoming?

But however she wanted to look at it, the reality was she felt a chasm beginning to develop between her and her family. Her dwindling naiveté was acting as a wedge between herself and the ones she loved. It made her feel uneasy. I need to be careful. I know that I don't fully belong in that other world and now it feels like I don't belong here either.

"Well, Henry," Anna said when Henry returned alone, "why didn't Albert come in?"

"He came because he wants to speak to Gertrude."

"Gertrude?" Jennie asked incredulously, her interest instantly aroused to even a higher pitch.

"Alone," Henry said shortly, thereby excluding Jennie with one word.

Gertrude left the room, wondering what Albert Bartel could possibly be wanting of her. She did not delude herself that it would be anything of a pleasant nature. Was he, as she was sure everyone else in the house surmised, going to remonstrate with her about some aspect of her conduct?

"Good day, Albert." She greeted him with the first-name informality which was customary with them, as she walked to the gate where he stood, uncertainly, waiting for her.

"Good day," he said as he fidgeted, not knowing what to do with his hands. "It's good to see you back, Gertrude. We hoped it was to stay but Sarah tells me differently."

"Why don't we go sit on those seats under the trees?" she suggested, hoping to put him more at ease, then wondering why it ought to be she who must put him at ease.

"I've come on a rather important mission," he said at last. "You're of age and can make your own decisions, so I didn't mention my reason for coming when I spoke to your uncle."

Gertrude nodded to show her appreciation of that small consideration, but hoped he would not be too long in coming to the point.

"I'm sorry to hear that you are planning on gong back to Winnipeg. Maybe after you hear what I'm going to say, you'll change your mind," he said hopefully.

"I doubt it, but, what?"

"Gertrude, have you never thought you'd like to get married and settle down?" Albert blurted, rushing to make his point while she was fully prepared for his further dallying.

"Why, yes." He had succeeded in startling her into answering before she could think. Then she hastened to explain, "I mean, everyone thinks about it sometime, don't they?"

"Yes, yes, of course," he agreed quickly.

"Is that why you came to see me?" She searched her mind for a likely prospect but could think of no one that she would remotely consider.

"Yes, I have come with an offer of marriage from one of our brothers. Abe came to me right after church and asked if I would ask you. I guess seeing you today, gave him the courage."

"Abe?"

" Yes, Abe Klassen."

"Abe Klassen?" Up until now Gertrude had remained calm, but this revelation sorely taxed her serenity.

"I think it would be a very good thing for both of you. You have both had to make your own living for a long time now. You could work together for yourselves." Seeing that she was somewhat shaken, he advised, "You don't have to give me your answer now. I'll return in a few days after you have had a little time," and he made as if to get up from his seat.

"Oh no, wait—there is no need to come back, besides I'm leaving tomorrow," she stopped him with a touch of her hand on his arm.

"But," and he leaned forward to emphasize what he was going to say. "But surely this is important enough to keep you here longer."

"No. I could never marry Abe Klassen," she stated flatly.

"How can you be so sure? You haven't had time to think

about it. And as a sister in the church, you know it is your duty to pray on it. I assure you God will give you a sign. You must listen! It has happened many times that a doubting sister was turned by prayer. You can not deny that."

"I know He would never tell me to marry Abe," she assured him and she thought of several girls she knew who had been pressured to marry against their will by just such tactics.

"But, Gertrude, you would have a home. You would be taken care of." Albert pleaded as though he himself were the suitor.

"I can take care of myself." Gertrude rose to end the embarrassing exchange. "There is no need to say more."

"Would you not like me to speak to your uncle?"

"No, no—please, don't do that." The appeal in her voice penetrated the fog of his bewilderment.

"Albert," she called after him as he walked dejectedly away. He turned with renewed hope on his face. "Albert, tell Abe, I understand." Through her annoyance, she felt a rising pity for Abe. Even in the best of circumstances, she would never have accepted him. And poor Albert. He took her refusal as a personal affront to himself.

Gertrude did understand. She was not flattered. Although she was ignorant of the fact that Abe had admired her for many years (she did not know that he had been tempted to ask for her before) she knew that he had an ulterior motive in asking for her at this time. It had happened about two weeks ago.

* * * * *

Gertrude, in the company of Tilly Rempel, was sauntering down Main Street. They had no special destination in mind, but were chatting and glancing idly in the shop windows as they went along. Suddenly her heart skipped a beat as she saw, to her dismay, a familiar face coming her way.

Gertrude nudged Tilly, "There's someone from home."

"Where? Where?" Tilly asked excitedly. "Is it that fellow with the scraggy beard, coming toward us?" Tilly had never seen any of Gertrude's people although Gertrude had told her much about them and had explained to her about the untrimmed beards and no neck ties.

"I only hope he doesn't see me," Gertrude murmured. But luck was not with her for at that very moment his eyes fell on her. His pace quickened and he came directly for them.

"We-e-ell, Gertrude….." Gertrude was immediately irritated. More and more of her people were starting to greet her in that manner. She wasn't sure what it meant. It seemed as though they were uncertain about how she was going to receive them but at the same time it also carried with it innuendos of disapproval. She didn't know yet that over the years, this grating greeting would become standard procedure and usually a preamble to unpleasantness. He stopped in front of her with a surprised look on his face all the while looking her over head to foot. Gertrude realized that, in his eyes, she must be quite a sight for she was wearing her jaunty suit and red hat. Her own surprise was in that she had never given a thought to the possibility of running into anyone from home. With another perfectly drawn out "We-e-ell", he held out his hand.

"Good day," Gertrude said shortly, taking his hand and then releasing herself as quickly as possible. "Ah—this—this is Tilly Rempel." They, too, shook hands.

"How are you?" He clasped his hands behind his back, sparring for time, and shifted his weight from one foot to the other, but made no move to leave.

"I'm fine. And you?" She began to sidle away. "It was nice seeing you."

"Say, how would you like to have a cup of coffee or something? There is a tea shoppe over there."

"Oh, no thank you. Tilly and I—"

"Please, don't mind me." Tilly interrupted her. "Go ahead."

"Won't you come, too?" Abe asked sensing an ally in Tilly.

"Alright," Tilly agreed.

Gertrude had no further recourse but to comply but she was considerably miffed.

They went into the tea shoppe and chose a small table and ordered rolls and coffee. Since they had accepted the invitation, Gertrude felt obliged to make conversation, while Tilly, aware of Gertrude's displeasure, occupied herself, eyes downcast, with stirring her tea. Gertrude asked about his family and about the crops and whatever else she could think of to bring up for discussion. His answers were short and sometimes vague. She decided that his talk was dull, but she noted that his eyes were bright with interest as he kept looking at her.

"You've changed," he said at last, after a lull which she had not been able to fill, feeling she had exhausted all possible topics.

"Oh? I wasn't aware of anything," Gertrude replied innocently.

"Well, you know, your clothes." He shrugged his shoulders elaborately. Then he occupied himself with his food but she felt a light touch of his knee at hers. She moved unobtrusively away but again she felt his knee nudging hers this time with undeniable pressure.

"I though maybe tonight, we—we could—," he began recklessly but floundered for words and to her horror, she now felt his hand on her thigh. She made no further pretence at hiding her annoyance. She hitched her chair out of his reach with an angry, noisy jerk that almost toppled Tilly who looked up in astonishment. People at the surrounding tables were trying not to take notice. Gertrude's unexpected reaction sent the hot colour to his face and he took a noisy gulp of his coffee which sent him into a paroxysm of coughing. Then without further ado, he pushed back his chair and mumbled incoherently something to the effect that he must leave to catch his train. He rushed past the bewildered cashier, not thinking to pay for their lunch and had a near collision with the door in his blind exit.

"What ever happened?" Tilly asked, wide-eyed and open mouthed.

"He thought he could get smart with me," Gertrude stated briefly.

"But I thought you were old friends," Tilly said lamely.

"No, not really. I've known him all my life but I've not had much to do with him. We worked at the same farm at one time but I never gave him any reason to think..." They looked at each other. It started with an exchange of smiles as the humour of the situation crept over them. Gales of laughter consumed them as they tried to compose themselves enough to pay the bill.

* * * * *

But now as she stood still, held by her thoughts, listening to the rhythm of the horse's hooves fading into the distance, she did not think it was funny. It was very clear that this proposal was in the way of an apology; a very clumsy apology at best, quickly conjured during her unexpected presence in Blumenort. More importantly, it was more than just an apology. It was also a means of cleansing his conscience. He used this opportunity to propose as an instrument for his absolution from whatever thoughts he had been harbouring when he saw her that afternoon. She remembered that he had mentioned getting together in the evening. What could he have been thinking? She had to admit that her city clothes and the environment were partly responsible for giving him notions. He must have known that she would not marry him, unless he thought her to be so naive as to accept him because she, too, felt guilty and a party to his attempt at flirtation.

She felt the entire episode to be a rather misguided, shoddy affair. It was best forgotten but she could not so easily dismiss her rising ire as she went back to the house. Besides everything else, Abe had succeeded in taking away the romantic aura of a woman's first marriage proposal, even though it could never have been accepted. She could not quite forgive him for that.

"What did Albert want?" Jennie asked bluntly as soon as Gertrude entered the door.

"It was nothing of importance."

"But, what was it?" she insisted stamping her left foot.

"Please, Jennie, I don't wish to talk about it."

"Why did he ask to speak to you alone?"

"Jennie!" Uncle Henry intervened.

Jennie was finally silenced but her scepticism was obvious. Gertrude would let them think what they wished. She was again thankful that Albert had not consulted her uncle in the matter. Had they known the gist of the errand, they would have undoubtably sided with the preacher and made things even more uncomfortable for her than they already were.

Gertrude was not sorry to leave Blumenort the next day. Her heart was heavy with disappointment. She had gone with an urgency she could not deny, to assure herself that nothing had changed. She had wanted to feel, touch, smell the fabric of her childhood. Ironically, she found that in spite of the changes, nothing *had* changed. Why then, was she not reassured and satisfied? She was forced to face squarely, the revelation that her disillusionment lay deep within herself. They were a good people and she loved them, perhaps even more so, as she saw their human frailties.

As her train speed down the track to Winnipeg, she, who had always been so sure of herself, making her own decisions, felt an unfamiliar yearning for fate to step in this time, if only this time, to do the choosing for her. If only there were someone—someone to share the tumult of the restive emotions within her. She had never been so alone or bereft of inner strength as now.

She closed her eyes and could see herself standing uncertainly in an opening of the veil which hung between her heritage and the rest of the world, her hand clutching tightly to its folds. She had only to step back and let it fall back into place,... or.....? She was standing on the threshold of her destiny.

Chapter Eleven

Upon her return to the Stanton's, Gertrude was touched by the somewhat less than formal greeting of Mrs. Stanton and the exuberance of Dodo's embrace. In a paradoxical reversal, she felt, for a short while, but only for a short while, for her position as a servant was never in question, that she had come home. She also sensed an undercurrent of relief in the reception given her which was further born out by Mrs. Stanton's next remarks.

"Did you have a good time, Gertrude?" she asked. After Gertrude's reply in affirmation, she went on, "I was afraid you would be so happy to be home, you wouldn't come back. Did they want you to stay? Did you want to?"

"Oh, yes, they wanted me to stay alright. But I didn't have any wish to, at this time. Anyway, I wouldn't leave here without giving you ample notice," Gertrude assured her.

"Well, I'm glad you're back, in any case. So is Dodo, aren't you dear?" she smiled fondly at her daughter. Gertrude held a secret admiration for the easy manner in which the Stantons used the many terms of endearment. "She asked many times every day, 'When will Gertrude come home?' It made me realize how much we have come to depend on you and how much Dodo loves you. Well—," Mrs Stanton, having dropped her reserve for a rare moment of open affection towards Gertrude, reverted to her usual air of flawless efficiency. "Now that you're here, we have lots to do. For one thing, we are planning a holiday trip to the lake in about two weeks. We would like very much if you'd go with us. There wouldn't be much for you to do there except look after Dodo. We plan to stay away about two weeks. Of course, if you'd rather go out to the country again—?"

"No, no," she answered quickly. "I'd not care to go out so soon again, I'd much rather go with you."

With that settled, Gertrude was swept into a whirl of preparation for the trip. She was relieved to have something new to occupy her time and thoughts. It would ease the depth of the disenchantment she had experienced during her short, bungled jaunt to Blumenort.

The day of the Stanton's departure arrived. They, with Gertrude in tow, boarded the train, with an unbelievable amount of baggage, each bag bulging to a point of near calamity. They traveled east out of Winnipeg, leaving the prairie behind them into a landscape of trees, rock and small lakes. From the windows of the train, they caught fleeting glimpses of various wildlife scampering into hiding, out of sight of the huge, man-made monster lumbering clumsily through their once secluded domain. By nightfall, they reached their destination, a small town on a huge lake. They were about a hundred and twenty miles from Winnipeg.

They settled in at their place of lodging and did little more than eat and unpack before they retired for the night.

All, except Dodo, felt the need to renew their zest for holidaying which had almost vanished in the hectic past few days. Their weary bodies had not been eased by the discomfort of the crowded train. Even the cushioned seats could not camouflage its bumpy, jarring progress. Tomorrow would be a new day.

It had become fashionable for the pleasure bound elite to congregate at lake side resorts where they could swim, go boating and otherwise socialize. The Stantons would undoubtedly meet a number of their friends who were members of their exclusive social circle, for this type of vacation was becoming a yearly event in most of their lives.

The new west had been occupied with the tasks of survival. But now, communities were moving beyond their crude beginnings and establishing themselves as thriving centres of agriculture and commerce. Winnipeg was becoming a centre for the western Canadian banking system. One of Canada's national railways had just built a magnificent luxury hotel and the second railway corporation was about to do the same in the next decade. Speculation on grain futures, not to mention the growth of large scale retail dynasties were making people rich. The Eaton's department store had just opened last summer. It was the second largest department store in Canada, the tenth largest department store in the world and employed over 1200 people. One year earlier, Ashdown's hardware store on Main Street had burned down and was replaced with a six storey building considered by many to be the finest hardware store in the country. Mr. Ashdown was establishing more stores in other western Canadian cities. There was talk that Winnipeg was about to become the Chicago of the north. So it followed, quite naturally, that people were becoming more pleasure conscious. Though the train reigned as the most important means of transportation for any distance, the emergence of the automobile was starting to play a part in this awareness of wider horizons. The number of automobiles on the streets of Winnipeg was growing and the era of searching for new diversions accelerated. Automobiles were still looked upon as a frivolous acquisition, and its practical benefits had not yet been revealed to a somewhat skeptical populous who nevertheless accepted it as a novel, singular plaything. It led to many short trips and outings which heretofore had been well nigh impossible by horse and buggy. As she looked around her, Gertrude took comfort in the knowledge that she was not the only one looking for a bigger, more exciting life.

As soon as breakfast was over, Gertrude was relegated to take Dodo to the beach. Mrs Stanton, losing patience with the child's impatience, cautioned Gertrude not to let her go into the water too soon. So Gertrude, sparring for time, waiting for the day to warm up, kept Dodo playing in the sand as long as possible; but when she could no longer restrain her, she removed her own shoes and stockings and waded in the shallow water's edge beside her. Although Gertrude held her skirt above the surface of the water, it became drenched almost to the waist with Dodo's carefree, undisciplined splashing. Gertrude did not mind. She would have liked to dip deep into the water herself, to feel the water against her body. By mid-morning, the beach was becoming more crowded with women and children and a number of men, in swimming attire. Gertrude had never been witness to anything like it before. Of course she had seen pictures—but—. Mrs. Stanton had suggested that Gertrude might like to take an outfit for swimming but she had demurred. Now that she saw them, she decided that she had been wise in refraining from getting one. She knew that she would feel much too self-conscious to enjoy herself in one of them. The costumes were considered very daring, although it was the style, not what they revealed of the ladies' natural endowments, that was responsible for that description. Indeed they covered the body remarkably well with the full bloomers which met the black stockings just below the knee, the tops, high at the neck and the sleeves, reaching the elbow. To complete the picture, they wore shoes. Gertrude noticed here and there some of the younger set had left off the shoes and stockings, which seemed the natural thing to do but she over heard two women discussing this latest innovation and referring to the young ladies in question as being "rather brazen". Gertrude noticed that, in fact, the mens' costumes were far more revealing than the women's leaving, she thought, little to the imagination, especially when wet.

Gertrude and Dodo shared a bedroom and after Gertrude had put the tired child to bed, she became aware that Dodo was unusually restless. She surmised that it was due to over exertion and her state of excitement. The day had been too long and strenuous for Dodo but she would have it no other way. When she was awakened a number of times in the night by Dodo's tossing and whimpering in her sleep, her concern grew. It was early in the morning when Gertrude was again awakened, this time by hearing her name called. She hurried across the room to her side.

"I'm thirsty, Gertrude, I want a drink."

Gertrude saw that her cheeks were flushed. It could, of course, be sunburn, but she put her cool hand on her forehead and cheeks and found them to be very hot. It did not seem to be the heat of a mere sunburn. She pulled the covers up close around Dodo's chin.

"You just lie still. I'll get you some water."

Gertrude gave her a drink and then hurried out into the hall and roused the Stantons with her insistent knock at their door. Mrs. Stanton came, sleepily to the door, and when Gertrude told her that she was worried about Dodo, followed her, at once, to her room. She agreed with Gertrude, that Dodo was surely coming down with something. In due time, they located the local doctor who left instructions that Dodo was not to leave her bed until he saw her again in the evening. So the second day of their holiday turned out to be quite different from the first. Gertrude spent the entire day at the little girl's bedside, while her parents looked in at regular intervals—each time listening to her pleas to go play on the beach. They could only promise her that tomorrow she would go. But when tomorrow came, the doctor advised them to return to Winnipeg where Dodo could be under the care of their family doctor. He told them that he did not think that it was any of the common childhood illnesses, but he would not commit himself to any specific diagnosis in the case. They hastily repacked all their belongings and returned to Winnipeg. It would be a long time before Dodo was again to play on the beach.

So their gay holiday, which had barely begun, was ended. Dodo was placed in hospital where she remained until the critical period of her illness had passed. To their utter dismay, they discovered, that her left leg was paralysed. Only then, did they know that she had Infantile Paralysis.

Dodo was sent home from the hospital in the care of a special nurse, who remained with her for another few weeks. But since Dodo much preferred Gertrude's attention to that of the nurse, her dismissal left Gertrude's routine in unprecedented disorder. The nurse had been an added irritation with her lofty demands but now Gertrude must assume a major part of the nurse's role. She was taught how to manipulate and exercise Dodo's withered muscles. The doctor assured the Stanton's that her leg would support Dodo's weight again but it would take time and patience. Meanwhile, Dodo had to be carried from place to place, for she was no longer bed ridden. Mrs. Stanton was expecting her second child, and she, in her delicate condition was forbidden by the solicitous doctor to lift Dodo. Mr. Stanton, who always openly adored his little daughter, took over her care in the evenings. It freed Gertrude but not for resting, for she had to utilize that time to catch up on the many things she had not been able to do during the day.

Chapter Twelve

The effect of Dodo's illness touched Gertrude in many ways. She willingly gave of her free time and in the beginning, most of her limited outside activities were obliterated. Later, when the demands on her, brought about by the unhappy situation, became less, she resumed her routine Thursday afternoons off—often with Tilly. Winter was again upon them. Both were averse to the cold, so they did not go down town as often as before. Somewhere along the way, Gertrude had lost much of the carefree, gay pleasure she had found in her earlier outings with Tilly.

As an expression of thanks and a reward for her diligence, the Stantons gave Gertrude a full week off at Christmas. Consequently, she went to Rosenort to spend the holiday season with her sister Katie and family. She vowed that she was going to enjoy herself, nothing more. She would not allow herself to become entangled in a web of uncertainty and soul searching as she had during her last trip to Blumenort,

Gertrude did not realize how much she had missed Katie until she saw her again. They clung together in a tight embrace. Oddly, Gertrude had grown ever closer to Katie—Katie with whom she had had so little in common in their early years. Perhaps as she felt her bonds with Annie and Jennie slipping away, Gertrude automatically moved closer to Katie in an attempt to fill the void. Whatever the reason, she was able to accept Katie for what she was in a way that was impossible for her where the other two were concerned. Maybe it was because she knew that a soft heart lurked beneath Katie's abrupt, brash manner. People outside her family judged her more harshly. They saw in her a wilful, unbending, strong-minded woman who stood resolutely at the helm of her family and who was not too timid to set her feet firmly and speak out on community and church matters as well. She strove to build up George's ego and public image and she deluded herself into believing that she was successful. For her husband and children, she had a protective, animal-like love, oblivious to their faults—permissive in the discipline of her children. There were three children now—two boys and one girl.

On the Sunday before Christmas, Gertrude attended church. As she took a seat, her eyes searched the congregation for familiar faces. It had suddenly become very important to see David Enns. When she saw him it took a long moment for her heart to resume its normal beat. He was even more handsome than she remembered. It was a wonder to her that some hopeful young maiden had not yet succeeded in capturing his heart. Why must the aisle between them seem so wide, she asked herself. She sighed, opened her hymn book and searched unseeingly, fumbling through the pages for the song that was being sung.

Father Enns, as Gertrude had quite naturally come to think of him through Katie (and also it was her way to distinguish him from his son John) invited Gertrude to their family Christmas dinner. So on Christmas Day, after church services, she went with George and Katie to the dinner. In the confusion of the large gathering, there was little opportunity for conversations of any length. She had a short exchange with Agnes who was curious about Gertrude's work in the city. Agnes was envious of Gertrude's initiative in leaving the Mennonite Community to work but Gertrude could only detect the condescension with which she deftly covered her envy.

"Maybe someday, after my sisters are older and can look after father and the rest of the work here at home, I might try my hand at working in the city," Agnes stated, but then she added, with what was meant to be sympathetic understanding, "the change must have been very hard for you. It should be much easier for me since I don't belong to the church." With that Agnes turned on her heel and left.

Why did she have to say that? Gertrude wondered. And, as if in answer to her thoughts, Peter was beside her. "Agnes doesn't always think before she talks," he said. Peter's smiling face was enough to make her forget Agnes. During their friendly chat, Gertrude looked up several times to find David's eyes on her before he joined them.

"It's been a long time since we've seen you, Gertrude," David said.

"Yes, I guess it has. I've been very busy and it's not easy to get enough time off to come out to the country."

"Do you like your work?" David asked.

"Oh, yes, very much. The people I work for are very

nice and they're good to me. They have only the one child—they call her Dodo. She was very sick this summer and she is far from well even now and takes a lot of care. I don't mind, though, she is such a sweet little girl," she hastened to explain because of the look of sympathy on both David's and Peter's faces.

"Are you staying there much longer?" David wondered.

"It will be a while yet. I had planned to stay only 'till spring, but circumstances will almost force me to stay at least into the fall."

"That's an awful long time." Peter looked almost comically crestfallen. "Surely you'll come back here before then?"

"I'll try," she placated him. "But I can't promise."

Gertrude skilfully turned the conversation away from herself to them. She did not need to feign a desire to know more about their farming operations, for there her interest was very real. The past season's crop yield had been excellent and they had plans to expand their acreages. Gertrude learned that David had bought two hundred and forty acres about half a mile from his father's farm, just past his brother John's place. "Are you planning on putting up any buildings?" Gertrude asked.

"Yes, in time but first, I have to break up the prairie and plant a windbreak—next summer I hope."

"Well, I see you have a very busy spring and summer ahead." They continued their conversation for some time, unaware that Peter had drifted away from them until they were summoned to the table.

During the dinner, while Gertrude was talking to Mary, she suddenly became aware, as she glanced around the table, that John was not present. Then she saw him through the doorway, sitting by himself in the 'guest' room. The sight of his lonely figure caused her to realize with sudden horror just what was taking place. It struck Gertrude, with an unpleasant shock, that her membership in the Holdeman church, made her a part of this inhumane attempt to punish John! She could not delude herself into thinking that she was only a witness, She was a participant. She had always known about not eating with Holdemans who had been thrown out of the church but this was the first time she had actually participated in the custom. Certainly, it was the first time in her experience that a family member was being punished. A deep sense of shame for herself and all the other Holdemans began to envelope her. She picked helplessly at her food, not knowing fully what she was feeling, let alone what she should do about it.

At the conclusion of the meal, Gertrude had gratefully escaped to the kitchen, going through the motions of helping with the clean up. She was still trying to make some sense out of what her own part had been in excluding John from the dinner. She was dimly aware that John and the children were now having their meal at the second table setting. The sound of animated voices from the dining room gradually pulled Gertrude's thoughts away from herself. She left the kitchen to seek out Katie. As she passed through the dining room, she saw that Agnes was sitting beside John, making the point again, that she alone, of all the adults, could eat with him.

"Well, John," Agnes spoke loudly. "Here we are again, the two of us—having our dinner, enjoying the childish banter."

Gertrude found Katie in the 'guest' room. "Look," she said, pulling up a chair. "Look at Agnes."

"Why?" Katie asked unnecessarily.

"Sitting there.....eating with the children....."

"Oh, she always does that," Katie said, the frown on her forehead deepening.

"She could have so easily eaten at the first table," Mary, John's wife who was sitting nearby, put in. "But, she has to make a spectacle of everything!"

"Sh.....shush," Katie cautioned quietly.

"She does it to make the rest of us feel worse," Mary, whose position was especially vulnerable, continued. "As if we don't feel badly enough already."

"But it's best to keep quiet," Katie hastily interjected. "It's all so embarrassing." Had Agnes eaten unobtrusively with the others, she would have been abetting them in their attempts at cloaking the procedure with a semblance of dignity but she found perverse pleasure in unfrocking them to reveal their painful embarrassment. Although Gertrude felt many of Agnes's antics in poor taste, she reasoned that it was no more than she and the rest of them deserved.

No more was said and Gertrude was finding it difficult to concentrate on the perplexing church matters anyway because her mind kept drifting off to other things. A warmth suffused her whole body as she recalled her exchange with David. The fact that he had gone out of his way to speak to her, was small, she reminded herself. But it had been the longest discussion they had ever had and quickly became identified in her mind as the highlight of her visit. As a result she left Rosenort with a lighter heart than she had felt for a long time.

Back at the Stantons, Gertrude tackled her work with renewed energy, even though she could see the demands on her were increasing daily as Mrs. Stanton's confinement drew nearer. She realized that she must take full advantage of her time off if she was to maintain her efficiency in her job. Tilly, sensing that Gertrude was again more like her old self, was happy to resume their weekly outings.

One Sunday, they went to a church in their neighbourhood. Gertrude felt an understandable furtiveness tingling up and down her spine as she stepped into the church, but her uneasiness vanished as soon as they were seated. She was greatly impressed with the fine, handsome fittings in the interior of the building. Her spirit soared when the organ music swelled to fill the church with its deep throbbing and then miraculously fell to a mere, hushed whisper. It moved her almost to the point of tears; she had never heard anything so beautiful. She was awed by the sight of the families filling in, sitting down together in the same pew—the father and mother sharing the same hymnal, surrounded by their children. This was the church in which the Stantons worshiped regularly. She was not likely to return, if only in deference to her own church but now she would be able to picture the Stantons in this setting as well as in their home.

Then there was the Thursday evening after Gertrude and Tilly had eaten supper downtown, when they were drawn to a building from which the sounds of singing floated out on the air to tantalize the passers-by. They looked up to see a sign stating that it was a revival meeting and that everyone was welcome. In truth, it was more the cold wind whipping at their skirts than the hymn which they happened to recognize, that spurred them to go in. At once a man came forward, a broad, toothy smile on his face, and shook their hands. Gertrude was not prepared for the pudgy softness of the hand which so greedily devoured hers and it repelled her. Unthinkingly, she swiped her hand against her skirt as the man ushered them to seats. The loud and lusty singing died down and the preacher began his sermon. Most of his script was not new to Gertrude. She had heard a lot of what he was saying many times before. Can't they ever think of anything new to say? But that was where the similarity ended . The preacher's voice was growing louder and more emphatic with every new sentence. His arms gestured wildly as he paced back and forth across the podium—sometimes like a high-stepping, graceful, well-bred filly, then with the heavy steps of a plodding plough horse. At intervals, he paused to pound vigorously on the pulpit. From here and there in the congregation came intermit, faintly muttered amens and a few hallelujahs, which gradually became more distinct and resounding as the participants became progressively more involved in the revival meeting. But it was when the people began to move forward, to the front of the hall, some falling to their knees, to moan and chant unintelligibly in their zeal, that Gertrude felt the blood drain from her face and her stomach began to lurch. She looked at Tilly and saw that she, too had become pale. In silent, mutual agreement, they slid out of their seats and hurried as quietly as possible to the door. No one noticed their departure.

Outside, they drew the sharp, cold air greedily into their lungs, to clear away the fog of strangeness and unreality which had threatened to smother them. It was some moments before they could speak as they hurried away from the meeting, not daring to look back.

"Well!" Tilly was the first to utter a sound.

"I do say!" Gertrude expostulated with equal vehemence. "I didn't expect anything like that! I thought a church was, well—a church was a church—if you understand what I'm trying to say. Every so often, we in the Holdeman church, do have revival meetings with guest preachers brought in, when our elders think the congregation is becoming too lax but they are nothing like what we just saw." Tilly nodded with equally confused understanding.

"I wonder, do you think if we'd stayed, would we have had to go forward, too?"

"Oh, Tilly." Gertrude was taken aback at the thought, "I hope not! I can say, though, that I was never so glad to get out of any place before."

As they made their way home, each remarked, in turn, on the cleanliness of the air.

It was Gertrude's sense of adventure, and eagerness to assess the latest fads and innovations which eventually caused her to capitulate to Tilly's pleas to attend a theatre. There were a number of theatres in Winnipeg. After Gertrude agreed to go they spent considerable time discussing which one they should choose. Their final choice fell between the two that also showed moving pictures along with their stage program. This way they could get a taste of both mediums of entertainment. Gertrude was much more interested in seeing the moving pictures which was the latest invention to confound her imagination. She had been reading about them in the newspapers and magazines. It eventually came down to The Dominion—an unromantic, staid name and the Bijou, a name which they could not even pronounce, giving it an aura of mystery. So they chose the Bijou.

As soon as the show started, Gertrude became too engrossed in the action to think about the question of moral approval or disapproval. The stage was vibrant with colour, song and dance. As the show progressed, and she began to understand a little bit of what theatre was all about, she found herself, involuntarily comparing it with the revival meeting which they had so recently attended. Then, before she realized it, she found herself drawing a parallel to the Holdemans too. Their dress, their demeanour, their abstinences, were they not designed to create an impression? Was it not all a show of sorts? Because of her unanticipated perplexity of thought, Gertrude was left with mixed emotions concerning the live show. But the moving pictures left her truly overwhelmed as they flickered and danced across the screen, the people gambolling frantically about, in jerky, rapid motions, the cars driving at speeds which she had yet to see on the streets. The pictures changed too fast for Gertrude to keep up with the explanations at the bottom, but she thoroughly enjoyed the movies, as she had heard them called. It was a fitting name.

"Of the two, I found the moving pictures the most interesting," Gertrude observed.

"Yes, they are really something," Tilly said by way of agreement.

"I wish I was better at reading. Most of the time I couldn't finish the titles at the bottom of the screen before they changed."

"Oh Gertrude," Tilly exclaimed. She hadn't realized that Gertrude's reading skills were not at the same level as hers. "If you would like, I could give you some help. I finished grade seven before my father made me go out to work."

"That would be wonderful! You really don't mind?"

Tilly was more than happy to comply, eager to be of some practical use to her friend. Gertrude, on her part, was amazed how helpful it was to receive some guidance from a teacher instead of relying solely on her own isolated struggle to decipher the written word. She was a keen pupil. Her confidence grew and by summer, besides reading newspapers and magazines she was starting to read books as well.

So, the winter passed. Spring, after several inept attempts to break through, arrived in full dress in the middle of April. With its advent, as though it had been planned, the Stantons were blessed with a son and heir, Robert Harold Stanton, the second.

In keeping with the latest trend of the more modern women in the city, Mrs. Stanton went to the hospital for the birth of her baby. In the two weeks while she was away, Gertrude, at the doctor's suggestion, redoubled her efforts to help Dodo walk again. At first, the results were very discouraging. Dodo's dependence on the people around her had grown to the point that she saw no need to help herself. Gertrude was almost at the end of her resources in finding a means to break through the child's indifference, when, one day, the doctor came to her rescue. He arrived at the house and with an exaggerated flourish, ceremoniously presented her with a pair of shiny, new crutches, emphasizing that they were just the right size for her. It was the novelty of her new 'toys', as Dodo dubbed them on sight, which started her on the way back to independence. The doctor explained patiently that she could not keep them for very long, so she must make very good use of them. He told her that there were many other girls and boys waiting for them, and they were just as eager as she to learn to walk again.

The day when Mr. Stanton brought his wife and son home from the hospital, Dodo, with Gertrude beside her, waited at the far end of the front hall. When her parents entered the door, she began to make her way, slowly, clumsily, towards them. Mrs. Stanton intuitively sensed that she was not to go meet her. She dropped to her knees, threw her arms, wide, and waited for her. When Dodo was a few steps from her mother, she dropped her crutches and flung herself into the waiting arms. Mrs. Stanton hugged her tightly while tears streamed down her cheeks.

"My baby, oh, my baby," she said over and over again. It was the first time that Gertrude had seen her mistress's composure break, even through all the pain and heartache of Dodo's long illness and the strain had taken its toll, she had remained calm. "Did you see, Harry? Did you see?"

"Yes Ellie," and he handed the baby to Gertrude and knelt to put his arms around his wife and daughter.

Dodo submitted happily to her parents embrace for some moments, then drew herself away, with proud dignity.

"But, Mama, I'm not your baby any more. We have a new baby now."

"That's right sweetheart," with an effort, she avoided repeating the term, baby, again. "That's right." She brushed the tears from her eyes. Her happiness was tinged with a wistful sadness for she knew that each new life marked the end of an old era and Dodo, in her way, was acknowledging that.

"Come, Dodo, lets go see your brother." Junior was already making his presence known in an unrestrained bid for attention as Gertrude was removing his outer blanket.

In a few months, Dodo discarded her crutches. Gertrude felt a justifiable personal triumph as she watched the daily improvements in Dodo's agility. Often, Gertrude had to restrain herself from picking the child up in her arms. She forced herself to ignore the pathetic pleading eyes in the small, pale face of the little figure. Although Dodo did not fully understand why she had to work so hard, she did her best to make Gertrude and her parents happy.

After her second and less than successful visit to Blumenort in May, the remainder of the summer was uneventful. As fall approached, Gertrude's employment with the Stanton's was coming to an end. She did not wish to stay with them indefinitely although they had asked her. Gertrude's anger about what had occurred during her last visit to Blumenort still remained with her and now, coupled with her sense of loss at leaving the Stantons, the struggle to gain a sense of belonging somewhere was becoming more intense.

The day before she was to leave, she went up to the room she had called her own for the last year and a half. It seemed much longer, almost as though it had always been—like a lifetime. Tomorrow she would leave it behind and her time here and all that had happened to her the while, would gradually diminish and shrink into a small package of times gone by.

Already she felt as though she didn't belong anymore as she walked slowly to the little window and looked out onto the street. The trees stood boldly bare and unadorned amid the colourful covering they had given the ground beneath them. The gnarled, stark limbs spoke of the many winters they had weathered and now they waited with eager, outstretched arms for what was to come. Did they never weary? She turned away from the picture for it served only to heighten her feeling of separation from her surroundings which automatically enveloped her when something was about to end. It was an armour against the hurts and regrets which she had schooled herself to deny.

She had just begun to pack some of her things, when she heard Dodo, with her hesitant step, coming up the stairs.

"May I come in?" Dodo asked politely, when she reached the door, for she was not allowed to go into Gertrude's room. She had been made to understand that she was to respect Gertrude's privacy.

"Of course, Dodo, please come in. You can watch me pack."

As soon as she was in the room, Dodo's formality crumbled and she threw her arms around Gertrude's waist and clung desperately to her. "Why do you have to go?" she asked, her voice muffled as she hid her face in Gertrude's skirt. "I want you to stay. Please Gertrude, stay," she pleaded.

"You, see, Dodo, I must make other plans. The longer I stay, the harder if will be for me to leave."

"But, Gertrude, I love you."

Gertrude hugged her closely and kissed the top of her head then gently loosened the grip of her thin arms.

"I love you too, very, very much." That was the first time Gertrude had been able to say that to anyone. She knew that Dodo had become more attached to her since her mother had become so preoccupied with the care of the baby, and it was a strong motive in her decision not to return to the Stantons. It was not what she wanted—to become too deeply involved with the people for whom she worked and still never really be a part of them.

Gertrude went on with her packing and as she moved about the room, she began softly to sing, to conceal the rising sorrow in her breast. She could see that her singing soothed Dodo's grief as she sat on the bed and watched Gertrude's every move. At times the little girl joined in with a quavering, childish tremolo, remembering some of the passages Gertrude had taught her. Gertrude's song gradually turned to an almost tuneless humming and she saw that Dodo had crumpled into a little heap and fallen asleep. Tenderly she straightened her to a more comfortable position and when her eyelids fluttered, she hummed a little louder to lull her back to sleep. It was the last lullaby she sang for Dodo.

Chapter Thirteen

As the train sped her on to Blumenort, every turn of its wheels was sending Gertrude deeper into the dark depression which had threatened to encompass her even before she left Winnipeg. Although the weather had turned quite cold, and the windows were catching a few short-lived drops of the drizzle which had begun to fall, she was hot and uncomfortable. The unregulated heat was geared to meet the requirements of the intense cold of the northland's winter, so the current passengers were forced to tolerate it in the meantime.

Gertrude had not anticipated the intensity of her sadness at the severance of her relationship with the Stantons. Dodo's tear-stained face pressed against the window as she waved when Gertrude left, would haunt her for many days to come—it would be left to time to bring recompense. But her departure from the Stantons was only one of the reasons for her melancholy.

She could no longer turn aside from the significance of the weighty problem which she was facing. The weariness of being in two worlds, was becoming intolerably oppressive. She longed to become a whole person again, not having her loyalties continually tested. Her first trip back to Blumenort had been difficult. By contrast, the visit to Rosenort at Christmas had been easier. The Ennses seemed more inclined to accept her for whom she was. She and Katie had been so glad to see each other that nothing else had mattered but she knew if she continued along the path of her Winnipeg life, sooner or later she would be expected to explain and justify herself to Katie too. There would be more questions. They would eventually turn into accusations and then what?

* * * * *

In mid May, Gertrude had made her 2nd trip to Blumenort. Mrs. Stanton, had delayed spring cleaning due to the birth of her son, but she still had not regained all of her strength, so could not participate as fully as she had the year before. The bulk of the work had fallen to Gertrude. Mrs. Stanton gave her 3 days off to recuperate so Gertrude decided it was time to make another appearance in Blumenort in the vain hope that she would find reason this time, to dispel the disillusionment she still felt from her visit in August. However, quite to the contrary, it became even more clear to Gertrude the extent to which things were continuing to deteriorate. They were making less and less effort to hide their disapproval. It hadn't been only Annie and Jennie. Aunt Anna and Uncle Henry were also putting on the pressure for her to return to Blumenort but one of her exchanges with Jennie was the most disturbing.

"I' don't think you are telling us everything about your life in Winnipeg. I've heard rumours," they were out in Aunt Anna's garden doing some preliminary work, getting ready for the spring vegetable planting.

"What kind of rumours?"

"Well, I don't really want to repeat what she said but you should know that people are talking." Jennie wasn't looking at Gertrude. She was bent down concentrating on extracting a couple of early weeds.

Gertrude had stopped hoeing and was leaning on its handle. "Jennie, stop this. It's pretty clear you want me to know, otherwise you wouldn't have said anything. Who is 'she' and what did *she* say?"

Jennie wasn't sure what sort of reaction she had expected from Gertrude but now she wished she hadn't said anything. After all she wasn't absolutely sure that there was any truth to what Helen had said. "Oh it was nothing."

"Jennie, as far as I know we have always at least been honest with each other. If you have heard bad things about me, you owe it to me, as your sister, to tell me."

"It was Abe Klassen's new wife, Helen. She said Abe told her that he had run into you in Winnipeg and that you looked like a hussy and that you had actually flirted with him over a cup of coffee. There, I've told you. I'm so embarrassed. I haven't told any one else, but who knows where else Helen has been spreading this story. If you are not concerned about your own reputation, at least you should be thinking about the rest of us who have to live in this community."

Abe Klassen! And to think that I actually felt sorry for him after I refused his proposal. How pathetic of Abe! If I defend myself I'll look just as pitiful as he. Gertrude was learning a first big lesson on how vulnerable she was in the face of those who would do her harm in order to protect themselves.

"My friend Tilly and I did run into Abe in Winnipeg and we did have a cup of coffee together. Abe's account of what happened is not what happened. He is lying. In fact, it was *he* who made a fool of *himself.* That is all I'm going to say. You can draw your own conclusions. Accept Helen's story or accept mine."

She hadn't had time to get to Steinbach to see Aunt Kathryne. Maybe Aunt Kathryne's influence would have helped calm her anger before the return trip to Winnipeg.

* * * * *

The burden of keeping such a big part of her life hidden was already becoming too heavy and it was only going to get worse. She felt she was being split in two. It wasn't just the strain of actually moving in and out of the two physical worlds. At night, after she turned off her light and lay awake for hours, she kept asking herself the same questions. Who am I? Where do I belong? Where am I going? She had been brought up to believe that much of the life she was now living was sinful. So why did it seem so natural to her? She felt no guilt and she knew that if she stayed in Winnipeg or some other city, she would drift farther and farther away from her people. In her attempts to think things through and get past the more superficial aspects of the situation, the whole picture was just becoming more complicated. She felt herself faltering.

Having decided to leave the Stantons, she needed a plan so, born out of a sense of fairness, more than anything else, the best she had been able to come up with was to return and live with them again, and see if she would be able to put her Winnipeg life behind her. By confining herself to Holdeman communities, finding suitable work would be a problem. She didn't like the idea of working for family members again. She would need to find job situations that were less confining but was that possible? Kansas had crossed her mind. Her brother Peter had found a new life in a Holdeman community there, could she? And Alberta. She knew of communities there including the one where Aunt Liza and Uncle Klass had bought their farm and where Bertha and her new husband now lived. She was accustomed to the handsome wage paid by the Stantons—much more than she could ever expect from working in a rural Mennonite community. These were obvious practical considerations that would have to be taken into consideration. But for now, she needed to focus on the implications of a return to life as dictated by her family. Were she to stay among the Holdemans, she would surrender totally. Their ways would have to again become her ways. She would force herself, once and for all, to accept the rules laid down by John Holdeman.

But, what if that didn't work and she were to leave them? In order to do this she would have to free herself; try to give up the love of the many people whom she had known all of her life. She did not know if she could accomplish such a task. If only the break would not need to be so brutal or the conformity so complete, but she knew there would be no half way resting place for long. The Holdemans wouldn't allow it and neither would her own integrity. Her thoughts kept going around and around. One thing she knew with certainty—there were fewer and fewer shadows left in which to hide. That was clear.

Her plan had been to go straight to Rosenort but in the days before leaving Winnipeg she decided she needed first to talk to her Aunt Kathryne. There had always been an unspoken understanding between them. Gertrude had not seen her on her last visit to Blumenort. In fact, they had seen very little of each other in the last two years. It was time. Maybe Aunt Kathryne could help her to break out of the circular thinking in which she was trapped and point out a direction that would guide her through the next few months. Uncle John picked her up at the station and they drove to the Loewens' house. Aunt Kathryne did not meet them at the door. She was sitting in the kitchen waiting for her. Gertrude was shocked. Aunt Kathryne, always a robust woman, was painfully thin. Gertrude had not seen her since her first trip back to Blumenort after starting her job at the Stantons. They had had a short visit after church. She was thinner but looked well, giving Gertrude reason to believe, at the time, that she was recovering from the poor health that had been plaguing her. Now her hollow face and bright eyes spoke a different story.

She rose to greet Gertrude. Gertrude was aghast at the fragility of Kathryne's skeletal body as they hugged. "I'm so glad to see you, Gertrude. It's been much too long."

"I know, I know." Gertrude had difficulty keeping her voice steady. Uncle John was standing behind Kathryne. During the embrace Gertrude's and John's eyes met for a brief second and everything was said between them about Kathryne's future. Gertrude knew at once that she couldn't burden Kathryne with her own struggles. However, as it turned out, Kathryne would volunteer some thoughts on how she saw Gertrude's future unfolding.

Gertrude was to stay for three or four days before going on to Rosenort. She decided to spend the entire visit with the Loewens. She would see Annie, Jennie and her brothers another time. Kathryne seemed to be in good spirits and did everything she could to make Gertrude feel at home. They spent leisurely mornings over their coffee. After dinner, Kathryne would have a long rest. Sometimes they would have afternoon tea and then Gertrude would prepare the supper which they lingered over until Kathryne was ready for bed. Gertrude got caught up on all the Steinbach and Blumenort gossip none of which was of much interest to her but she knew that Kathryne enjoyed sharing the local news. Kathryne wanted to hear everything about Gertrude's adventures in Winnipeg. Gertrude realized that her aunt wasn't asking just to be polite. She seemed genuinely interested. She had many questions which led Gertrude into talking about areas of her life that she had not been sharing with any of the other members of her family. Her resolve to protect Kathryne from her own inner conflicts melted away.

They began by talking about what Gertrude saw and did in Winnipeg. This seemed to move them naturally to Gertrude's questions about religious faith. As Gertrude began to reveal her private doubts about some of the Holdeman teachings, Kathryne did not reply with anger. She listened quietly. She told her aunt about her growing feeling that much of what the Holdemans believed to be so vitally important, she really didn't think was important at all. They talked about sin. So much of what she had seen and done during her life in Winnipeg was deemed by their church to be sinful. More and more she had been thinking that many of the outward behaviours demanded by John Holdeman had no place in religious dogma. Why brand things as sinful that would so much better be left as simply matters of individual taste? Why shouldn't people choose for themselves how they spend their leisure time, what they read, how they dress, whose hand they shake? It angered Gertrude to think that so much time and energy was spent on enforcing and monitoring what to her seemed like trivia. What about the more important sins—like the sins that involved hurting other people? She longed for a God that—she still didn't know.

"I know that I have very little time left."

Katheryne raised her hand to stop Gertrude from interrupting. "No, please don't protest. We must be honest with each other."

As it turned out, Katheryne too, had questions and doubts.

Katheryne began speaking as though her thoughts were coming from somewhere far away. As she spoke her face gained a little colour and lost some of the strained look that had been so apparent upon Gertrude's arrival. "I feel much differently about what you are saying, much differently than I would have felt three, even two years ago." She swallowed with difficulty, clearing her throat. "Knowing that I am coming to the end of my life is changing how I look at things. I have seen many retreat even further into our Holdeman faith when they know their time is near. For me it's been the opposite. I've been thinking of the big world out there that I have devoted my life to shutting out. I've been thinking about the belief we hold that heaven is unavailable to anyone who does not belong to our church. We must represent only a tiny fraction of the world population." Now there was almost a hint of a twinkle in her eye. "If we are right, heaven must be a very small place." Some of the old strength returned briefly to her voice as she continued. The words were coming easily now. She took Gertrude's hand and looked intensely into her eyes. "Surely there are good people out there who don't wear black shawls on their heads, who read all kinds of books and listen to beautiful music—music that I can only imagine—who use what the world has to offer to fashion a good life, who worship in other churches; all things that I have never done." A sigh passed her pale lips. "I've lived the Holdeman way all my life. I couldn't change any of that now. It's too late. But you—you have a whole lifetime ahead of you still."

They sat quietly without speaking for a long time.

"I hadn't thought about my brother Johann for years but I've been thinking of him lately. Now I regret refusing to see him when he returned to Blumenort with his new English wife. What was gained by that? You were very young at the time and wouldn't remember. We were *all* so very young then," she said wistfully. "Has anyone ever told you about him?"

"I didn't even know that I have an Uncle Johann."

Kathryne told her about Johann's errant ways and his refusal to repent bringing about his excommunication. She then explained about his visit 2 years later as it had been described to her by Gertrude's mother and how everyone else in the family had refused to come to the Penner farm to meet with him and his wife Penelope.

"He sent a short letter to your uncle and me after your mother died. I don't know how he heard of her death. The note was so short but it broke my heart to hear about the pain he was suffering. In spite of that, I put my church above my feelings for him. I clung to the belief that we had done right by shunning him and vowed to put him out of my mind forever."

"Do you still have the letter?"

"No, I kept it for a while, but eventually, I tore it up and threw it into the stove. I wish now I still had it."

"So do I," Gertrude said, almost in a whisper.

"You haven't shut out the rest of the world. I expect you have been doing even more things than you are telling me about. I can't condemn you for that. But I do fear for you. Those who are born into the Holdeman faith and who choose a different way of life do not have an easy time of it. I won't be here to lend you a helping hand but God is being good to us by giving us this opportunity to talk about these things now before I'm gone." Gertrude began to sob and Kathryne put her tired arms around her, rocking and comforting her as though she were a small child. "You are strong. You have always known the difference between right and wrong in a way that goes far beyond any of the Holdeman notions. I know that about you. I know that you will choose a life that is right for you and that will please God."

Two days later, they said their final good bye. Their sadness threatened to overwhelm them but it did not because they shared the feeling that they had made the best possible use of their short time together. They had not held back. There would be no regrets in the days to come. Neither would think that too much had been said and more importantly, that not enough had been said. As time went on, Gertrude would come to realize with increasing gratitude just how precious Kathryne's gift to her had been. She had never experienced such intimacy so willingly and lovingly given from another human being. It was new to her. She would never be quite the same again. Something had opened up inside of her—something that would help her in forming the loving relationships that were still ahead.

Back on the train, starting the journey to Rosenort via Winnipeg, she used the time to reflect and try to prepare herself—for what, she didn't know. Thanks to Kathryne, Gertrude was feeling an unfamiliar sense of freedom awakening in her. The plan to leave her Winnipeg life behind and give herself fully to the Holdeman way again in a last attempt to fit in was starting to make less sense. She had surprised herself many times during their talks because she was able to express her thoughts with a new kind of clarity.

As their time together came to an end, it almost seemed to Gertrude that her aunt knew which path Gertrude would take. With a wry grin she said to herself, well, we'll see how this all holds up after a few weeks in Rosenort!

When the train was almost at the little station where she would be met, probably by George, the excitement which she began to feel at seeing her old friends again, drove her dismal thoughts to the back of her mind. In thinking of David, she was filled with the deep, tender regard she held for him. Ever since the last time she had been with him, she had had the growing conviction that he, too, was stirred by a magnetism which was drawing them together. Nevertheless, she refused to build up any hopes where he was concerned until she would see him again; it was so many long, long months since they had last met.

Gertrude was surprised to see that it was Peter Enns who had come to meet her. He explained that George had been unable to come, so he had asked Peter to do him the favour of fetching her. He assured her that it was not a favour at all but a privilege and a pleasure. He took her hand and assisted her up into the buggy. When she was settled, he tucked the lap robe around her knees. While he untied the horse and hurried around to his side of the buggy, she wondered at his polite and gracious manner. He was not like any of the other young men she had known—even his speech was different. It was easy and at times almost flowery. It was not the way of the young men of their heritage. They were usually brusque and taciturn in the presence of women. Of course she also knew that the Enns boys had had more schooling than most but she suspected that there was more to it than that.

It was several miles to her sister's home, but Peter did not seem inclined to hurry his horse, so the journey took some considerable time. They talked of many things and suddenly, after she remarked on how good it was to see the spacious, open countryside after being so long in the closeness of the city, he quoted a snatch of lovely, lilting poetry which elaborated on the beauties of nature.

Gertrude looked up in surprise, "That's very pretty. I didn't know you liked poetry," she stopped, not knowing what more to say. "Did, did you learn that in school?"

"No, I didn't, " he looked at her, his eyes searching her face, wondering how much he could tell her, then seeing genuine interest, he said proudly, "I wrote it myself."

Her eyes widened. "I didn't know," she almost stuttered, "that you wrote poetry."

"Very few people do. I never let anyone read my poems, that is, except David. I have given him some of them to read," he explained. She began to see Peter in a new light, and the poetry bore out her earlier thoughts regarding him. It was the first time that David's name had come up between them since Peter had picked her up at the train, and it brought the colour to her cheeks. The intimacy of the conversation and then the mentioning of David's name had caught her off guard.

Peter took Gertrude's blush as encouragement to continue. "I have even written a poem—I have written a poem, for you," Peter confessed hesitantly, shyly. His eyes glinted with eagerness, pleading for her approval.

"But, Peter," Gertrude began, her confusion mounting again, "you shouldn't have. I don't know what to say." Through her acute embarrassment she was struck by the disconcerting thought that he may have shown the poem to David. If that were true, it could come between them just as they were on the verge of a relationship which could very possibly become important.

"I have never shown it to anyone, nor will I, except someday, to you." Peter went on, not sensing her discomfiture but unknowingly allaying her fears that David had seen it.

"I'll be happy to see it, then," Gertrude assured him, after her breathing became normal again. "Thank you for thinking enough of me to write a poem for me, but I don't see that I deserve the honour. You really shouldn't have done it."

"Oh, but I wanted to," he said simply.

Fortunately for Gertrude, they had reached the turn in the road which brought them to the end of their trip. She felt that she couldn't handle any further intimacies.

After Katie met them at the door, Peter returned to his rig with a bounding step and sent his horses into a gallop, whistling a merry tune as he waved farewell.

"I didn't know his horse could run that fast," Gertrude remarked abstractly and then stood lost in thought watching him go.

Katie's gay laugh brought her back and she gave Gertrude a sly look, "Ooooh?" she drew the tiny word out into a long upward sweep. "I thought you were rather long coming from the station. He seems to be in high spirits today, I wonder why?" and again she laughed. "Who could blame him? You do look very well—such rosy cheeks." With that she dropped her banter and welcomed Gertrude to her home.

Several weeks passed. Shortly after Gertrude's arrival they experienced a beautiful 'Indian Summer'—so welcome a characteristic of the north but now it was clear that winter was well on its way. One day in mid November, Katie decreed that there was to be no further malingering. The heater was to be set up that very day. The cooking range, alone, could no longer keep them warm. She had mentioned it to him more than once but George disliked the chore intensely and had kept putting it off hoping that, by some miracle, it would be accomplished without him. But today, from Katie's tone of voice, he knew that the time had come and he must bow gracefully to her edict.

It *was* indeed an unpleasant undertaking. Short lengths of tin stove pipes had to be joined together and attached to the stove. From there, they were led straight up almost to the ceiling and then made to follow a path parallel to the ceiling around the room before being turned up again and guided through a hole in the ceiling. The trail of the pipes continued on up through one of the upstairs rooms to the roof where they were connected to the chimney. In this way, a maximum amount of heat was distributed throughout both floors of the house. It took more hands than were available to hold up the pipes as they were being secured with wire from the ceiling, but they did their best.

Katie and Gertrude were up on chairs, their arms stretched high, holding up the pipes. George had struggled to fit the pipes into the heater, and was now fighting to get the last support wire in place before leading the pipes through the ceiling to the second floor. It was while they were in this awkward tableau, with George muttering under his breath, amongst which the word "sinful" was distinctly audible, that they heard someone coming on to the yard. George eagerly dropped his work and was about to go to the door.

"George!" Katie shouted, without restraint, while she and Gertrude fought to hold onto the pipes which were threatening to give way. "You come back here at once and get these pipes through the celling! We can't stop now—hurry," she pleaded in desperation. Then she shouted, "Come in!" The door was thrown open and there stood Father Enns smiling broadly. "Oh, Father," Katie said more calmly, "come in and sit down. We're almost finished." Father Enns sat down and as was his way, he threw one of his long legs in a wide arc, crossing his knee and twisting his foot around the calf of his other leg. It never ceased to amaze Gertrude but it was evidently his favourite sitting position, and only then was he ready for conversation.

"If I had my overalls on, I'd help you, George," he said, seeing George's flushed face and observing his annoying predicament. "But I decided, since I was coming over mainly to see Gertrude, I had better look nice," he said, looking down at his best suit which he had donned for the occasion. From her lofty position, Gertrude smiled at him fondly.

"I might as well tell you why I came, Gertrude," never being a man to dangle a point, "I've come to ask if you would marry my son." He spoke as though he were offering her the world. Gertrude's heart almost stopped, then soared expecting something other than what was to come.

"My son, Peter, is asking for your hand….."

"Peter?" she asked incredulously. At first, she was not certain that she had heard right. "Peter," she repeated almost a whisper. This time it wasn't a question. She knew that she had heard correctly. For a moment she was immobilized, then her hands flew to her cheeks and the stove pipes went clattering down, falling apart and spreading black soot all over Katie's clean floor. She looked quickly from Katie to George. They were smiling their approval, oblivious to the havoc she had created out of all the work they had painstakingly done. They must have known! That's why Father Enns didn't ask to speak to her alone. They had all been so sure of themselves!

Gertrude jumped off her chair and blurted, "Oh, no….. oh, no…..I could never…..never marry Peter….." With her hands still covering her face, she ran from the room and up the stairs.

Just before she closed her door, she heard Katie saying loudly into the dead silence, "George! I thought I told you to clean all the soot out of those pipes before you brought them in! Now just look at what you've done. What a mess!"

Gertrude sat down on her bed and leaned her hot forehead against the cool iron of the bedpost. She could no longer hold back her tears and her shoulders shook with the deep sobs welling up inside her. As though from a great distance, she heard the outside door closing, and Father Enns's rig leaving the yard. Then she heard the creaking of the stairs as someone came slowly, hesitantly up the stairway.

There was a light rap at the door. "Gertrude?"

"Yes.....come in," she managed to say.

Katie came in and sat down beside her. Slowly, she stroked her sister's hair, "Gertrude, don't cry like that, please don't cry so. I've never seen you cry like this before....."

She gradually became quieter. Katie waited patiently until she knew Gertrude could speak.

"But, Gertrude, what happened? I thought you were very fond of Peter. Father did ask us before what we thought."

"It's not that, I am fond of him, but....." She looked at Katie for the first time. Katie's worried puzzlement deserved an explanation. "I have always liked him—from the very first. He reminded me of Joseph. He seemed just like a brother. I must have been looking for something in Peter that I had lost in Joseph. I have never though of him as anything else but a brother."

"But, Gertrude, should you have been so quick to say no? Shouldn't you have given it some thought?"

"Oh, Katie," Gertrude looked almost horrified. "What must Father Enns think of me? I was terribly rude. Oh, my, I'll never be able to look at him again." His reaction suddenly seemed more important to her than Peter's. She had not even thought of how Peter might feel when he would be told.

"I don't think you have to worry about Father. I'm sure he will understand. But I still think you should have thought about it. You know Peter must love you, or he wouldn't have asked for you and you could learn to love him; you would have a home and the children you've always wanted. You couldn't ask for a better man."

"But that's not the way I want it. I would rather have nothing. Why, you know he's younger than I am," she began wearily counting the ways, "he's short and small built. He would always look smaller than me," she spoke tonelessly, automatically, trying to think of excuses. She couldn't bring herself to tell Katie the real reason for her refusal.

"All that wouldn't matter, if you loved each other. There isn't that much difference in your age." Katie was trying hard to understand, reaching out for hazy fragments of reason, examining them carefully, wondering what else she could say.

After a lengthy silence, Katie asked suddenly, "Is it someone else? Is it, Gertrude, is it—David?"

Gertrude nodded miserably.

"So that's it! You know, I used to think that but lately we all thought that you and Peter—anyway, Peter always asked if we'd heard from you and he was so excited when we told him you were coming home. Why, George even made up an excuse so Peter could meet your train." Many things were becoming clearer to Gertrude but it would never alter her decision.

Several days passed, with Gertrude silently resigning

herself to a dreary fate. After all, she reasoned, David had always held himself aloof from her. How could she have let her foolish heart run riot? Just as she was beginning to reassemble some of her usual serenity, Father Enns, once again wearing his best suite, made another appearance at the door.

"Gertrude, I wonder if I could have a few words with you?" he asked after the barest of preliminary observations on the weather. "Alone?" He looked at Katie and George who had greeted him in an unusually subdued manner. Katie started for the door at once but seeing George still in his chair, she threw him a glaring look and with a pull at his shirt sleeve, hustled him out of the room.

As soon as they were alone, Gertrude said hastily, "I want to apologize. I beg you to forgive me for my strange behaviour the other day."

"There is no need, Gertrude. It should be I who begs your forgiveness. You see," he explained, "Peter had made his intentions known to me quite some time ago. He asked that I come to you at the first opportunity. I talked it over with Katie. We both agreed that you and Peter had a special relationship. We were sure you shared his feelings—that you probably were actually waiting for his proposal. So with all our good intentions and in our zeal, we forgot the most important person in the whole story. To think that I actually asked in front of Katie and George *and* while you were standing on a chair holding up the stove pipes! So please, won't you forgive my clumsiness?"

Gertrude could not but admire Father Enns.

"There is nothing to forgive. It's over now and it is best forgotten," she said and to avoid any further embarrassment she hurried on, "but, please, before you say anymore, I haven't changed my mind."

"But that isn't what I came for. You left me no doubts as to how you felt," he assured her and at her sigh of relief, he wondered just how to word his next plea. To parry for time, he went on at some length in explaining to her that he had been the go-between in many marriages on behalf of the young men, yes, and older ones, too, in his services to the church. Quite often the young ladies refused at the first meeting but he was seldom mistaken as to which of them would change their mind, and most of them did, he added with satisfaction.

"Now, for the reason I came to see you. It may be hard for you to understand at first but hear me out. Now it's David who wants to marry you."

"David?" Gertrude said with difficulty. The incredulity of the affair was deepening. If it were not so serious, it could have been a comedy unfolding before her eyes.

"As soon as David heard that you had refused Peter, he came to me. I think that your quick 'no' gave him the courage. I was astonished but, as you can see, here I am."

"But....." Gertrude started to say something more, but he stopper her.

"No, Gertrude, don't say anything. Think it over and when you have made up your mind, I'll be waiting."

"I promise." she said meekly. She did not want to make a fool of herself a second time.

Father Enns rose to go, then turned back to her.

"If it will make it any easier for you, I'll tell you one thing. David told me that he had had this on his mind for a long time, long before he knew that Peter felt the same way."

He left her with the words that he would be very happy to have her as another daughter if her decision made it so.

Peter's proposal had jolted her into the realization that her feelings for David were not merely a passing fancy. Yet she was unable to accept the strange turn of events without misgivings. She was plagued by doubts. Her self-confidence was sorely shaken. How simple it could have been had David asked for her hand in the first place, she sighed, and she would have accepted him with dignity and decorum. In her present uncertainty, she was not sure that she could marry him at all.

Several days after Father Enns's last visit, Katie and George decided to take the children and visit their grandfather. Uncharacteristically, Katie did not invite Gertrude to join them. Gertrude was in no frame of mind to go out anyway, especially to the Ennses, so she was relived to have an opportunity to be home alone. She wondered how she would ever be able to face them again.

After they were gone, Gertrude wandered listlessly about the room still in a quandary about recent events. She stopped to look out of the window. The bleak picture of the oncoming winter, the patches of snow, where the strong wind had chased it into hiding, the bared trees and the creaking of the woodshed door which someone had carelessly left open, sent her back to the stove to put more wood into its hungry, greedy mouth. She was reaching into the woodbox when she heard a knocking at the door. She wondered who could be coming here at this time. She really didn't want to see anyone.

Gertrude straightened up, forgetting that she was still holding the piece of wood in her hand and went to the door. She opened it to find David standing there. Gertrude was too stunned to speak. They stood and looked at each other.

"May I come in out of the cold?" David finally asked. Gertrude had been unaware of the cold swirling into the door. "Or are you going to keep me out with that piece of wood?" She looked down uncertainly and when she lifted her head and saw the grin on his face, she couldn't hold back a small, wavering smile herself.

"Well, come in then, at least to get warm," she stepped aside, "but there is no one else at home."

"I know, Gertrude, that's why I came." She looked at him inquiringly but she had regained some of her composure and was determined not to lose it again. While David removed his heavy jacket, she indicated a seat and she, too, sat down and waited.

David told her that he had come to clear up what must have been puzzling to her, so he would come right to the heart of the situation. Things had not gone at all to his liking. After Gertrude refused Peter's proposal, he, David, had wanted to rush right to her and make his own wishes known. But Father Enns had restrained him. That would not be fair to Gertrude. She needed some time to collect herself. He agreed that, in that, his father may have been right. And as was their custom, his father maintained that it was his place to go ask Gertrude. In that, David felt that he was wrong but he would not argue the point. Further more, his father said that since he had made the first blunder, he felt impelled to smooth it out as best he could. David could not deny him that opportunity.

"But, David, I don't understand. Why, if you felt like this, why, didn't you ask for me, first?" Gertrude interjected.

"That is another thing I have to explain. You see, when

you were here last Christmas, I made up my mind to marry you, if you'd have me. I had thought about you, often, long before that but there was something about you that day….. One day when Peter and I were in our room….. we were both reading. I could not keep my mind on my book. I decided I must tell someone about my hopes or burst. But I didn't know how to start. Suddenly he spoke of you and I felt that now was my chance but just as I was about to speak, he blurted out that he was a going to marry you someday. He had already asked father to ask you."

David went on to say that he had been too astounded to say anything but it led him to examine what he knew of the relationship between Gertrude and Peter. He remembered that many times he had seen them talking and laughing together. How he had envied Peter! They seemed to have so much to say to each other, while he was tongue-tied in Gertrude's presence. He convinced himself that Gertrude must certainly prefer Peter to him. So he said nothing.

"Oh David." Everything was falling into place. She began trying to explain, haltingly, that since Peter's proposal, she had felt the same way—that David could not possibly feel toward her the way she felt toward him. They dared to exchange a smile as they started to feel the constraints which had held them apart for so long start to melt away.

"I couldn't wait any longer to see you, Gertrude. We have wasted so much time already." David reached for one of her hands and held it between his. She looked down at his hands, they were long and slender, the hands of a builder of dreams. "And, Gertrude, I do love you and only hope you feel the same way about me."

"Yes, David." She could not so easily say she loved him.

She knew that would come but he had spoken the most wonderful, beautiful words she had ever heard.

"I came to ask you to be my wife. I just couldn't wait for father to come and ask you again. But, before you answer me, I have one more thing that I must discuss with you." Gertrude waited expectantly while David searched for the words to begin what he must say.

"It's about the church. I haven't agreed with it, almost from when I first joined. But I had no idea what could replace it for me. John and Agnes had been reading the books of Emanuel Swedenborg and other writings examining Swedenborg's ideas. They were quite excited about what they were discovering. So when John asked me if I would like to read some of the material, I agreed immediately. George got curious, thinking he might be missing out on something. He started reading too. It's hard to believe now, but at first, George seemed even more enthusiastic than I. Evening after evening John and I talked into the night. Sometimes Agnes and George joined in. Like John and Agnes, I really feel as though I have found what I have been looking for but not George. I have a feeling Katie laid down the law, especially after what happened to John. It's like George has now become more Holdeman than John Holdeman himself.

"John began to openly challenge the church elders. There is no room for dissent in the Holdeman world. So far the only people I have talked to about actually leaving the church are John and Agnes but my silence can't go on much longer. Worrying about Father has held me back. John's excommunication was heart breaking for him. But it's only a matter of time and they will do to me what they did to John."

"Oh, David! How awful!" Gertrude burst out.

"Oh, I'm so sorry." David, misinterpreting her reaction, let go of Gertrude's hand. "I didn't know how you would feel about it but I….."

"No—no," Gertrude interrupted quickly, stopping him from going on and this time she took his hand in hers. "I don't mean that your feelings about the church are awful. I have been dissatisfied with our church for a long time too. What *is* awful is the thought of you going through what John went through—that terrible situation with your family and all the rest of it."

"Yes, I know and I've thought a lot about it and what has been happening to John is only one of the things that I can't accept in the old church, there's so much more.

"But right now, the thing that worries me most is, if you marry me, you will be dragged right into the middle of what surely will be a big mess."

"That's one thing you must never worry about. And I'm not afraid of what might happen as a result of all this—really, I'm not," she emphasized. Gertrude was allowing herself to hope that maybe, like David, she could find in Swedenborg's teachings what she had sought for so long. She needed to find out more.

"I don't know anything about Swedenborg."

"It is too much to go into now but I find it a beautiful religion and it has opened my eyes to so many things. From now on, we can explore his teachings together. It is going to be so wonderful!"

They sat quietly for some time.

"Knowing all this, will you still marry me?"

"Yes, I will. And whatever happens it will happen to us together. I am so happy."

David's deep sigh of relief brought a smile to Gertrude's lips

"Yes, I'm happier than I have ever been. Somehow I just felt inside of me that you must feel the same way as I about the old church. For me, it is the most important thing, next to you, in my life." He reached hesitantly toward her and touched her cheek, then seeing her eyes fill with happiness, he took her face between his hands and softly kissed her lips.

Gertrude and David decided that for now, they would leave things just as they had always been. David would come with his father for Gertrude's formal acceptance of the marriage. The announcements would be made in the council and in the church. Gertrude chose Christmas Day as her wedding day. She would stay with her friend Margaret Fehr. She knew that this would cause an outburst from Annie but she would deal with that quickly before going to the Fehrs. She didn't want to have anything to do with treading the tight rope that their relationship had become, distracting her in the days preceding her marriage. From there she would go to the church of her childhood to be married. These plans, they would make with Father Enns, for he was ignorant of the fact that David had come to Gertrude. David did not wish his father to think that he had gone beyond his authority. David wanted to share the joy of his marriage with him without any reservations, for soon enough, his father would be confronted with David's denial of the teachings of the Holdemans and everything else to do with the Mennonite religion. He wanted to spare his father that grief as long as possible. It was David's one regret that he must hurt his father in the same way as he had seen him hurt when John left the church but he knew of no other way.

Katie and George knew that David was going to see Gertrude that evening but Katie had grave doubts as to the outcome of their meeting. She had stretched the rules of propriety by allowing David to come. She meekly carried the weight of her share in the extraordinary occurrences of the past few weeks so she felt she had no recourse but to agree to David's request. She reasoned that the people involved were long past being children and with a decisive turn of mind, she felt it was time to bring the muddled situation to a conclusion, whatever that was going to be. As soon as they returned home and Katie saw Gertrude's face, she knew that all was well.

When the formalities and plans were completed, the two sisters fell excitedly into the preparations for the wedding. George had to take them to Morris. There they carefully shopped for the material for the dress Gertrude would make for herself. They chose a length of deep, wine-red coloured woollen material. Gertrude bought shoes with a well turned heel which laced high above the ankle. They did not forget the linens and lawns for the undergarments, nor dainty laces and ribbons to trim them. Only Gertrude and Katie would know that they were there and it would remain their secret. Katie was delighted to be a part of the conspiracy. Finally Gertrude bought a square of black silk which she would hem by hand, fashioning it into her head covering.

The marriage services of the Holdemans were plain and simple. The ceremony of vows was the culmination of the long sermon which preceded it while the bride and groom sat side by side at the front of the church—the first and only time they would be able to sit together in church. But the holiness, the excitement, the anticipation of what was to come, were all present. There were no planned celebrations, only informal family gatherings in honour of the event. The gifts were in the nature of small momentoes from the nearest and dearest, reminders of that most important day.

So the days sped and dragged, dictated by the mixture of emotions which coloured their passage, until a week before Chirstmas, when Gertrude left for Blumenort to stay with the Fehrs. Her only regret was that Aunt Kathryne would not be there to share her joy. Kathryne had succumbed to her cancer shortly after Gertrude's last visit to Steinbach. Gertrude had already given a detailed account to David of the last time she and Kathryne had been together. The new sense of freedom which Gertrude had felt after leaving her aunt was renewed in the telling of their meeting. David listened intently wishing that he had had the opportunity to know her. They would both feel her approving presence during their wedding ceremony.

The marriage of Gertrude Penner and David Enns took place as was decreed, on December the twenty-fifth, in the year nineteen hundred and seven.

For Gertrude, the decade which followed that day, was rich with experiences. It brought her happiness of undreamed heights. It was a time of rapid change which brought with it its own special kinds of adventure. All this was interspersed with days of quiet serenity and the simple pleasure of living

Chapter Fourteen

The first year, so exciting, so hectic, so wonderful, drew to a close. David and Gertrude's marriage had been launched. It had been filled with the hard work of building up their farm and seeding and reaping their first crop. It was filled with becoming acquainted with each other and loving each other and every moment of the time they spent together. Gertrude had established a warm relationship with John and Mary Enns and their large and growing family. For the first time since she was a small child, she had the feeling of being part of a large, diverse family full of people of all ages.

Gertrude was astounded by their pace of living. They had kept their hired help long after the threshing and ploughing had been done. To sell their grain, it had to be hauled by wagon to the nearest railroad. The farmer had to rent a box-car, fill it and have it shipped to points of handling. They returned with their wagons filled with wood and coal. They also had many of their staple foods shipped in, which, too, had to be carted home. But now the extra help was all gone. The privacy they had so enjoyed during the first months of the marriage was restored. It was winter again and the Ennses second year was underway. It began quietly enough.

They were not lonely. They went to church most every Sunday and if they did not go visiting, they had guests. During the week, when the men had work to do together, the women, too , would get together at one or another's home with their children in tow. Gertrude and David did not need the stimulation of the company of others for them to enjoy themselves. They would have preferred to be left to their own devices much more often. Katie who had never been able to make close friends since she had come to Rosenort, made no secret of how proud she was to have her very own sister near by with whom she could associate freely and intimately.

One afternoon in mid-February, Gertrude stood at the window looking out. It was a winter of many snowfalls and winds. Between the house and barn a high drift of snow was growing every day. The snow was dense enough to support a pathway across its top, so instead of shovelling a path to the barn through the drift, David had carved steps from the base of the drift in front of the house leading to the path on the top with more steps to go down to the barn door at the other side. Gertrude could just see over the top to the south and west. The wide open country looked like a big sea with the ripply water laying static, unmoving, as though it had been frozen in a gay moment, while over its surface the loose snow drifted ceaselessly, restlessly until it would find a barrier which would stop its flight. The vastness of the panorama was almost frightening and a shiver ran through her body. She heard David come up behind her.

"Isn't it beautiful?" he asked. Gertrude looked up at him, in surprise. She saw the reverent awe in his face. Her head just reached his shoulder and always his towering height sent a warm, comforting glow to her heart. She turned again to the window to see if she could see it as he saw it.

"Yes, maybe—maybe it *is* beautiful," she said softly, wonderingly, and the view took on a miraculous, new light as David drew her close and she laid her head on his shoulder.

"Look," David broke into the silence after they had stood, not moving for some time, "there's someone coming from the south. From here It looks like George's team." In the winter time, they could cross the frozen creek which ran close to George's farm, and cut across the field to make the way much shorter between them. "You know, I think it's Katie. She's in the open sleigh-alone. I better get dressed and look after her team."

"I'll stoke up the fires. She'll be frozen. It's so cold out today." Gertrude put wood in the cook stove and pushed the kettle to the front where it began at once to sing. The kettle always stood, filled, simmering, at the back of the stove, ready to be put into action at a moments notice. David picked up the coal pail and dumped coal into the heater in the main room and opened the dampers so the fire would begin to roar cheerfully up the chimney. "You didn't have to do that; I could have—," she said to him but she was pleased at his thoughtfulness. "I wonder why Katie would be coming by herself."

"I'm sure she must have come for 'women talk', so I'll do some things that need doing in the barn for a while."

"But don't stay out too long. I'll make some coffee."

Katie hurried to the stove as soon as she came in and held

her hands out to the welcoming heat. Gertrude pulled up two chairs and opened the oven door. There was nothing more soul satisfying than to sit back, relax and prop your feet up on the oven door and besides it was the quickest way of warming cold feet. Usually confidences flowed easily in this comfortable position but today, the silences were becoming longer from each pleasantry to the next.

Finally Gertrude said, "Katie, I can see that something is bothering you. You might just as well tell me what it is."

"Well, there has been talk. I only want to know from you if it's true. If you tell me it isn't, I'll be satisfied." Katie was trying to unearth a hope out of the futility she knew it to be.

"What is it?" Gertrude prodded, "I can't tell *you* anything until you tell *me*."

"You see, it's on account of John. I always knew there would be trouble." Katie began to circumvent the issue. "I know that he and David have always been close but now John spends entirely too much time here."

"How can you say that? He and David have always been more than brothers. They are the closest of friends. It's only natural that now, since David has his own home—"

"But, you see," Katie broke in, "that's just the trouble. People are bound to talk."

"Just what do you mean by 'talk', Katie?" Gertrude was losing her patience. "What on earth do they have to talk about? *And,* I don't mind saying that I'm very fond of John too, since I've gotten to know him better."

"You know that we are supposed to keep a certain distance from those who have been thrown out of the church—no business dealings—no close friendships and such like. Well, we all can see that you are not following those rules. But worse than that. The talk is that you and David are not keeping the shunning on—no!—let me finish. They say that you eat with him at your table when he's here and it's the same thing when you go to his place. At first, I flatly denied it. I told them that we had all been together lots of times and I had never seen anything like that. But the talk did not stop. So yesterday when a couple of John's boys were over and they mentioned that you had been at their place for dinner the day before, I asked them straight out if it was true—if you all ate with John at the same table?"

"Well?"

"They said it was. But I want to know from you. Is it true, Gertrude?" Katie persisted, still hoping for a denial.

"Yes, It's true," Gertrude admitted without elaborating. "But you shouldn't have asked the boys. They should not be drawn into this."

"How could you, Gertrude?" Katie began to wring her hands in agitation and the frown on her forehead deepened. Gertrude's reproof had fallen on deaf ears. "How could you? You know just what this leads to. It will surely be brought up at the council. You don't know how far it might go!"

"I know, Katie. I know. But we can look out for ourselves."

There was a prolonged silence. Gertrude knew that Katie was brooding about something more but she was determined not to help her out. Let her speak in her own good time.

"Gertrude," Katie finally asked, "how could you let David get you into this thing?"

"Oh, but you're wrong there. David didn't get me into anything. It was the most natural thing to do, to invite John to our table. We didn't even discuss it beforehand. Anyway, David and I both agree that the practice of shunning is wrong. It's *all* wrong! And you might as well know that I have had many doubts and questions about Holdeman practices even when I was a young girl, long before I ever met David."

Katie looked aghast. "I know that you don't really believe what you just said." She brushed aside Gertrude's avowal as unworthy of comment, as though that put an end to that. "It was up to you, Gertrude, to put your foot down when you saw how things were going. I know I would never have let George talk me into anything like that. I would have set him straight in a hurry!" she stated emphatically.

"Maybe you can handle George that way. He seems to want you to tell him what to do but I would never treat David that way," Gertrude said quietly.

"Well!" Katie looked shocked. "I didn't know you felt that way about George!" She picked up at the mote which might be critical of George, her defence of him, always within reach, ready to be put into action.

"I wasn't criticizing George or you either, Katie. I think a lot of George. We're just different people, that's all."

"I *do* know that." Katie was deflated, ashamed of her hasty retort to Gertrude's innocent, but pointed remark. "Anyway, I thought it my duty to warn you, I didn't want you to be hurt by something that wasn't your fault."

"I know you have my best interests at heart. I am grateful for it."

After Katie was gone and David returned to the house, he looked searchingly at his wife. "You don't look as though you had a pleasant visit with Katie. And I must say she looked very unhappy when she came out."

"No, I guess it wasn't very pleasant," she answered slowly.

"She was worried. It was about the shunning." She was searching for a way to say what she had heard, less bluntly than it had been told to her.

"Oh, you mean, about our eating with John?"

"Then you've heard about it too?" Gertrude was relieved.

"Yes, but I didn't think it was important enough to repeat."

"Well, Katie thinks it is. She says it will very likely come up at the council."

"Does she?" David thought about it for a while. "You know this is new for them, their church, I mean." Significantly they had begun, without thought, to refer to the church and its members in the third person. "They used to bother Mary about obeying the church rules . They were never sure what to do about her. I know that many thought a mistake was made when she wasn't put out at the same time as John. But this is a very different thing concerning you and me. Well, we'll see. I certainly won't deny our not keeping the shunning if it comes up at the council."

* * * * *

"Well! She certainly didn't deny anything! Oh George, what are we going to do? Besides having no guilt about eating with John, she actually said that she was questioning our church before she met David! I don't believe that for a minute. I think she just made that one up to further aggravate me. I don't know if she knows what she is playing with. Our faith is what gets us into heaven. Surely she can't be willing to gamble all that away. Maybe I should try and talk to Annie and Jennie about this. Ach!..... what good would that do? They are too critical of Gertrude as it is.

I just don't know what to do. If she is excommunicated, what will happen to our relationship? We have become so close in recent years. I can't imagine it."

"It will go before the council in a week or two. There will be a warning. They will be given some time. If I know David, he won't back down at the start. Then, things will come to a head and people will speak out against those books they have been reading. It will become clear how wrong those ideas are and once it comes to that, Gertrude and David will see the error of their ways. I've never been able to understand John. His head has always been somewhere up in the clouds, even when we were little children, but David—he's a different story. He is practical. He will come around when he is faced with the consequences of continuing to break the rules and when he does, so will Gertrude. No one ever leaves our church because they choose to. If they are excommunicated it is to punish them for sinning so that they can repent and come back to us. Gertrude and David are smart. They will repent before the church has to take the last step."

Katie was listening closely, somewhat taken aback by the confident tone in George's voice. Maybe he was right.

George patted Katie's hand. "This will all work itself out. I know it will. Things will get back to normal. You just wait and see. Now, what's for supper?" he asked with a smile.

* * * * *

About two weeks after Katie had alerted Gertrude to the developing situation, an afternoon council meeting was announced at the Sunday morning's service. When

Gertrude and David were leaving the church, they sensed the tentacles of coolness spreading through the congregation. Though they were cordially greeted, no one asked them over for dinner, which in itself was unusual. They in turn, invited no one. They did not tarry.

It was a cold day with a strong wind blowing from the south. It was still a source of wonder to the pioneers in the north country, that the southern winds were more vicious and penetrating than the north winds. The days on the calendar spoke of March, yet there was no sign of spring. As they approached their rig, the horses nickered a friendly 'hello' and with the snow swirling around them, Gertrude and David climbed into their covered sleigh. They were grateful for its protection, not only from the weather, but from the curious eyes of the others.

David had built a light, wooden frame on top of a low box on sleigh runners. The frame was covered with canvas and had sliding panels for doors. They were completely closed in except for the small opening through which they passed the lines to guide the horses and the small isinglass pane through which the driver could peer out to see where he was going, though much trust had to be placed on the good sense of the horses. At best the little window gave them only a partial view. Though it was an improvement from riding in an open wagon box transferred onto runners, it had a number of drawbacks. It gave some people an uneasy sense of suffocation. Then there was the ever present danger of the rig tipping over. Though it was virtually impossible for anyone to get hurt in these minor mishaps, because the occupants were so thoroughly bundled in heavy clothes and blankets, it was still an unpleasant experience. Nevertheless, the covered sleighs were very popular and a boon to travellers in the wide open spaces so characteristic of this area. Gertrude remembered with longing her childhood home with the protection of the bushland and the closeness of the farms. "Well, I guess that's it," David said when they were some distance from the church.

"Do you really think so?" Gertrude asked wistfully.

"What else could it be? You saw how everyone acted. But don't look so sad, Gertrude. They can't hurt us."

"I know—but—," she could not shake the depression that was pressing in on her.

They were silent, swaying with every motion of the sleigh. Suddenly the horses veered slightly off their course and one side of the runners sank into a patch of soft snow beside the hardened track. The horses, used to that type of an emergency, stopped at the first warning, and the sleigh started to tip, ever so slowly, gently, but without a doubt, to land, with a spray of flying snow, on its side. Gertrude and David looked at each other, helplessly, accepting the inevitable as they tumbled into a soft mass of tangled wrappings. The humour of the situation and their comic expressions broke the tense atmosphere which had filled the sleigh. David's ample form began to shake with laughter and Gertrude's merriment rose and mingled with his. They laughed until they were almost too weak to unravel themselves and climb out to right the sleigh. The laughter relieved some of their pent up tension brought on by the announcement of the afternoon council meeting.

David went back to the church alone that afternoon. When he saw Gertrude's reluctance to go back, he told her it would perhaps be better if she did not go. "I think they more or less just want to feel us out, just as I want to feel them out," David said. "I wish I were wrong, but I think this is only the beginning. And I like to think of you safe, waiting for me here."

The feeling of being protected and sheltered from care and harm was still new to Gertrude and she luxuriated in it. As soon as David was off the yard, she heard the familiar scratching at the door. She hurried to let Skipper in. Skipper had been David's constant shadow since he was a puppy several years before their marriage. He had, without question, followed David to his new home. He was seldom in the house but when David was away, he insisted on entry. He would follow Gertrude about the house and when she sat down, he settled at her feet. Gertrude felt the comfort of his presence. The honour of being accepted with no reservations by Skipper, essentially a one-man dog, filled her with humility.

Gertrude settled down with a book, but her anxiety, her impatience for David's return, would not let her concentrate on what she was reading. She listened for the sound of his approach and made countless trips to the window, even though she knew that Skipper would be alert to David's coming, long before she and take his stand at the door.

When Gertrude saw Skipper's ears perk up, she reached out and petted his head. He laid his nose on her lap and submitted to her caress but his tail was wagging furiously in his eagerness to go to the door, even though he knew it would be some time before his master would come in.

"What would I do without you, Skipper?" she asked him absently. "We're much alike, you and I, both waiting for his return, every minute he's away." She gave him an extra pat and let him go.

"Hurry and tell me," Gertrude said quickly as she greeted her husband, "what happened?" Her anxiety had mounted until she could scarcely contain herself once David was in the yard. For her, the time it took for David to lead his horses into their stalls, could have been an eternity.

"It was nothing to get excited about," David assured his wife. "It was very much as I expected," he began telling her as he removed his outer clothes and they sat down to their lunch. "The church was pretty full. George and Peter were there, but not Katie. Father spoke first. He talked about how important it is to obey the church laws. He said that a church could not exist without them and you could not be a good member unless you did your very best to carry them out. He spoke in very general terms and what he said made good sense," David said, then he added, "but then Father always does."

"Yes, he does." Gertrude agreed. "And he didn't say anything else?"

"No, he made his talk short. Father likes to stay in the background when any of us are involved in church matters. From then on, Henry Esau did the talking. He repeated most of what Father had said but then he came to the point of the shunning. That, he said, was especially important, especially here in Rosenort where it is our misfortune to have a brother in our midst who has been put out of the church."

"Oh, dear."

"Then Henry went on to say that from several sources it has come to the ears of the elders, that there are some members of this church who are being lax in that area. This, he said, could not be allowed, and those who knew their failings must correct them."

"But he didn't say who they are?"

"Not then. He sat down and he and Father talked quietly together. Then Henry said that if anyone had anything to add, they were free to speak. Several people got up and said things to the effect that if they had not been good members and if they had sinned, they asked to be forgiven and from now on they would do better. Isn't it funny, Gertrude," David digressed, "that it's always those who could never do anything wrong, who will get up and say that sort of thing?"

"Yes." Gertrude nodded her head in agreement.

"Then Abe Plett jumped up—his face all flushed. He demanded to know just who they were talking about. He said that it was not right to blacken everyone's name because of a few back-sliders."

"Wasn't it just like Abe to do something like that?" Gertrude remarked after a while.

"It certainly was," and David couldn't help laughing. "I've known him since we were boys together, and he always was a troublemaker. He could never let well enough alone." David could still hear the gasp that went though the church. The gasp was followed by complete silence while each one became studiously preoccupied with their own thoughts, some looking down at their hands, some looking straight ahead. Everyone had known when they came that the talks were aimed at David and Gertrude but, that this meeting was only meant to be an indirect warning. They were displeased with Abe's interference.

"Then did Henry tell them it was us?"

"He couldn't do much else. I got up after and said that it was true that we had not kept the shunning on John. But Henry cut me off and said he was sure that we would see that we had done wrong and ordered everyone to pray for guidance, so that the right paths would be found. With that he dismissed the meeting. He gave me no chance to say more."

"And that was all?"

"Yes, that's all that was said. But it goes much deeper than that," David said thoughtfully. "I could feel that there was much left unsaid. You see, our not keeping the shunning was the one concrete thing they could jump on, a way to bring out in the open something they still do not quite know how to handle. This meeting was meant to give us an opportunity—a chance to turn back to the church. By focusing on the shunning they were trying to make things as simple and easy as possible for everyone. You have to admit that most of them hope we will see it their way. They sincerely believe that they and their church are right and we know that you can't take away anybody's right to believe in the church of their choice and to live by it. But, Gertrude, it's fine for you and me to say that about them but to say to them, that it's our right too, is like talking to the wind. They claim that their church is the only true one, so, with that, they take the right away from us. They quote from the writings of John Holdeman as though they were the word of God, not just one man's opinion. How can one argue against the word of God? There can be no further discussion."

"Yes, it seems hopeless to think that a reasonable agreement can be made doesn't it?"

David nodded his head sadly.

Things seemed orderly and serene on the surface but something intangible, something vital had changed. Gertrude sensed a kind of artificiality creeping between them and the others. Those whom she felt most close to, she thought, were acting slightly aloof while the people who meant little to her—were they being overly friendly? At first it caused her to feel ill at ease, however, she decided it was best not to spend a lot of time thinking about this. After all, the Holdeman church was steadily losing what little influence it still had on their lives. The more they learned about the Swedenborg writings, the less credible the old church was becoming. Part of her new life must be to leave them to react however they saw fit. She would not do anything to try and ingratiate herself. The reality was, she must learn how to start detaching herself; more food for discussion with David.

Meanwhile, John was corresponding regularly with the circuit ministers of their new church, so as the weeks passed, Gertrude and David spent much time talking with him and Mary about all the new ideas that were flooding into their lives. The four of them and Agnes got together to read and discuss. The exhilaration they felt was like a tonic. As a result, David and Gertrude were finding it more and more difficult to tolerate the messages delivered in the Holdeman sermons every Sunday morning. Their attendance was becoming less and less regular. John was arranging for two of the ministers to come for a visit sometime in the late spring. They looked forward to this with great expectations.

*   *   *   *   *

The spring was late. David hired an extra hand in the beginning of May and by the end of the month they had all the crop in the ground. Gertrude said she would not need a hired girl until harvest. There was not a lot of extra activity on the farm this year and she felt the need to be left alone with her work.

One day in June, the beauty of the day invited Gertrude to leave her noon dishes unwashed, to enjoy its perfection away from the demands of the household. Gertrude's eye measured the new height of the trees that were planted the year before. Their rapid growth was already softening the harsh contours of the farmyard. The shade they threw was negligible but she was not looking for shade. She loved the sun. She sat down on a patch of grass beside the row of trees, turning her head away from the weeds in the vegetable garden. She would pull them later.

Suddenly she thought of a day—a day so much like this—and when she closed her eyes, the time between then and now, slipped away. She was walking with Tilly, into the shop where she had bought the red hat. They were both wearing their new clothes but somehow the buying of the red hat stood out in her memory. It had become a symbol of the beginning of her freedom. She had left it behind, with deep regret, just as she had left the rest of her Winnipeg life behind. David had never seen her in that hat. Maybe, she thought, in a lighter vein, if he had seen her wearing it, he would have swept her off her feet in one romantic gesture and they wouldn't have wasted so much time. She sat for a while longer savouring her fantasy. David was out in the field for the afternoon. His return would be the highlight of the day for them both. A perfect conclusion to such a perfect day.

Gertrude had not noticed that someone was coming down the road until she looked up just in time to see Katie coming at a smart clip in her one-horse buggy, and turning onto the yard. It had been a while since they had seen each other so Gertrude hurried back to the house. "Hello, Katie," Gertrude called as soon as Katie had brought her horse to a stop. "Where are the children?"

"I don't always have to take them along," Katie said curtly, as she tied the lines loosely to the buggy so the horse could graze aimlessly, at will, on the grass outside the fence around the house.

"Oh," Gertrude said uncertainly, not knowing just how to take Katie's attitude, but seeing that her sister looked hot and harried, she suggested that they sit on the shady side of the house. " I'll get you a drink of water." I might have known, she told herself, as she went into the house, that Katie had something on her mind when I saw that she had come alone.

"Isn't it a beautiful day?" Gertrude asked lightly as she returned with Katie's drink.

Katie gulped thirstily, then said shortly, "I hadn't noticed."

"Dear me, Katie, do you have to be like that?"

"Do I have to be like that? That's funny." She gave a short mirthless laugh, "It's *you*, Gertrude….."

"Me?" Gertrude decided not to say more.

"Why, Gertrude, why couldn't you be satisfied with things as they were. Everything was going so good. I was so happy to see you married. Why? We became sisters twice over—to have you so near by—why couldn't you have left things as they were?"

"For goodness sake, calm yourself. What has happened to set you off—to make you so upset?"

"Well, there are a number of preachers here from the other Holdeman church across the river and they had a meeting yesterday. Everybody knows that something is going on when they get together, so I told George to go to Father last night and ask him about it. I was certain I knew what it was about but I wanted to know for sure. I *had* to know." Uncharacteristically she made no attempt to excuse her curiosity but took off the straw hat she had been wearing and wiped the sweat off her brow. She sat for some time vigorously fanning herself with the hat. "I was right," she said at last.

"Yes, Katie? You were right about what?"

"That it was about you and David and Mary. Mary was brought into it, too," Katie said wearily, as though it was hardly necessary to say it at all. "It's sure Mary won't be able to sit in her comfortable seat much longer—belonging to the church but doing just as she pleases." For the first time, Katie expressed resentment against Mary which she had successfully kept hidden until now. "They are going to call several council meetings next week. We'll all have to go, you know."

"So it's come to that," Gertrude said slowly, looking at the white, still clouds dotting the blue, blue sky.

"And Gertrude, unless you do something, unless you say that—that you will give up this other religion—tell them that you are sorry, they are going to put you out of church! You can't let them do that. Please, Gertrude. Gertrude I love you! I know David won't stop this—it's up to you." This was not like Katie.

Gertrude turned back to her and was surprised to see tears rolling unchecked down her cheeks. She was about to reach out and touch Katie's arm and then checked herself. Instead, she asked, "What started all this?"

"It was those two circuit ministers from that Sweden.....that Swedenberger bunch who came to visit John a few weeks ago. Of course, many people saw John pass by when he took them home from the train. That sent tongues to wagging. Then, naturally, Agnes had to get in on it and go to John's place while they were here. That's how it all came out, that you and David came there, too, that you had all discussed religion. And the worst part—the ministers led you in a service with readings, prayers and singing! Oh Gertrude! Then," Katie went on, her emotions rising, "Agnes had to say that you had invited the ministers over to your place and that they had spent the next afternoon with you. John took them back to the train, so no one need have known about your part. But no, Agnes had to tell all about it at home—while they had company. So it didn't take long to spread all over the country."

"It's all true enough," Gertrude said, "and by the way, it's not Swedenberger—it's Sweden*BORG*."

Katie was not at all interested in the finer points of how to refer to these people. She continued, "But if Agnes had just kept her mouth shut, nothing need have come out."

"It's better this way. It had to happen sooner or later. I'm relieved that it has."

Deflated, Katie got up to go. "I'll never understand you, Gertrude."

"You don't have to hurry off." It was a small measure of comfort to offer but she could think of nothing else to say.

"I have lots of things to do at home. I left everything just the way it was. I couldn't stand it, I had to see you."

Then, in a last burst of renewed energy, Katie, with absolute certainty, made her final thrust. "Unless you do something, God will punish you. You will be damned! I will not be damned along with you! If I have to choose between you and God, it won't be you!"

Gertrude was stung. Katie's words were meant to dissuade Gertrude from her path but in fact they had had the exact opposite effect. She replied with equal certainty, "Your God is no longer my God."

The sisters had opened a chasm between them and they both knew it.

Gertrude silently watched Katie climb into her buggy. Her shoulders were bent in sorrow. After she was settled in her seat, she picked up the corner of her apron and wiped her tears and loudly blew her nose. Then, without a backward glance, she slapped the horse with the reins and they were off.

Chapter Fifteen

Gertrude had retained her reserve throughout Katie's brief, but paralyzing visit. But now that Katie was gone, she felt it crumble away. Katie was finally starting to understand what really was at stake here— complete departure from any agreement on the meaning of God and God's word. Though it was only a short time until David would return from the fields, it seemed like hours. She prepared the supper mechanically while her mind strayed far from her tasks.

Finally, she heard the familiar sounds of David and Skipper's homecoming. She listened impatiently: the clinking of the harness rings, the calls of 'whoa Nell, whoa Daisy' to halt the frisky horses in their playful spurt of exuberance, brought on by the knowledge that their work was done, the resounding, but companionable slap on their firm, muscled rumps which sent them to drink noisily at the water trough followed by the dull staccato beat of their hooves on the well trampled ground leading to the barn. She heard the hollow echo as they marched along the wide floor boards of the barn, each to his own special place to munch on the oats which was their reward.

At last, the evening ritual was done. Gertrude had grown to love these homely sounds, for they meant the return of her man at the end of the day but today she did not listen to them with her usual serene anticipation, but wished only to hurry them on.

As soon as David came through the door, she related, with ill-concealed emotion, the details of Katie's visit. During the next day, David was loathe to leave Gertrude's side. He knew how shaken Gertrude had been by Katie's departing words. He sent his man to do the field work and he did not leave the yard. They waited for word of a council meeting, but no one came by to give them any news.

The evening of the second day, Henry Esau drove into the yard. David and Gertrude stood at the gate waiting for him to halt his horse beside them. Henry refused their invitation to alight from his buggy, pleading the necessity of hurrying home to tend to his chores as he had been gone most of the day. "There is a council meeting tomorrow afternoon, and we would ask that you come," Henry stated. It was nearer to being an ultimatum than an invitation. He left without waiting for an answer.

They were dismayed by Henry's brusque manner, especially since he had been a life-long friend of David's. It was not Henry's way. They discussed all possible angles as to the reason for it but came to no conclusion. When later that evening, John, accompanied by Agnes, came to see them, the disclosure that there had been a general council meeting that day, brought the picture into much clearer focus. Agnes declared that had she known of it, in time, she would have informed David. Very pointedly, the David Ennses had not been told of the meeting—the others had banked on a very slim chance that they would not accidentally stumble onto the fact of its being held. Agnes further disclosed that from what little information she had been able to pry out of Peter and Martha who had gone with Father Enns, there had been rather heated debates concerning David and Gertrude's defection.

"They gave me no details, though because I have made it clear to them that I'm on your side," Agnes explained.

"But I should have been there," David said. "Don't I have the right to tell them how we feel?"

"That is just what they didn't want, David. The preachers already know how you feel but they wanted to draw out the people. Had you been there, many would not have spoken freely," John said. "And those who have been puzzled by recent events now know what stand to take. They have as good as been told how to think. It's really very sad.

"If this were a court, and as far as I'm concerned," John continued, "it is a court, the people are the jury. Their job is to judge whether we have sinned or not but it's a travesty, because the verdict has been determined beforehand. That's what I mean when I say, it's sad. I know," John ended with the acceptance of painful experience, "I've been there."

"Yes, I have not forgotten that," David said.

"Did you find out if there were many there, Agnes?" Gertrude wondered.

"It sounded as though most all the men were there—some of the women, too, but many stayed away. I dare say, they will all be there tomorrow. Many came from across the river, too."

The silence hung heavily in the room, then Gertrude heard a small, chocked voice asking, "Were—were any of my family there?" She had not meant to ask and she was fearful of the answer. Just as a sensitive node on the body draws one to press it in a perverse compulsion to assure one's self of its pain, so she must know if her brothers and sisters had come.

"I'm sure there were some of them there," Agnes said with a gentleness such as Gertrude had never seen in her before. "I asked Martha and she said there were many strangers —strangers to her, that is, but she said that there were some with a strong family resemblance to you. In her opinion they had to be your relations." Gertrude's face paled as she realized what was happening. They had come and she had not seen them.

Gertrude and David walked out with John and Agnes and as they said their goodbyes, Gertrude could feel wave after wave of emotion take hold of her insides. She couldn't wait for the departing slap of reins. She swung around and ran back into the house. David remained at the gate a moment longer, seeing off his brother and sister, then he rushed after her. Gertrude was in the middle of the kitchen. She was gripping the back of a chair to steady herself. At the sound of David bursting into the room she looked up and in a rising voice, she shouted, "Oh David, David, what are we all doing? They are here and they haven't even come….."

The force of Gertrude's feeling immobilized David just inside the doorway. For a moment, neither moved. All was in suspension. Hesitantly, she loosened her hold on the chair and in another second was in his arms.

"Oh please forgive me, I'm so sorry, I should never have let myself go like that. We are on the brink of our freedom from all of this. I must not lose sight of that."

"No, my dear, beautiful Gertrude," he held her close, "always let yourself go with me—that's what I'm here for."

As she became calmer, Gertrude knew that she had at long last found someone with whom she could share the secret recesses of her innermost self. During the short time of their marriage, she had, without thought, given more and more of herself. Their intimate bond would give them the strength they needed to get through the crisis that was moving in on them and then—then—they would begin their new life. As David held her, she made a silent vow to herself and to David, "I will never let them know how much they can hurt me." The Gertrude whom the Holdemans were to know from then on was born. By her adversaries she was interpreted in different ways—as arrogant, proud, indifferent, cruel, vile. She would be held up to young Holdeman children as an example of a woman gone wrong, someone who had given herself to evil. The vow and the memory of David's arms around her at that moment were to sustain her throughout the rest of her days.

The next day the sun rose into a clear, cloudless sky. David and Gertrude were wakened when the first rays reached their bedroom window. The days were at their longest and it was too early to get up, so they lay in each other's arms without speaking—they felt no need to speak. When at last David got up, he urged Gertrude to try and get more sleep. He would prepare the breakfast for the hired man and himself. But she could not sleep, she could not rest, she must hurry and put her house in order. While she was putting it into its most impeccable state, her ears were constantly tuned to every sound outside of the house. Surely they would come this morning—they had not found the time to come yesterday. They were her brothers and sisters—today they would come. They would listen and show some respect for David's and her situation. They would understand. They would agree that they could still be a family even though they were following two different religions. Then, she had to remind herself that that was probably wishful thinking. No one had given the slightest indication, so far, that they were going to accept what she and David were doing. I must stop this. I'm just putting myself into a tug of war of my own doing.

The morning wore on, her house was finished, spotlessly awaiting. The ticking of the mantle clock grew progressively slower and louder, etching each second indelibly into her brain. It was not until she had begun listlessly to make the noon meal, that she heard a rig coming. She dropped what she was doing and went to the window. It was Jacob Unger with Annie and Jennie. Hurriedly she brushed back a stray tendril of her hair and straightened her apron. She saw that David had come from the barn and was shaking hands with each of them.

Gertrude, with a broad smile of welcome, watched them come to the house. Jacob led the way with Annie following meekly after him, then came Jennie, with long strides—chin thrust forward. Jacob took Gertrude's hand and shook it for an inordinately long while as his shifty eyes darted quickly from one object in the room to the other, passing fleetingly across her face but never stopping to really look into her eyes. Frivolously, she thought that he was making the most of the handshake which was likely their last and she had difficulty suppressing a giggle which was threatening to rise up and push its way past the smile which had already become fixed. Annie threw her arms around Gertrude.

After disengaging herself from Annie, Gertrude turned to Jennie. "How glad I am to see you!" She was about to embrace her when Jennie extended her hand and gave her a limp handclasp, barely touching her cheek in a brief kiss, but her eyes were cold and quickly averted.

Gertrude offered them chairs and said that they had come just in time, that she had the dinner almost ready. But they told her, in embarrassment, that they could not stay. So Gertrude left everything as it was and they engaged in an abbreviated, stilted, unsatisfying visit. No one came even close to talking about the council meeting and what it was going to mean to the future of the Penner family. When they felt it was enough, they got up to go and none of them were sorry to put an end to it.

"Is that the way it's going to be, David?"

David looked at Gertrude and knew that in spite of her composure, she had been deeply wounded. In an attempt to ease the hurt inflicted by the visit he said lightly, "I'm afraid so—all except for the handshaking—there won't be any more of that." Falling in with his repartee, she told David that she had come near to disgracing them both. She had almost lost control of herself during Jacob's lengthy handshake because a thought in very much the same vein as David's had crossed her mind. The need to find humour in adversity seemed to come upon them with more and more frequency.

* * * * *

Katie could not keep away from the window overlooking the road down which she knew her sisters would be coming when they returned from the David Ennses. The table was laid, the dinner was waiting when at last she spied them in the distance. She made no further pretence at being busy but stood transfixed at the window until they were at the door. She did not know what she was expecting, they could not have performed a miracle, or could they, perhaps?

"Tell me, how is Gertrude?" Katie asked anxiously. Though it was only a few days ago that Katie had gone to warn her of what might happen, it seemed so very long ago.

"She is well," Annie answered laconically for the men had come in with them. She silently indicated that they would talk later. They sat down to the meal and ate hurriedly, the men speaking of things to do with farming, the sisters impatient for them to finish and be gone.

"Oh, Annie, what happened over there?" Katie burst out as soon as the screen door slammed shut behind the men. "Did you say anything to Gertrude about.....?"

"No, there was no chance."

"But couldn't you have made a chance? I was so hoping ....."

"Before we went I was so sure I would be able to talk to her about things. I had planned exactly what I was going to say but when I saw her, the words just wouldn't come. She smiled and welcomed me but, at the same time, she seemed like a stranger somehow. In any case, I know I would have cried, she's never liked that, and things will be hard enough for her today." Then Annie added with the authority of her position as the eldest, "It seems to me, you could have done something about this, Katie. You being so close. You must have seen this coming." Annie petulantly turned the focus back on to Katie.

"I tried. I spoke to her several times but she wouldn't listen." Katie's failure weighed heavily on her shoulders.

"You couldn't have tried very hard." Jennie put in her first observation with an unmistakeable note of sarcasm. "But then, Gertrude has always done just as she pleased."

Katie did not like Jennie's callousness, and decided to ignore it but Annie nodded in agreement.

"Yes, Gertrude has always been different. But this is surely David's fault," Annie said, convinced of its truth.

"No—no—," Katie contradicted, "I don't think so, not at all. I've tried to tell myself that but I know it's not true. She told me that she has been dissatisfied for a long time—about many things. At first I didn't believe her. I thought she was just trying to provoke me, but thinking back now I know that I closed my eyes to a lot of things, telling myself that once she got married she would put her doubts behind her and forget about all that stuff."

"Her going to Winnipeg to work, is what started it," Jennie stated plausibly.

How Jennie had envied her! The helplessness of the envy had at times flared into moments of bitter hatred. Even now, today, she envied the love she had seen in Gertrude's eyes when she looked at David. As a young and vulnerable child, Jennie was left on her own to understand why she and Gertrude had been separated. At the time, no adult had thought it necessary to explain why she was being moved to the Friesens. She knew that she had had parents just like other children but that hers were dead. Death was still something of a mystery to her and in her confusion, she felt by dying they had abandoned her. Then on top of those feelings she tried to deal with the loss of Gertrude. Why had Gertrude not stopped them from taking her away? She felt betrayed. Perhaps if Aunt Anna had been more approachable she could have helped, but left on her own to stew in her loneliness, Jennie felt deserted, first by her parents and then by Gertrude. In her isolation, those feelings were allowed to fester unchecked and played an important part in shaping her personality and outlook on life.

As she grew into adulthood, Jennie naturally pieced together a more realistic understanding of the situation that they had all been in but in spite of her best efforts, she could not totally rid herself of the feeling that Gertrude had rejected her—Gertrude, whom she had looked up to and loved as her protector.

The envy that Jennie felt about Gertrude's move to Winnipeg was also laced with anger. Gertrude was making a new life for herself and Jennie knew she could never be part of it. Why hadn't she been content to stay in Blumenort? Did she think she was better than the rest of us? The religion they had shared since birth was one of the few things they still had in common but now it looked like Gertrude was casting that aside too. Why wasn't God punishing Gertrude for her sinful ways? Instead it looked as though He was rewarding her with a perfect life. It was too much.

"No, its not that either." Katie said, "it goes back even further than that."

"I think you are right, Katie. I remember," Annie spoke softly, "when mama knew she could not live, she whispered to me, 'Take care of Gertrude, take very special care, she is not like the others'." They were quiet, each with their own thoughts—Annie and Katie, their grief momentarily renewed at the memory of the loss of their mother—Jennie, rueful at not being able to fully share their sorrow, only knowing their mother from the stories of others.

"I've tried," Annie continued, "through the years I've tried so hard, but whenever I offered her guidance about how to behave more like a good Holdeman, she rejected my advice. And now it's too late," Annie said hopelessly.

On the many occasions when Annie had reminded Gertrude of their mother's final message and explained to Gertrude that even their dying mother knew of Gertrude's weakness, Gertrude refused to believe that was the meaning of her mother's words. Their inability to prove one way or the other what mama *really* meant, only contributed to their sisterly frustrations.

Annie continued, "If we can't be like sisters anymore, I just don't know if I ever want to see her again. What is going to happen to her today? Oh dear God, what's going to happen today?"

"Whatever happens, I think it serves her right," Jennie said shortly.

"Jennie!" Katie shouted at her. Then to change the subject, she asked, "Did you tell her that you are getting married soon?"

"No, I didn't." Jennie answered sullenly.

"Why not? It might have helped somehow. Now I'll have to be the one to tell her," Katie wailed.

"I don't see why. If she gets put out of the church today, she has no right to know 'till it becomes common knowledge."

"How can you say such a thing? She's your sister!" Annie cried.

"And besides, why is everybody so sure that they will be put out of church? They might change their minds," Katie said hopefully.

"Who do you mean might change their minds, the church or Gertrude and David? Oh, what's the difference?" Jennie flung out in frustration. Before Katie could answer, she left the room.

When Jennie had told her earlier of her forthcoming marriage, Katie had been very disturbed. The man, Edward Harrison, was many years her senior, a notably mild mannered man of delicate frame and health. He had pursued her unsuccessfully for a number of years and Jennie had openly derided him, laughing at his persistence. Katie had heard of this, and she disapproved strongly.

"Annie," Katie began, now that they were alone, "how does it happen that Jennie finally decided to marry him?"

"Uncle Henry and Aunt Anna, together with the preachers, decided that things had gone far enough. They don't like it to be known but Edward said if he couldn't have her, he didn't want to live." Annie said confidentially.

"You mean.....?"

"Yes, he said he would put an end to it," she whispered.

"Oh my, I guess they couldn't let that happen. Imagine, a church member, too, but of course, the Harrisons weren't born into our church. That's not the way it should be—for Jennie, I mean." Katie's logical mind come to the fore. "Surely she could have waited for someone else." They did not know that underneath Jennie's brash exterior, her self-confidence was badly shaken. She had wronged him from the beginning by subtly encouraging him, pleased with her power to make him miserable. That none of the young men around her had ever given her any indication that they were remotely interested in her, had long been a source of secret humiliation to her and it rose up to taunt her, adding to her dilemma. But it was the weight of the guilt, which forced her to give way to the pleas of her elders.

"We had best get started on our way to the church, Annie."

"How I wish I could stay away. But I couldn't stand it—the waiting—"

Annie and Katie went out of the house to hurry the others on their way and were surprised to see them waiting at the gate. Katie looked up at the cloudless sky. It promised to be a hot afternoon.

Chapter Sixteen

Gertrude was oblivious to the quality of the day. She was only aware of the time which seemed to be standing still. Already it seemed an eternity since this morning's painful visit from Annie and Jennie and the worst part of the day was yet to come. It was with relief mixed with apprehension that she closed the door behind her to go to the meeting. A surge of weakness swept over her as she made to climb up into the buggy but she felt David's hand at her elbow. His touch assured her that she was not alone, something she still needed to remind herself of from time to time. They did not take the section road, but took the short-cut which was their private road to John's place.

"Why did you take the four-seater today, David?" Gertrude wondered. "It seems so much extra clatter with just the two of us."

"Well, since we have to cross John's yard, I thought we'd ask Mary if she would like to go with us."

"But you know, she said she wouldn't go."

"She might have changed her mind. Somehow I wish she had."

"I wish it was that simple—that we could stay away, too," Gertrude said speculating on the idea. David agreed, but they both knew that they had to go. A second-hand accounting would never satisfy them. Then too, they could not afford to give the impression that they were afraid to face their adversaries.

"Do you have any idea why Mary is so set against going?"

"It could be that she just doesn't want to go without John but I think that she still hopes that if she stays away, they might just forget about her—at least put off….."

"But, David," Gertrude broke in, "why? Why wouldn't she want to have it over and done with? Why didn't she want to be out of the church with John right from the start?"

"It's hard to say, but I've had the feeling for a long time, that Mary has never really wanted to leave the old church. At the time when John was put out, she stood beside him, yes, but with bowed head. She kept her silence, and she has kept it ever since. I think, to her, the question of what a church believes, is not important enough to cause the friction that now exists between her and her family."

"She has never said anything about it to me."

"No, I guess she wouldn't, she doesn't speak of it to anyone. I think she says very little, even to John. But it comes out in other ways and John is very well aware of it," David said. "I remember once when he was in an especially dark mood, he spoke about it to me, and he wondered if it would make Mary happier if he would return to the church. From that and other things, I know that he has been very unhappy too but his convictions about religion are too strong. They will always stand between him and any compromise."

"Oh, I'm so sorry." Gertrude said compassionately.

They found that Mary had not changed her mind about going, so they went on. The rest of the way, David deliberately held his horses to a slow pace. He bade Gertrude to sit back and relax against the pillow he had put at her back. There was no other vehicle in sight, but the road looked well traveled with many new wheel marks and hoof prints left in the dry, loose dust which lay in a thick layer on the hard tracks beneath it. It was a simple deduction that they would be the last to arrive.

They were not wrong, for the church yard was haphazardly crowded with restless horses left harnessed to their rigs or tethered loosely. Here and there were small groups of people who had not yet gone in, knowing the heat would soon be almost unbearable inside. Others had hurried in to get their choice of positions on the long, hard benches. The familiar hum of mingled, unintelligible voices floated out of the windows. The impression of undisturbed communion was masking the portentous reality of the occasion.

Gertrude, defying convention, walked toward the church with her arm through David's. Her eyes were unfocused, unseeing, until she became aware of someone's approach. She looked to see that it was Joseph and two more of her brothers right behind him. Only Peter was missing. So, they were all here, all except Peter. Had they come to give moral support…..?

Her brothers were a sombre trio as they each shook hands, in turn, with both of them. Gertrude noted that Joseph, who was the smallest of her brothers, nevertheless, looked the most distinguished. All he needed was a splash of grey at his temples to complete the picture. Age would be kind to him. His handsome face wore the small, well-shaped beard proudly—a badge of honour. Was it just a little bit too manicured? She inquired about his bride of a few months and he told her that she was not feeling well enough to have come with him. Isaac's face was lined and weathered, making him appear older than he actually was. His rather shabby clothes and his long, thick beard, scraggly at the edges, more in line with John Holdeman's guidelines for beards she thought, served to emphasize his scowl, giving him a grim, forbidding aspect. His usual jovial manner, though he had always been very impersonal towards her, was not in evidence today. Joseph and Isaac moved away and when Abram came forward to take her hand in his big one, she felt the first real warmth extended her that day. His lips held a small, uncertain smile and his eyes looked into hers with unspoken, suppliant questioning. It took her a moment to realize why he looked so different since she had last seen him. It was the still soft growth of hair framing his face. He had begun to let it grow with his recent conversion to the church. She cringed knowing that today would be a cruel, harsh initiation into the darkest corners of the church. It was unfair to his tender, vulnerable nature. It struck her that he was beginning to look more like Papa than any of his brothers.

Linking arms again, they went through the door. The din inside ceased abruptly, replaced by an expectant hush that was swallowed by the dead, sweltering heat that filled the church. Though every window was thrown wide and the door propped open, there was no hint of a breeze. The only sounds were those which drifted in from the outside. Flies droned as they swooped in wide, precipitous arcs, past the open windows, some flying in momentarily, then back again to the outside world, others remaining inside to harass the occupants. The horses could be heard in the distance as they swished their tails and stomped their feet restlessly, occasionally whinnying softly in secret communication.

An elder standing inside waiting, led them to the front benches that had apparently been left empty for them. As they followed him, Gertrude saw her three sisters sitting together. It brought back a poignant memory of their childhood and she wondered if Annie and Katie had remembered to leave enough space between each of them so they could slide close together and make room for her and Jennie. She remembered that she and Jennie had always been the last to arrive but today, Jennie wasn't entering the church with her. She had her own place beside Annie and Katie. Katie was sitting next to the aisle and when Gertrude passed, she reached out and caught her hand, pressing it reassuringly. So Katie remembered, too. The implication of the two unoccupied front benches, one on each side of the aisle, was clear but now it was David's turn to defy convention. Without hesitation, David chose to sit beside Gertrude. The last of the stragglers who came in behind the David Ennses, were quickly seated. After that little flurry died down, the mood of anticipation resumed.

Henry Esau stood at the pulpit and was about to speak, when the clear, precise notes of a meadow lark's song rang out, trumpeting a prelude to pageantry. Henry, his mouth open, was drawn hypnotically to look towards the window. Heads turned automatically to follow his gaze. Faces mirrored annoyance, relief, blank surprise at the interruption. Breathing seemed almost to stop as Henry waited for the birds next song but a rustle of wings told of its sudden flight. Henry Esau, clearing his throat loudly, commanded everyone's attention back to the business at hand.

Henry asked John Enns to lead them in the opening prayer. It was to be Father Enns's sole contribution to the meeting. He prayed eloquently for guidance, peace, leniency and compassion, knowing full well that his words were flowing over the heads of most of his flock into nothingness. David felt the underlying sadness in his father's supplication and his heart went out to him, yet he knew of no way to shield him from further hurt.

Henry again had the floor. "Brothers and sisters," he began. "We are gathered here today because of a very grave situation in our midst. We have to make an important decision. We didn't want it to come to this but we have discussed it and see no other way. We can't put it off any longer!" he said emphatically. "There are three—yes, three of our number who have not lived by our laws. The laws of our church. They are brother David Enns, his wife, sister Gertrude Enns and sister Mary Enns. We have come to put before you the acts of sin they have committed and you must make up your minds whether they are to be expelled from the church.

"First of all, there is the shunning of expelled members. Avoiding shaking the hands of these unfortunates, and the not eating with them at the same table are very necessary *but,* it is also very necessary not to have close association with them! This can be difficult. I know that this is the hardest law to follow. I know, too, that most of you have been guilty of not obeying it at one time or another," Henry looked balefully at his congregation. The nods and murmuring indicated that most of them were willing to accept some of the guilt, if only to take the edge off their subsequent righteousness. "I too, have failed in my duty. I should have been an example to you," he admitted gravely. "But, let me remind you, brothers and sisters, that all these things are very important. They are the means of bringing those who have strayed, back into our midst. We must make them want to come back—back where they belong, back where they are not shunned. That is not to say that we shall not help them when they are in need, yea, as charitable Christians, we must help them but with long arms, with long, long arms." He stopped as if to renew his energy.

"But that is not all, my brethren, these three have committed another and far greater sin! They have taken up with another religion!" Henry shouted. "They have denied the beliefs of their Mother Church." He paused to let his last statement of accusation sink fully into place, then he continued in a lower key. "It is true that many people do not belong to our church and they are to be pitied. Yes, they are to be pitied. *But,* to have been a part of—to have been one of the chosen few of God's chosen church," here he paused, looking first at Gertrude and David and then around the rest of the room, shaking his head and making no attempt to hide his incredulity, "knowing that it is the only church which can offer true salvation and then, to deny this church like these three have done—can you and I condone this? They must be punished! But we are only the means to punish them. It is God who punishes them through us. He tells us to punish them and we must obey Him. Our conscience is clear. We are only obeying a God-given duty.

The time has come!

"Mary Enns is not here, but David and Gertrude Enns may speak," he said more quietly. He nodded curtly in the direction of the two in question and sat down and wiped the sweat from his brow. His shoulders sagged with the weight of the cross he had to bear.

"Friends," David began after he had risen to his feet and turned to face the gathering. He was conscious of their wary uneasiness. "It is true, like Henry has said, that we have not kept the shunning. He calls that a sin. How can you believe that a law like that is made by God? These laws are only made by people—by people just like you and me. Surely we have come far enough to leave these man made rules behind? How can you call it a sin to take the hand of a beloved brother and eat with him? And it is true," David went on, "that we have found another religion. We believe in it sincerely and have found in it many things which we did not find in the Mennonite church. That it does not agree with the teachings of John Holdeman, does not make it wrong.

"But Gertrude and I have not come here to argue about what you believe or what we believe. We do not condemn you for your beliefs and we would wish that you not condemn us for ours. We have come only to ask that you allow us to withdraw from your church. We know that we do not belong here anymore. We will go to the church we have chosen but let us remain friends with our neighbours and relatives, as we have always been. We love you no less for believing in another religion. Why do you want to punish us for believing in ours?" Seeing the blank, unreceptive faces before him, David felt the futility of his plea. He said no more.

Henry raised himself half-way up out of his chair and nodded to Gertrude, "If you have anything to say….."

"David has spoken for both of us. I have nothing more to say," she said simply, clearly.

"Is there anyone else who would like to say something?" Henry asked.

Whispered conferences followed Henry's invitation. Then a voice spoke out, rather timidly, "I think David may have a point. I don't think we should be too hasty. He should be free to—to—" While he was groping for words, the under-current of whispering became louder and a stronger voice took up the slack. The hesitation of the dissenting voice had been too long.

"Free? Free to do just as he chooses? Who does David think he is? We are supposed to change our ways all of a sudden, just to suit him?"

Others joined in.

"No, no, we can't give in now. Where would it all end?"

"That's right! We have to stick to our laws."

"They are God's laws, like Henry says."

"And to say they are not, is blasphemy."

"They will be punished until they repent."

They were not finished, there was more, much more. David and Gertrude sat quietly, unmoving, hardly breathing. They did not look to see who spoke. While at first they recognized the voices, they began to lose their individuality, coming at them from nameless faces, melting together into one big, dissonant chorus battering at their defenceless ear drums. After the first weak attempt in their favour, no one else dared speak out against the overwhelming tide of condemnation. Then, through the dark malignancy which permeated the atmosphere, a voice caught Gertrude's attention. Yes, it was true. It was Joseph! But what was he saying? He was saying that he had read some parts of the books. Oh, dear God, let him say something good. Let him speak up for us.....

Albert Bartel leaped out of his chair. "Joseph Penner, you, a member of my flock, do you mean to say that you, too, have read the writings of this—this infidel?"

"Yes, I have." Joseph said coolly. "But wait, it's not what you think. I have read them only to prove to myself and to you how far these people have fallen. The beliefs which have blinded and misled Gertrude, my own sister, and her husband are much worse than I would ever have believed if I had not seen it with my own eyes."

"How could he?" Gertrude murmured to David. "How could he?" David grasped her hand. He pressed it until his knuckles were white. Gertrude felt no pain.

Ah, now at last they would hear something. They would no longer have to be satisfied with rumours and supposition. As quickly as they had been ready, in the feverish pitch to which this meeting had risen, to loose their wrath on Joseph, at his opening words, they now gave him their rapt attention. And Joseph did not disappoint.

Joseph expounded at some length. In his desire to belittle, he had carefully chosen passages to read which he knew would be particularly abhorrent to the Holdeman congregation. He ended with the sweeping statement that this man, this Swedenborg, had set himself up as a God! His own books were his bible. His followers did not need the bible! With that, he sat down. The ominous darkness deepened.

"Brother Joseph is right," someone spoke suavely out of the heavy silence. David looked around to assure himself that it was actually his brother George. "He is right to bring out into the open the evil we are fighting. More of us should have read those books before we came here today." By advocating that more members should have looked at the books, he was obviously wanting to soften the impact of his next revelation. "I must confess, that I, too, have read some of them but only for the same reason as Joseph."

David was so astonished, that whatever else George said was lost to him. George was twisting things to suit his own purpose. David was remembering the eager interest with which George read the writings. He had shown a clear, comprehension and understanding of the material. Then, like a swift changing of the wind, he had completely reversed his stand.

The fear that his errant behaviour might be discovered, had remained a burden to George. With the recent eruption of this long dormant situation, his apprehension had increased. What if John or David, or even Agnes, especially Agnes, said something that would implicate him? Any number of unforeseen repercussions could damage his secure position in their society—the society in which the church and the community could never be divorced. He had spent many sleepless nights. Then he got an idea. Maybe he would be able to turn this to his favour. By the time he and Katie had their talk back in February, he was feeling more confident. So far he hadn't been exposed and if his luck continued he would make it through the next few months. He still hoped that David and Gertrude would come to their senses and everything would blow over and get back to normal, but if not, the inevitable final council meeting would present him with the perfect solution. He knew what he would do.

When George finished his damning indictment and sat down, he knew his strategy had worked. Anything further that might have been said, would have been an anticlimax. The preachers, realizing this, put an end to the open meeting. Henry Esau then turned to Gertrude and David. "This is your last chance. Will you now renounce these heathen beliefs you call your new religion, repent and remain in the true church?" No one breathed, waiting for their reply. David and Gertrude looked at Henry in stony silence feeling no need to give him an answer.

The voting began, with each one in turn, as was their custom, giving his oral vote.

Gertrude's head had begun to throb. The proceedings became an undecipherable cacophony. Even though some of the votes were barely audible, the reverberations merged into one loud, endless, "Ye-e-e-s." They did not realize that the voting was over until one of the visiting preachers stood at the pulpit, declaring that they were no longer members of the Church Of God In Christ Mennonite Church. His closing remarks were empty and pointless. The pre-vote question was repeated but this time as a statement of hope that they would soon repent and come back to be one of them again. It was almost laughable.

After the final prayer, none made a move to leave, so Gertrude and David, alone, walked the interminable length of the aisle, a narrow path through the dense, black hostility. Their feet were leaden, they were barely conscience of them moving but as soon as they reached the open door, their footsteps quickened. They could not get away fast enough. The horses led them, instinctively, in the right direction and they had gone quite some distance before the sounds of the meeting breaking up caught up with them.

"Oh, David, David, I didn't know it was going to be that bad. They were so cruel—and the hate, I felt as though it would smother me."

"I know, Gertrude, I felt it, too. I'm afraid we'll never be able to forget this day."

A cloud covered the sun. Gertrude looked towards the west and saw that more clouds were gathering. Suddenly a breeze rose up and as it passed, it touched her cheek like a cold hand. She shivered and involuntarily looked over her shoulder.

Earlier in the week, much to David's joy, Gertrude had told him she thought she might be pregnant. The possibility of their first child being on the way was on his mind and prompted him to say, "I hope our children will never have to go through anything like this."

"Hope, David? I *know* they never will! I will see to that!"

"But if they grow up here, in this community, they will have friends amongst the Mennonites. They will not have seen the ugliness we saw today….."

"Don't say that, David. I will not keep them in ignorance. They will know exactly what happened today."

"But we must not become bitter. We can't let ourselves."

"You are much too kind and good, David, to ever become bitter or vindictive but I'm not so sure about myself. I don't know if I will ever be able to forgive them. They did not even listen to what you said. They went right on tearing us apart. But I was proud of you—so proud."

"Oh, don't think I'm that good. The hate you spoke of before, I felt it, too, and I hated them more than I have ever hated anyone."

"You know, I have the feeling that we will not stay here. I don't think I want to raise our family here." The thought had never occurred to her before but suddenly it struck her very forcibly that she would never want to raise her children where they would be touched or influenced by Mennonites.

"I agree with you, but it would be very hard to pull up our roots here. Things may not look so black when the strong feelings have cooled off. We'll see." David slapped the reins smartly to hurry the horses on. He felt an urgency to put more distance between them and the ugly scene.

When they came into John's yard, John and Mary were waiting for them at the gate. They asked them to stay for supper but David said that they must hurry on. They were anxious to get home before the rain would start. The clouds were coming up fast. David gave them the briefest outline of what had transpired that afternoon. When Mary heard that she, too, had been put out of the church, despite her absence, her faced blanched. She took John's arm to help bolster her against the weakness that flooded her body but she said nothing. Gertrude felt a pity for her which she had not felt before because she had never understood Mary's lack of open support for John.

"Poor Mary," Gertrude sighed after they resumed their journey.

"Yes. Poor Mary," David reiterated. "She has lived with the dread of this day for so long. It will be especially hard for her to get used to the way things will be now. To live day after day with the hope that things will go back to what they once were has been difficult for her, but I suspect now, to be faced with the prospect of an unknown future outside the Holdeman church will be even worse. She doesn't share our hope for new and better things to come." Gertrude look up at David. She could never cease to wonder at his insight into things which had always puzzled her.

The storm was almost upon them and the wind was beginning to lash at them. David urged the horses into a run and they reached their yard with the first large drops of rain cutting into their cheeks. Gertrude hurried into the house. David unhitched his team and rushed them into the barn.

In a few minutes David came in wet and breathless. "My, it's good to be home." He encircled his wife's waist with his arms, lifted her up off the floor and twirled her around the room. "Let it rain—let it storm—what do we care?" Gertrude's laughter filled the room. He set her down but did not release her. "I don't think I've ever felt so—so—what is the word.....?"

"Free?"

"Yes! That is exactly it! I don't think I've ever felt so free!"

"Oh, David, David, I don't know how to tell you what I'm feeling. All I know is that I love you more than anything and that's the only thing that matters." He gave her a tender, lingering kiss which told her all that she would ever want to know.

"Now," he stated with satisfaction, "what we need most is a good, strong cup of coffee." He let go of Gertrude and went to the cook stove and busied himself with building the fire.

Gertrude bent over the basin to wash her hands before she would lay the table. Her hands were not dirty but she felt a compulsion to scrub them with extraordinary vigour. She straightened up to reach for the towel and caught her reflection in the small mirror which hung over the wash stand. She had forgotten that she was still wearing the shawl. Strange that they had not torn it from her head while they clawed at her dignity, her pride, her restraint. With deliberate movements, she hung the towel back on the rack and without taking her eyes off her image, she began, slowly to untie the knot beneath her chin. She stripped it off her head, brushed back her hair, and holding it by one corner, she walked determinedly to the stove. She lifted the lid with her free hand and for a brief second, held the shawl, poised over the fire, then, just like that, let it drop. She watched with fascinated gaze as the flames licked into the edges of the square of black cloth, then consumed the entire piece. It lay there for a moment, a thin black layer of ash. Then, bit by bit, the ash fluttered up the chimney with the rising heat to float away into the rainswept sky.

She had made it through the narrow opening and now the veil of her heritage, that had shrouded her for so long, closed behind her. Its folds dropped into place with finality.

David and Gertrude, 1911

Gertrude, Helen and Elma, 1917

Gertrude, Arnold and Benjamin, 1917

Some of the horses, 1917

Anna and Benjamin, 1916

The new house, 1918

Gertrude driving her Model T Ford with Arnold, Elma & Anna

Gertrude and her children shortly before leaving for Texas, 1919

Gertrude in her Texas citrus orchard, 1919

Chapter Seventeen

It was mid-summer of the year 1915. Excitement was running at a high pitch in the David Enns household. The sky was clear, not the tiniest wisp of a cloud to mar its blueness. That was all that mattered. Rain, today, would have been near disaster, for this was the day that they were getting their first car. Three days ago they had received notice from the company that it was to arrive at the railroad station today. The days since the message had arrived, were swollen with anticipation and preparation as though they were expecting an important, long-awaited guest. But their waiting had a dream-like quality to it which would not become real until they could see the car, touch it and, yes, ride in it.

Both David and John had capitulated to the persuasive arguments of the local salesman for the Model T Ford. Once the order was placed, they referred to it flippantly, though affectionately, as the Model T, which was the popular term widely used. David and his hired man Neil, had left early in the morning so as to be at the station when the automobile arrived. They planned to uncrate it right there and then, David would drive it home. Gertrude was understandably a trifle apprehensive of David's first trip alone at the wheel but then, he had assured her, as the salesman had assured him, that driving was a simple matter. He had given David explicit driving instructions and had let him drive his own car. Of course, it was all in the interests of sale, but it was comforting nonetheless. In the early afternoon, Gertrude went anxiously to the window to see if there was any sign of David. She saw nothing to the east from where he should be coming, so she looked to the west to assure herself that no rain clouds had appeared on the horizon.

* * * * *

It was a day several months ago, in the early spring, when she had first heard the sound of a motor car on the road. This was indeed a novelty as no car had ever passed by before. None of their neighbours had one, although there were some owners in Morris and, of course, she had seen quite a number of them in Winnipeg. She was even more astonished when she saw it turn into the yard at the same time that Arnold and Helen came rushing in from their play, too excited to speak coherently. "Yes, yes," Gertrude murmured though not listening to them, preoccupied with her own burning curiosity.

The young man at the wheel stopped in the middle of the yard and jumped lightly to the ground. He pushed his straw boater to the back of his head and seeing no one about, he strolled toward the house. As he came closer, Gertrude recognized him as a fellow living about five miles to the south. To her, he was merely a nodding acquaintance but she was aware of his reputation as a rather wild fellow whose escapades with the girls were widely circulated. His special prey, apparently, were any of the the latest school teachers to come to the neighbouring districts. They rarely stayed for more than one year so Harvey could follow his amorous pursuits with little fear of making too much of a commitment while, at the same time. satisfying his taste for variety. He, on the other hand, knew from his Mennonite neighbours, of the Enns's questionable reputation as people who had fallen away from the fold. That, in fact, was what motivated him to make this call. Perhaps these 'worldly' people were in the market for a new automobile.

Gertrude opened the door to his insistent knock. She stood self-consciously in the half protection of the shadow of the door. Much to her immediate chagrin, she realized that she was feeling awkward because of her misshapen body heavy with the child she was carrying. "Good morning?" she said with an inquiring inflection.

"And a good morning to you too, Mrs. Enns," he said with a broad smile. "I'm Harvey Ferris. I am the salesman for the Ford Motor Company in this area. I wonder if I could interest you and your husband in looking at one of our automobiles?"

"Oh?" she said momentarily taken aback. But now understanding what accounted for his overly friendly manner and his free use of her name, she relaxed a bit. "Oh," she said with more self assurance, "I think not."

"But won't you come out and just look at it?" he invited, appraising boldly what little he could see of her.

The nerve of him she thought, the way he's looking me up and down—and in my condition! Well, he's not going to get the better of me. "You'll have to speak to my husband but yes, I'll take a look." With that she stepped outside the house and followed him to the car. It did look quite remarkable—much different up close, sitting in your own yard than at a distance, driving down the street in Winnipeg. Arnold had followed his mother to look at the car too and at Harvey's invitation was sitting in the driver's seat, hands on the steering wheel, cruising down the road at high speed accompanying himself with all the appropriate sound effects. "Mr. Enns is not far from the house. Arnold, run and fetch your father. Tell him a car salesman is here to see him." In the interlude before David's arrival, Gertrude, having completely forgotten about her self-consciousness but being careful not to appear too enthusiastic, chatted with Harvey about the many desirable features of this Ford automobile.

David and Arnold appeared and Gertrude, thinking it best to leave Harvey to David, excused herself and returned to the house and watched the proceedings with interest from the kitchen window. Harvey, wanting to appear casual and relaxed, took off his jacket, revealing his natty vest and the fancy arm bands over his shirt sleeves. He flung the jacket carelessly over the back of the seat and hitching up his pant leg, he placed his right foot on the running board showing off one of his new powder blue spats. Plainly, David was listening avidly to Harvey's every word. Arnold was the diminutive image of David, imitating his father's physical stance and acting as though he understood it all.

After Harvey left, the family was trying to have their supper but the topic of the car kept dominating the scene.

"But, Gertrude," David argued, barely touching the

food on his plate. Gertrude had decided she best provide the voice of caution. He was finding her dubious to the point of exasperation. Maybe I'm overdoing it she thought.

"Think of all the time a car would save. Why, it would take less than half the time to go to Morris or the village stores just for starters and then, the summer picnics….."

"Yes, the summer. It might be alright in the summer," she observed taking him up quickly, thinking it was time to show more interest. But then, "What about the mud in the summer—then the snow—," her practical mind was taking over again.

"Well, I'll admit, we might not be able to use the car in the winter, but, the mud, that, I am sure would be alright. I've heard that a Ford can get through the mud just as well, if not better, than any horse and, as a matter of fact, I've even heard they can be driven in the snow too."

"But, David, wouldn't you feel much safer with a horse? You know, if something goes wrong, a horse will take you home—and he's a friend. You can always talk to him if you're lonesome," she added laughingly. "No one would notice if you muttered to your horse, but to a car…..?" She would find, in the future, that a great deal of talking *was* done to the Model T Ford, the language at times decidedly colourful.

"You're right, a horse is a very good friend, but we're not getting rid of our horses—not for a long time yet," ignoring her attempt at levity. "But when you think about it, the car is probably safer than a horse. When you have trouble with it, you just stop the car or it will stop by itself more than likely." David reminded Gertrude of the many tales of run-away horses they had heard through the years and recalled some of their own frightening experiences as well.

"But," Gertrude parried, "no one else around here has one."

"Oh, Gertrude, for goodness sake, why couldn't we be the first? If we wait much longer to buy one, we won't be the first. It won't be long before everyone will have one. You'll see."

Gertrude felt relieved that her arguments were falling flat. She was sure that they would eventually buy the automobile. The thought of it was beginning to excite her.

David along with John, whose interest was as great as David's, had several more sessions with Harvey, listening to his persistent sales talk, before they put in their orders for the Model T.

The startling thought that they had committed themselves to becoming car owners passed and was almost forgotten for a time. The normal hectic activities of spring rushed in at them on the very heels of their momentous decision. Then it was the birth of their fourth child, a lusty, healthy son, which became the centre of their attention.

* * * * *

But now, with the imminent appearance of the Model T, the period of waiting which had lain dormant, resumed its earlier intensity.

Gertrude had put the two younger children to bed for their naps after lunch and now, needing relief from their persistent questions, she sent the other two out to play. It was not that she didn't sympathize with their impatience for it well nigh matched her own but she did not wish to transmit her growing anxiety to the little ones. They had only been outside a short while when Arnold came running and shouted through the screen door, "Mama, Mama..... Papa's coming."

"Papa's coming....," Helen parroted unnecessarily at the top of her voice.

"Hush, children, you'll wake the little ones," Gertrude cautioned them, but she was too late. The unmistakeable sounds of their awakening came from the bedroom. Alas, even her babies would rather take part in life than waste the daylight hours sleeping. She helped Elma off her bed and picked up baby Benjamin.

"Hurry, hurry," Arnold and Helen chorused and hopped about. Elma ran out and made clumsy attempts to mimic them.

"Coming," Gertrude called. As soon as the screen door slammed shut behind her and Benjamin, the other children, suddenly quiet, crowded around, clinging to her skirts. They gazed, spell-bound as their father came charging down the road at unbelievable speed, in their new Model T. A huge cloud of dust behind him tapered into the far distance. Being the novice at the wheel that he was, David neglected to slow down sufficiently and the car tilted precariously as he turned into the yard. In the resulting, momentary confusion, he braked too suddenly and the car came to a shuddering halt.

The chickens, picking contentedly about the yard at mysterious bits of food, now scattered in all directions. They ran for cover with flapping wings and lowered heads, screeching their protest wildly. The horses in the pasture, kicked up their heels in a skittish burst of playfulness, then came curiously to the fence, tossing their manes, their tails swishing, neighing in questioning astonishment. They viewed the contraption with suspicion. Only the cows declined the opportunity to be stirred out of their calm serenity and went on with the rhythmic chewing of their cuds. Their liquid, brown eyes looked with tolerance upon the unpredictable human race.

"Well, here she is!" David said proudly after he turned off the engine. "Come on, look at it, it's ours!"

Gertrude stood, still frozen in her tracks, but the children broke away and followed their father's suggestion, scrambling all over the car, in and out, examining it in great detail from every angle. David took Benjamin out of Gertrude's arms and led her closer. They stood silently looking at the car, oblivious to the little gremlins so busily intent on satisfying their childish curiosity. They saw only the beauty of the black, shiny new coat it wore so regally and the brightness of the sun beams reflecting from the glass of the windshield and headlamps. There it was beckoning them into the future. "It's beautiful, David," Gertrude sighed. David looked so pleased. Gertrude made sure that he knew she unreservedly shared his enthusiasm.

"Would you like to take a ride?" David asked almost shyly as though he half expected her to demur.

"Oh yes, let's all go." Gertrude agreed without hesitation. With the unexpected collapse of the last bit of her opposition, David, who had so stoutly defended the positive side of owning a Model T, found himself wondering what he had let himself in for. The audacity of taking his family for a ride in this machine, with all its hidden eccentricities of which he, as yet, was in blissful ignorance, stopped him for a moment—but only for a moment.

"Come on then, children get in the back seat," David called out. They jumped in without any coaxing and bounced gleefully on the springy seats. "Now, none of that, children. You just sit still."

"And that's exactly what Papa means. Sit still, don't you dare move! Don't touch the doors while we're driving, or they might fall open.....and you'd fall out. Oh—," and Gertrude clapped her hand over her mouth. The thought held images which had not occurred to her before. "Arnold, now remember, you're the oldest." She resumed her motherly duties firmly. "You look after your sisters, especially Elma, you know she's the littlest." Arnold dutifully reached over at once and took a fistful of Elma's dress and pulled her up on the seat beside him. Gertrude thought his gentleness left something to be desired, but she would not scold him.

"Come Helen," he ordered with his new authority. "Sit down." Helen answered him with a rebellious kick on his shin. She glowered at him balefully, but she did sit down.

"Oh, dear me, Helen. Poor Arnold. Now I want you to behave yourself, or you'll have to stay home." Helen's bravado was over so Gertrude added, "And anybody else who doesn't mind, is going to stay home next time." That was enough to forestall any subsequent notions. Indeed this awe inspiring creation was to hold their respect for a long time to come. Had the threat of not being allowed to be a part of a family outing in the Model T ever been carried out, it would have been the cruelest of punishments. Luckily, the mere suggestion invariably brought about swift reversals of raucous behaviour.

Gertrude was about to step into the car when David stopped her. "I better see how much gasoline is in the tank."

Calmly he removed the front seat, and there it was! He screwed a small cap from the tank and took a metal stick with numbers on it and dipped it down into the very bottom of the tank. He studied it carefully after he withdrew it and seemed satisfied with the results. "You see, it shows the gallons." he remarked off-handedly.

"Oh, my." Gertrude was appalled at the mere thought of sitting on a seat with a tank of gasoline beneath her. "What a place for the gasoline," she remarked weakly. She had visions of it exploding and sending them flying unceremoniously into the air.

After David's reassuring words on the subject, she was finally settled in her seat. David turned the switch. He set the levers at the steering wheel, then went to the front of the car and began to crank vigorously. The motor popped and sputtered but David kept on cranking until it ran weakly. He let go of the handle and bounded back to the steering wheel where he pulled down the spark lever before the motor had a chance to die again. With his hand bearing down heavily on the lever, he sent the motor into a wild, vibrating roar. He climbed in and toned it down with a pleased smile on his face while Gertrude set her feet firmly, clutched her baby to her breast and steeled herself for the take-off. To her surprise, they leaped backwards with a jerk. David looked at her and laughed at the comic expression on her face. Obviously she had been prepared to go forwards. He turned the car until it pointed to the road and they shot forward. The Model T, as well as its passengers, relaxed and the family began to enjoy the first of many rides they were to take that summer.

The automobile was a manifest example of the fast pace of the changing times. The war in Europe, lurking in the background of their lives, did, in fact, do much to hasten technological development. The advances in more effective machines of war, spilled over into a wide range of innovation in the post war era which lay just ahead. Wireless communication of signals was being utilized by the armed forces which a few years later was to evolve into the ability to transmit voice and then music—the crystal set— the radio. In the next ten years the impact would be felt by farmers with important strides being made in new and improved farm implements—trucks—tractors—discs—cultivators—harrows. Occasionally all activity stopped as everyone paused to watch a flying machine pass overhead. Young boys would fantasize that some day one of the aeroplanes would land in their pasture and the pilot would invite them to go for a ride. This was still ahead of them. Right now the Enns farm was prospering due to several years of cooperative weather conditions. They were unaware of how the boom years after the war were to influence their lives.

* * * * *

David watched the events that led to the outbreak of World War I with keen interest. Had he been a younger man without dependents he would have probably been among the first to enlist but the reality was, with the birth of their latest child in March, 1914 he had four dependents. That coupled with his age and the fact that the government was promoting farming as an essential component of the war effort, he was forced to accept his lot but not without some regret.

Gertrude often thought of that day in August in 1914 when David had returned from a trip to Morris and brought her the news that war had been declared. He told her that excitement was at a fever pitch and several of the boys in the town had already joined the Canadian forces to fight for the British Empire. David had brought home the Winnipeg newspapers which held the glaring headlines. She begged David to read aloud to her while she was preparing supper, for she must hear all the details at once. She could not wait. She would look at the papers again later, re-read them. They discussed the distressing situation, wondering how it would effect their lives, hoping that it would be quickly resolved.

"Well, at least, we won't have to worry about you going to war," Gertrude remarked after they had been quiet for some time.

"I know I'm too old, but….."

"That wasn't exactly what I was thinking of. Mennonites are……"

"Gertrude!" David exclaimed. "Have you forgotten?" Gertrude stared at him in surprise. "Have you forgotten that we're not Mennonites anymore? That agreement they made with the Canadian government, it no longer applies to us. And thank the Lord, for that!" David said emphatically. "How can it be right? We live here in this country, we take all it has to give, shouldn't we do our part when there's trouble? That's why I wish I were younger. Oh how I wish I were ten years younger."

"Oh, I'm so sorry David! Yes, sometimes I *do* forget that we aren't Mennonites anymore. You're right, of course." She wondered if he would think harshly of her if he knew that she was secretly glad that he wasn't ten years younger.

She felt the need to explain herself further. "Just now we were talking about you and then my mind went to all the other men in our community, realizing that they would not be joining up. That's when I forgot for a moment that we are not all the same people anymore. I'm sorry, David," she said again.

"I know, I know, Gertrude, I understand," he said more kindly. "You don't have to apologize to me. It's that we've never had to face anything like this before."

"Don't you think that some of the Mennonite boys will join up anyway? There are many who would be the right age to go and most of them haven't joined the church."

For a couple of years prior to the onset of the war, it had been evident to David and Gertrude that there was an increasing number of young people who were delaying joining the church. Instead they were sampling more and more, the ways of the non-Mennonite world around them. It was, of course, more noticeable among the young men who had more freedom to move about than the young women. They could be seen wearing stylish, sporty clothes including neckties. They frequented portrait studios to have their pictures taken. There was more socializing going on between the young Holdemans and Kliene Gemeinde. Some of them gravitated to the two Enns farms for afternoons and evenings of friendly visiting. David and Gertrude understood their visits to be part of their rebellion. Although they wished their motivation had been otherwise, they returned their friendship. David and Gertrude privately applauded. They even allowed themselves to think about the possibility that a new generation would succeed in forcing the Mennonite churches into new leniency. The community's reaction to the declaration of war put an end to Gertrude and David's optimism.

The Holdeman churches had gone through these kind of pendulum swings before. The elders would cope by organizing a week of revival meetings with guest pastors brought in from other communities whose job it was to bring the young locals back into line. The outbreak of war had made the situation even more urgent. It was time to repeat the strategy. The visiting pastors were called in.

First one, then another, then two more, made the decision to join the church until a veritable stampede occurred among the remaining dissenters. Upon orders from the elders, the clothes were destroyed, the pictures burned, the cigarettes thrown into the trash. There was no more fraternizing with the Ennses, no more friendships with their Kleine Gemeinde peers, no more going to the moving pictures, no more listening to phonograph records (which had been a favourite pastime at the Ennses). Most important of all, the threat of having to take part in the war was raised and condemned. With just one week's worth of revival meetings the young people were folded back into the safety and harsh restrictions of their mother church.

The same people who had sought out their friendship now passed them with down cast eyes.

After the first shocking impact of the news that war had been declared, it took on the aspect of a dark, ominous cloud in the distance. War news was sketchy, most of what they heard was hearsay, allowing them at times to almost forget that it was there. Only when David went to Morris and brought the Winnipeg papers home did they get a clearer picture of what was happening. They saw the casualty lists and though they were to them unknown, and faceless, they read each name carefully, grieving silently for the young lives robbed of their brightest years. The remote unreality of the distant battlefields where they fought and died was heightened because neither they nor any of their kin were there.

Life must go on despite all else, especially when the needs of young children require constant attention. Life for Gertrude and David resumed a near normal course just as life had not stopped after the brutal day of their final, physical severance from the Holdeman church. Their first child had been born the winter following their excommunication and their second child arrived two years later. And now their new baby, Elma, was demanding her share of attention too, At first they hoped that in continuing their associations with their relatives and friends, they would surely soften their attitudes towards them. They were wrong. They found that the once well trodden path to their door was now becoming overgrown with weeds. The few who came stepped lightly lest they disturb the growth. Even Katie kept her distance, remaining true to her word that she would not allow herself to be damned along with her sister.

Obviously, Gertrude heard that one or another of her brothers or sisters had come to Rosenort and she had not seen them. When they did come to see her, their visits were so short and stilted that she wished they had not come at all.

There were the times when they were driven by loneliness to go out to call on one or another of their neighbours and found there a gathering of the clan. How quickly the babble was stilled at their approach. There were the times when they felt the sting of the round-eyed curiosity from the children with whom, in their demoted state, they were relegated to eat at a separate table in the kitchen. For some reason, children, who were not yet members of the church, were not required to practice the shunning rituals. There were the times during these meals that the children's unguarded questions and remarks (the kind that come only from the young) made it clear that Holdeman parents were holding David and Gertrude up to their offspring as examples of people who had chosen a life of sin.

Because of their common tribulation, David and Gertrude drew closer to John and his family; but there was one other who remained constant throughout this difficult period—that was Father Enns. He never altered his habit of calling on them regularly. His visits were short, but that was his way. The children loved their grandfather who seldom came without a few pieces of candy or liquorice or perhaps a handful of peanuts, for each one. But not until he announced solemnly that he had brought them a surprise, did they search through his pockets until they found the special one where it was hidden. He shared fully in their childish delight in finding the cache. None dared to question the wisdom of Father Enns's continued visits, for he occupied the most venerable of positions among his people; that of being beyond criticism or reproach.

David and Gertrude were coming to the conclusion that their relationship with the Holdemans was reaching an impasse. It must come to an end and end it did. But it took one last, cruel incident to bring it about. It happened on a summer's day, a little over a year after they had left the church.

* * * * *

"David," Gertrude called from the bedroom, "Look at the calendar. Isn't it the fifteenth?"

"Yes," David answered, walking to the bedroom door. He stopped for a moment, admiring the tableau of Gertrude looking down, with a small smile, her eyes shining in adoration at her little son who was drinking greedily from his mother's full breast. He was loathe to break in on a reverie which, he thought, had no place for the banal world measured by dates on a calendar, a moment made to be etched into his book of favourite memories, then, reluctantly, "Why do you ask?"

"Oh," Gertrude looked up startled. "Oh," she laughed, "because the fifteenth is Katie's birthday and I had almost forgotten it."

David sat down beside Gertrude and took his son's hand in his. Arnold's eyes turned to look at his father but a frown of annoyance furrowed his brow. He was not to be diverted. Then as if to compensate, he curled his tiny fingers around David's big one with a firm grip. "So little—and so determined— already he has a mind of his own. And so beautiful," he said, his voice filled with the awe of the miracle of life in so tiny a creature.

"Yes, I think he's the most beautiful baby I've ever seen," Gertrude interjected proudly. "Have you ever seen such hair on a small baby?"

For a moment, Gertrude remembered her thoughts just after the pain of birth when she was told that her child was a boy. She felt that she had been given a heaven sent gift. She had dreamily, envisioned how she would dress Arnold and all of her children yet to come, in beautiful clothes. She would probably sew most of them herself. She would make sure they all would grow up in a world so different from what hers had been. They would fit comfortably into the big, exciting world that so long had been a mystery to her as a child.

She brought her thoughts back to the moment. Smiling at David and Arnold she felt more at peace then she had ever thought possible. Arnold was now asleep in her arms so she laid him back on his blanket and covered him. Gertrude and David returned to the kitchen.

Then Gertrude suddenly remembered Katie's birthday again. "Don't you think it would be nice if we went to Katie's this afternoon to wish her a happy birthday? I could bring her a little gift and take some of those cookies I baked yesterday."

Gertrude still harboured the hope that she and Katie might regain some of what their relationship had lost. Why should Gertrude not make the first gesture? Visiting Katie to celebrate her birthday might be a start. The principal issues remained clear and clean cut, but the feelings surrounding them had become muddled, murky, as the hurts between them mounted. Though the Ennses had felt directly wronged when refused a graceful exit from the church, none could emerge guiltless or unscathed out of a conflict which, as it smouldered over time, would flare up unexpectedly causing new injuries to all who were involved.

"If you think it would make you happy—," David agreed, though dubiously. He was unconcerned about his relationship with George for it had always lain shallowly on the surface. He had long since dismissed George's eloquent betrayal at the council meeting for what it was. But it was another matter where Gertrude and Katie were concerned. He knew how close they had become in later years. It went back to the time of Katie's marriage.

Gertrude rummaged through her bureau drawers and picked out a length of print which she knew Katie would like and wrapped it up. She filled a box with the cookies. She placed the packages neatly on the kitchen table. Arnold had fallen asleep, so she would leave him to the last, but she laid out his clothes. She picked out a tiny blue sailor suit with a wide white collar that had a border of two blue stripes.

For herself, Gertrude chose to wear her newest blue silk dress. She had found no occasion to wear it before. She slipped the dress over her head, then buttoned the tiny buttons at the front waist. The buttons continued all the way down the skirt between the two rows of small tucks. She straightened out the large, white lace collar and at her throat, she pinned the delicately carved gold brooch David had given her for her last birthday. After rearranging her hair, she put on her straw hat which was trimmed in a ribbon to match her dress. She set it carefully at the accepted, most pleasing angle.

When all the preparations were completed to Gertrude's satisfaction, they set out in high spirits. David complimented her on her appearance and her fine looking son. He had not seen her so gay and relaxed for a long time. He hoped that nothing would spoil her happiness today.

When they reached the George Ennses, it was plain to see that they already had visitors, but that was nothing strange, for it was still common to invite dinner guests after the church services. Katie met them at the door.

"Oh, Gertrude—and, and David—it's you—," Katie looked unduly flustered.

"We came to wish you a happy birthday, Katie," Gertrude said holding out her gift. When Katie saw the parcel, her agitation clearly mounted.

"Well. Well, thank you," the reluctance in her voice was unmistakeable as she took the parcel. "But, come in."

She led the way into the kitchen, explaining hurriedly, "A few folks came over—for my birthday. Annie and Jennie came, and, oh, yes, Joseph. Oh, well, it's just a little family gathering." Then she gasped and her hand flew to her mouth, her eyes horror-stricken, but it was said. Her words carried clearly into the kitchen. The guests were crowded around the long table. A plate with a few last slices of birthday cake, fallen into a tired, crumbly heap glowed eloquently in their midst. When they saw who had come in, their questioning faces changed to mirror Katie's embarrassed consternation. Her last words were still echoing about the room. 'It's just a little family gathering—family gathering—family gath.....'

"You are right, Katie, it *is* a family gathering," Gertrude said clearly, shattering the silence into little, sharp, tinkling fragments. "So, of course, we shouldn't have come." She handed Katie the cookies. "Here, you might need these." She and David turned to go and the room suddenly came to life. The grown-ups clamoured from the table, leaving only the children who were not to be diverted from eating their cake, which was a rare treat, finishing what their parents had left, as well as their own.

"It's good that you came," Annie said too loudly, her voice rising above the tumult. She made her way toward her sister. Glancing briefly at Arnold she said, "My, what a lovely boy," but quickly stumbled on to say, "we were coming over to see you too, but now—come, have some lunch.....," she blustered, "we were finished anyway."

At that Gertrude and David who had already started for the door, turned again.

"How convenient," Gertrude said, "that you have finished your lunch, anyway."

"We, Katie, didn't mean—," she began to explain, but the cold, unemotional look on Gertrude's face stopped her. It became too much for her and forgetting momentarily about the shunning, she threw her arms around Gertrude and began to sob. Gertrude stood motionless, her arms hanging at her sides. She saw Jennie at the far end of the room. Jennie's eyes fell at once to the child she was holding in her arms. The child was her first-born, whom Gertrude had never seen. Then Joseph glided smoothly up to them. He stopped, his hands clasped behind his back.

"We-e-ll, Gertrude," he began, drawing the words out to just the correct inflection. Gertrude's eyes flashed angrily at him. It was the first time she had heard this term of address from Joseph. It had always rankled her, even in her youth. In the early days she thought of it as some kind of veiled disapproval but didn't fully understand why. During this last year, however, there had been no mistaking the meaning. Now it was delivered with hands resolutely remaining still at their sides or elegantly clasped behind their backs, inauthentic smiles pasted on their faces. Mingled with a smug tone of superiority, the disapproval was unmistakable . But to hear it from Joseph and in such polished perfection......

"We thought it would be nice to celebrate Katie's birthday and make our last visit here at the same time," Joseph said. "Did you know that Margaret and I are going to Kansas to live?" he paused to give Gertrude a chance to answer, but she remained silent, so he continued, "you know there, where Peter lives. So, now we get to see you, too, before we go. How nice."

"Oh?" was all Gertrude said and Annie backed away, dabbing at her eyes and blowing her nose.

"Well!" David said, taking his wife's arm, "now you've all seen us and you won't have to take the trouble to come to our place. Come, Gertrude." Again the room fell into silence.

"Gertrude, wait—," Katie cried, taking a few steps, following their retreating backs, holding out an imploring hand, "please wait.....," but Gertrude's step did not falter. As though she had not heard, Gertrude did not look back. Katie's hand fell limply. "I'm sorry," she whispered, almost inaudibly, "I'm so sorry."

David took a long way home. He let the horses take their own leisurely pace stopping from time to time to snatch a mouthful of grass. They looked at the vast fields of grain, the slight breeze teasing it into almost imperceptible movement. At one point David stopped the horses and jumping down, picked a few handfuls of the grain, assessing its growth, measuring its potential yield, counting the days until it would be ready to cut, before climbing back into the buggy. It looked like it was going to be another abundant crop. The weather had been kind to them these last years. After a time, Arnold, in Gertrude's arms, fell sound asleep. Looking down at him fondly, she said softy, "Our baby." and moved closer to David.

They did not need to tell each other that a part of their life had ended, that they could not hold on to something that was over, that they must build from a new foundation, that they, again, were pioneers, striking out for something new, but in a different sense than their forbears. David and Gertrude's children would be the first generation of this bright, new heritage which they would build together. Perhaps the Holdemans would, in time, learn how to allow those of their membership who wished to leave, to do so with less pain and anguish on both sides. Maybe that would be part of the legacy left by the John and David Enns families. What would eventually fade into the dim shadows of the past might, at the same time, become the paving stones for a brighter future.

"You know, David, what I would like to have?" Gertrude asked.

"No," David answered, "but you shall have it—that is, if its not too unreasonable," he teased.

"Ever since I worked at the Stantons, I've wished the time would come when I could have it. Well, the time has come, and it's a gramophone!"

"Oh, is that all? Such a little thing—a gramophone! Of course, you can have it. The first time I go to Morris, I'll look for one. I thought you would want something big."

"Well, maybe I should have asked for a pump organ instead." Gertrude laughed at her absurdity.

"Would you really like an organ?" he asked, looking at her in surprise.

"More than anything else, but, then, I wouldn't ask for one. Why, I can't even play on one! But I'm sure I could learn to play—a little. Even simple songs sound nice on the organ."

"We'll get one. Maybe not right away, but we'll get one." David promised. "Maybe If we have another good crop. Let's get both; an organ and a gramophone!"

Gertrude had finished feeding Arnold. Their hired girl, Anna, who had returned from her Sunday's outing while they were away, laid the table for supper. They ate with little conversation. The wall of numbness which had initially protected them from the scene of the birthday celebration, was beginning to crumble, revealing the significance of what had happened. David saw the deepening sadness in his wife's face.

"Gertrude, why don't you change your clothes and come out with me while I do the chores?"

Gertrude's face brightened. "Maybe that's a good idea." Women often worked side by side with their husbands in the barn. David had never let Gertrude do any of the barn chores since they were married but sometimes she followed him about because they enjoyed being together. "If Anna will look after Arnold."

"Of course." Anna agreed at once. She could see that something was troubling her mistress. "I'll put him to bed as soon as it is time."

Gertrude watched while David threw the hay down from the loft and spread it evenly in the mangers. The mother cat and her family of half-grown kittens were milling around their feet yowling in distress, their hunger unendurable, now that they knew their milk was coming. Skipper sat sedately at Gertrude's feet, making no effort to hide his disdain for the cats' performance. He was waiting for David to open the back barn door which was his cue to go for the cows.

"Go, Skipper. Go get May and Bess." The dog bounded out and when he reached the varied herd, he made no mistake in cutting out the two he had been told to get. Skipper was especially watchful of May for she was wont to display a stubborn streak. But in eyeing her too carefully, he failed to see one of the horses streaking by and he was thrown by a flying hoof, then tramped under the pounding feet. Skipper yelped in pain, then lay still.

"David!" Gertrude screamed. Her anguished call brought him running out of the barn. He saw what had happened and they both hurried to the beloved dog. Skipper looked up at David. David stroked his head. He nuzzled weakly at David's hand and licked it begging his forgiveness for having failed him.

"That's alright, boy, that's alright." The light in Skipper's eyes slipped away and he was gone.

Gertrude broke into a wild torrent of sobs, the tears streaming down her cheeks. David carried Skipper into the barn and laid him carefully on a bed of straw. He would bury him later in a special place under the trees in the windbreak at the back of the farm yard. Gertrude's sobbing became quieter, but her tears did not stop.

"Gertrude, Gertrude," David comforted her. "We'll get another dog." He had never seen her cry like that. She had not cried before but in her tears for the little dog, she released all the pent-up anguish of the past few hours. She cried for Annie and for Joseph whose love had been so shallow. She cried for Katie who had spoken thoughtlessly. She cried for all of them who by their silence echoed Katie's final words of renunciation. She cried because she didn't care anymore. And she wept for the dog who had never questioned their love.

Chapter Eighteen

Within a few days, David decided to go to Morris. He insisted that Gertrude accompany him. He agreed with her that he was quite capable of buying the gramophone but he needed her help in choosing the records for it.

After they made their purchases and stowed them in the buggy, they strolled down the street. While looking into the shop windows they spied a poster propped up in one of them. They stopped to read it and found it to be an announcement of a Chautauqua coming to town. The list of performers meant little to them, but it was a tantalizing invitation.

"Oh David. I think we should go. What do you think?"

"You know—my very thoughts. What a very good idea!" They looked again at the poster and took special note of the dates when it would come.

They did attend that Chautauqua and several subsequent ones in other summers. It was the heyday of the Chautauqua and some of the the world's brightest stars travelled the circuit. They crossed the country, pitched their tents in the small towns and gave of their talents to many people who otherwise would never have heard of them.

One of the most memorable performances they saw was that of Harry Lauder, the man in the kilts from Scotland. They were very impressed and enjoyed his singing and his wit no less for having some difficulty in deciphering what they heard through his thick Scottish burr.

Another artist whom they would never forget, was a pianist with the astounding name of Ignace Paderewski. His handsome, aesthetic features were emphasized by his great mane of hair. But all else was forgotten when he started to play. Gertrude was transported into a world which had hitherto been unknown to her. She was dazzled by his brilliance, his deft fingers. She had never seen anyone using the entire keyboard before. Nothing she would ever see in later years, would ever quite equal that experience.

David stopped at John's farm, on the way home and invited the family over for the evening to initiate the new gramophone but they hurried home to have their own first hearing. It was an instrument designed for the pure entertainment of the listener and they were not disappointed. Many happy memories were built around it. When Arnold was old enough to start taking a real interest in the music, he was enchanted and fascinated by what came out of the small box and he refused to be convinced that there were not little people inside.

When the John Enns family came, the little house was filled almost to bursting. The older children took over the operation of the new music box. Winding the machine and seeing how long it would play before it ran down, and changing the needles at frequent intervals, was an important part of the total enjoyment and had not yet fallen to the status of tedious annoyance. As the younger children began to nod their heads, they were put on the bed in the bedroom until they would be roused to go home. The music and chatter did not cease the entire evening.

Gertrude and Mary watched from outside the circle, discussing the things of house, garden and family, which despite their sameness from day to day, nevertheless, were constantly a source of rich and interesting conversation,

David and John withdrew to the quietest corner they could find but their conversation ran in a different vein than that of their wives. As they talked, a plan to form a formal affiliation with the new church of their choice began to take shape. It was time. Among other things, they were concerned for John and Mary's older children, some of whom had already entered their teens. Their eagerness to embrace and enjoy so little a thing as the gramophone, was touching. It was glaring proof of how starved they were for something more than they were getting. As parents, they must give them something to replace what they had taken away. They must take concerted steps to become part of a new community. They began holding meetings in each other's homes. During the summer for a change of scene, they held some of the meetings in their new district school house. which had been built just a few years ago. Agnes was a colourful member of the small circle from the beginning. Then when the John Eidse family, who had been members of the same church for some time, moved into the community with their large family, some of whom were grown up, their numbers swelled considerably. John assumed the duties of a lay minister, a talent he had inherited from his father, no doubt. From then on, it became the custom for a Swedenborgian field minister to visit them several times a year to perform the services and duties of an ordained minister. His first task was to baptize Agnes and all the members of the John and David Enns families.

* * * * *

There were many Sunday picnics during the summer. They would pack their lunch early in the morning, then from their church meeting, they set out until they found an apt spot, very likely on the bank of a river. There was often swimming. The winter brought indoor parties, holiday dinners, and skating on the small creeks which wound through the countryside. There were a few Swedenborgian families scattered to the south of them. Distance was a problem but in the summer they would meet each other half way to spend an afternoon together. They would make a special effort to congregate when their field minister was paying a visit. John and Mary's older children were meeting other young people their own age. After the Ennses acquired their Model T's in 1915, they looked forward to future summers. Others in their group would, no doubt, follow suit. Get togethers would be so much easier.

Eventually the organ which David had promised Gertrude, was purchased. It was set in a prominent spot in the small house and Gertrude was pleased and proud of the modern effect it added to the room. But for some time it proved to be an object of obstinacy and frustration. Gertrude, who could read the notes to sing, attempted vainly to transfer them to the organ. She would begin by pumping the pedals energetically, but in her concentrated search for the right combinations which eluded her, her feet would slacken and the sound died away. When at last she conquered that difficulty, she managed to pick out a few tunes by ear but it gave her little satisfaction. David discovered, upon discreet inquiry, that there was a teacher of music in Morris. He arranged for Gertrude to take a short course in reading music for the keyboard. She was an adept pupil and before long, she could play simple melody lines accompanied with the appropriate chords. She played her favourite hymns and bought sheet music and albums of the popular songs of the day. They discovered that between David's respectable tenor and Gertrude's beautiful contralto they were naturally able to harmonize even though they had been taught that singing in harmony was a grave sin. They got great enjoyment out of performing duets at the centre of many gay singalongs.

It was almost an idyllic existence as though they lived on a small enchanted island, being only dimly aware of the sea around them, the tides rising and falling, not yet touching them. They celebrated the arrival of their second child Helen and their third, Elma. Gertrude was enchanted to have two daughters following in the footsteps of their son. They savoured the pleasure of each passing day but with the underlying knowledge, which held a faint tinge of regret, that it could not last indefinitely. Gertrude and David's love sustained them. Their children were as yet their very own. But before they knew it Arnold would be starting school and discovering that other relationships and interests were very important, that there was more, much more beyond the life of their little family. Knowing this and seeing the time when they must begin to start letting him go draw nearer, the nagging certainty that they would have to make more and bigger changes stayed with them.

David and Gertrude got into the habit of taking a day trip into Winnipeg two or three times a year. They cherished these excursions. They would leave their children in the care of Anna or some of the Enns family. This gave them the opportunity to be together with only each other's company. They left first thing in the morning and drove to the railway station to catch the early train. Before the Model T, they would leave their horses in the station's stable in the care of the station agent for the day. Once they had the car they simply left it parked on the side of the road outside the station. In Winnipeg, they would separate for a time, David attending to farm business or just roaming around, enjoying city life, Gertrude usually spending a few hours in the Eaton's department store. What a magnificent place! It covered an entire city block and soared nine stories into the sky. She could spend hours there, shopping and looking at everything. Then they would meet at one of Winnipeg's many fine restaurants and have a lunch that sometimes went on for several hours. This was their time to share ideas about the farm, talk about their children, make plans—generally assess the state of their lives and what they hoped for the future. If they had time before catching the train home, they would take in a vaudeville show and sometimes the moving pictures.

Today, they were having lunch in a quiet corner of one of their favourite restaurants just down Portage Avenue, east of Eaton's. They had finished their main course and hadn't decided yet about desert and coffee. "In a year, Arnold will be old enough to start school. We used to think that maybe by the time our children were ready for school we would have sold our farm and moved on to another life."

David nodded pensively. "Yes, we are going to have to start thinking more seriously about that again. We've been so busy making a new life for ourselves here that we haven't been thinking so much about making a new life for ourselves somewhere else. Our farm is doing so well. We have made more money in the last four years than I had ever dreamed of. And don't you think we have done a good job of cleaning the Holdemans out of our daily lives?"

"Oh yes I do. But, I still wish that Katie and I could find a way to be friends again. I don't know. I miss her. When I think of hardly ever seeing her, it makes me feel sad." She drifted off for a moment.

The waiter had cleared the table and left the dessert menu. "I know, lets have some apple pie and ice-cream," David suggested hoping to bring a smile back to Gertrude's face.

Gertrude brightened and countered with, "Yes but before that, let's have a glass of sherry and then do the pie and coffee."

"You have such good ideas, Gertrude." (Neither of them had any inkling that in a couple of years the sale of liquor would be banned in Manitoba.)

The sherry was ordered and served.

Gertrude returned to the topic of Arnold's schooling. "I've been talking to Mary about our school." The new school, built several years ago had been moved to a new location just two miles north of the Enns farms. "One good thing about our school, at the moment, is that there are no Holdeman children attending. That will change in the near future. The Friesen farm is in our district and they have had their first two children and Mary thinks that another farm in our district will be up for sale soon and possibly bought by a Holdeman family. Right now, besides John and Mary's Peter, Margaret and Edward the other children are all from the German Lutheran farms to the north of us."

"That will give Arnold a chance to make some new English speaking friends," David said. Although Arnold spoke the Mennonite dialect, his parents had been meticulous at making sure that he was equally fluent in English. "We've also talked about building a new house. We can't stay in our little place much longer. It's overflowing. The children need their own rooms and so does Anna. She is spending more and more time with us and she can't continue to sleep in the kitchen. We certainly have more than enough money to build something nice."

It had been a long lunch. The sherry was finished and the pie and coffee served in plenty of time for them to get back to the train station. No important decisions had been made. No important decisions needed to be made today. They were still young. They were in love. The world was theirs.

* * * * *

The summer of the Model T did much to widen their scope of activities and to hasten them into a new world. They were, first of all, impressed with how quickly they could travel the miles which had seemed so long before. They enjoyed the heightening of the breeze around them as they sped along, the top down, feeling the warmth of the sun. They leaned how to raise the top quickly at the fist sight of rain. Then, when the storm became too severe or the air too cold, they discovered the little black, leather curtains with the isinglass windows, folded neatly under the back seat, which buttoned around the outside of the car.

In a short time, they became reasonably proficient in coping with various mechanical difficulties which cropped up quite regularly. Indeed it was all in the spirit of the adventure surrounding them, and the delays which they encountered did not disturb their equanimity.

Although the first flat tire was viewed with some alarm and apprehension, they soon became experienced veterans in the art of handling so minor a mishap. Invariably, as soon as the car was stopped at the first hint of a flat, everyone tumbled out of the car. The tools to repair the damage, were stored under the back seat. Since the car had to be jacked up, the passengers preferred the solid ground under their feet to the uneasiness of being perched up in so precarious a position. But the children, fearlessly, motivated by curiosity, clambered back in, for they had discovered that the mysterious cavern under the seat was a veritable treasure trove of lost items and toys and sometimes even a coin or two which they were always allowed to keep. The inner tube was carefully patched and the tire returned to its wheel. The jack was then released and the car settled back on its four wheels. It remained to bring the tire up to its original shape with each member of the party taking turns at the hand pump. They watched anxiously lest it flatten again before they resumed their journey, satisfied that the operation had been successful.

"Gertrude," David asked one day after they had the car only a few weeks, "wouldn't you like to learn to drive?"

"Oh, David," Gertrude could not help laughing at the absurdity of it. "What an idea!"

"Don't laugh. I mean it. You could go to the store or the neighbours, take the children for rides when I'm busy."

"But I can still take the horse and buggy, you know. And besides, wouldn't it look funny—a woman driving a Model T?"

It did not take much more persuasion on David's part, however, for Gertrude's reluctance to evaporate almost as soon as the seed had been planted. So she became David's pupil. The first lesson was a composite of false starts, wrong turns, sudden stops, liberally punctuated with laughter. With the first small triumphs of success in manoeuvring the car, she lost her initial nervousness and became a confident driver. Her reservations at being seen driving, by the neighbours, disappeared. She dauntlessly covered the countryside and passed through the small villages, making no excuses for the cloud of dust she left behind.

It was a sad day, late in the fall, when they regretfully put the Model T in the garage for the last time and closed the door on the summer of what had proved to be the happiest and most carefree time of their lives. The day when they would bring her out of hibernation in the spring seemed very remote indeed.

Chapter Nineteen

The day broke slowly, emerging with difficulty from the thick grey pall which had settled over the countryside during the night. It aptly depicted the darkness which hovered over the world in this year of 1916. David and Gertrude rose early and though it was mid-March and the days were lengthening, Gertrude lit the lamp, but its glow did not reach the dark, shadowy corners of the room. The lamplight which gave the room a cozy warmth in the evenings, now was only making a cold, ineffectual attempt to light the room. The sun rose and for just a moment, peeked at the world before withdrawing behind the gloomy mantle of clouds. The day crept stealthily upon them.

Gertrude had laid the breakfast table. The porridge had finished its bubbling, and was waiting, with the simmering coffee, at the back of the stove. The ham was still sizzling, its aroma permeating the room. Gertrude was waiting for David and the hired man to come in from the chores. She went to the window and looked across the fields. The snow had thawed just enough to reveal the black earth which had blown in with the strong winter winds, mingling with the snow, leaving all the land, as far as the eye could see, with a mottled, blackish, lumpy covering. On the far horizon, the scene melded together and the line where the earth gave way to the sky was lost.

When they were sitting at the table, Gertrude was startled by the stuttering, jangling ring of the telephone but she made no move to answer it. It would be for David. She drew back from using the phone unless it was absolutely unavoidable. It instilled in her a tinge of apprehension. The phone lines had not been carried out to the farmers, though telephones had become general in the towns and cities across the country. But David and his brother John had strung wires between their two farms, since it was but a small fraction of a mile between them, and put in their own phone boxes. They used this new contrivance sparingly, mainly when there were plans to be made which involved them both or when some bit of news could not wait until they would see each other. The annoyance of shouting and repeating what was said, far outweighed the pleasure of its use.

"I suppose that's John," David remarked unnecessarily as he pushed back his chair. "We've been talking about getting together and cutting up our fire wood for some time now. I expect that's what he'll be calling about. I suppose one day's as good as another," he explained before he picked up the receiver.

From David's side of the conversation, it appeared that his surmise had been correct. Gertrude also gathered that David was to take the stationary engine. The engine had a large flywheel. The saw with its smaller wheel would be positioned several feet from the stationary engine and then the two wheels would be connected with a large belt. In this way, the engine powered the saw.

"I'll go over in about an hour. I should be finished with all my chores here at home by then," David told Gertrude, as he resumed his seat at the table for a second cup of coffee. "And tomorrow, we'll likely move the outfit over here and do our wood too. So we'll be having a few extra men for dinner."

The phone call had awakened the children and Gertrude turned her attention to their getting dressed and washed for the day. At the same time, she made plans with Anna for the extra baking they must do for the next day. Anna had come back to them a few weeks earlier, just as she had done for a number of years now. The children loved her and Gertrude could rely on her implicitly.

While Gertrude was buttoning baby Benjamin's shirt, the thought came to her mind that he was almost ready to walk out of her arms, that he would not be her baby much longer. He was only ten months old, but his innate manliness shone through all his actions. Soon he would scorn being petted and cuddled. Gertrude loved her children more than life itself, but she hoped wistfully that she would not have another child, at least not for a long time. She had borne four in the seven short years of their marriage. It had taxed her strength greatly. She prayed only to be able to look after the ones she had, not like her mother who with her ninth child had died in childbirth. She had had nothing more to give and left her family for others to look after. Gertrude caught her thoughts up sharply and gave Benjamin a big hug, remembering how only this morning, in the half-light, they had been awakened by his gurgling and they looked over to see him standing up in his crib. When he saw that he had succeeded in rousing them, he laughed and said clearly, "Papa?" It was his first word and David had looked so pleased and proud as he lifted him out of his crib and played with him for a while before the day got underway.

Later the older children were scuffling at the window, each determined to have the best view as they watched their father and Neil loading the engine on the low, flat sled. Neil too had come back early this year. David was anticipating a busy spring. Benjamin was watching his brother and sisters with avid, lively interest. When with excited squeals, the three at the window, indicated that the men were finished, Gertrude lifted Benjamin and held him up to the high window in the door so he could see, too.

David looked up and waved back at his family. He was about to step on the sled, when he laid his reins down again and came back toward the house. Gertrude opened the door for him.

"Have you forgotten something?" she asked with concern.

"Yes, I have." David answered with mock seriousness. He put his arm around Gertrude and lifted her chin up with his other hand. He looked deep into her eyes. "Why are you so sad today, Gertrude?"

"Oh, David," she said in a low voice. She had not realized that she was so transparent. "Somehow I wish you weren't going today," his attention to her every changing mood always touched her.

"Why, Gertrude, I'll be home soon. But if you really want me to stay, I could phone back."

"Oh, of course not. I'm being foolish," she interjected hastily, "I'm just silly."

"You're never foolish, Gertrude, That's one of the many reasons why I love you. Tomorrow will look different, you'll see. Now let me see you smile." She complied, almost shyly.

David kissed Gertrude and enveloped her and Benjamin in one big hug.

"Papa—Papa?" Benjamin remembered his new accomplishment and called his father's attention to himself. David stood back and shared a hearty, comradely laugh with his youngest child. The moment was theirs alone, and Gertrude did not intrude.

"Take care of Mama while I'm away little man," David said, tweaking his small son's cheek playfully. Then calling good-bye to his other children and with another quick kiss on his wife's cheek, he was gone.

"Good-bye, David," Gertrude called, wistfully, after him, but her call did not rise above the children's lusty farewells.

Despite the life about her, after David left, time dragged for Gertrude . They ate their early noon meal and though the children went back to their usual, noisy play, Gertrude took little notice. When she saw Anna reaching for her coat, Gertrude stopped her.

"Anna, let me go. I'll get the wood. I need some fresh air, anyway." She did not add that she wanted more than anything to be by herself for a while. The feeling was strange to her, for her family was such an integral part of her, that to want to get away from them, was, alas, to want to get away from herself. Was that what she wanted? She did not know. She could not explain her own feelings—her disquietude.

Gertrude was surprised at the soft air that touched her flushed cheeks as she stepped out of the hot kitchen. Despite the lack of sunshine, the snow was mushy and starting to mix with spring mud. Her feet sank into the slush on the path to the wood shed. She stopped mid-way there, and she drank in the air, hungrily, to fill her thirsty lungs. When she had satisfied her need, she stood, without moving and listened, she heard only the stillness—the stillness which was pressed down by the leaden sky. There was not even a hint of a breeze. The atmosphere had the strange hollow characteristic which carried sounds over a great distance. From somewhere came the distance tapping of a hammer, from another direction, the echoing of barking dogs, then faintly, from yet another source, came an answer to the first dog's mating call. If spring was not here, it was not far away. Soon all the male dogs in the neighbourhood would be congregating around the edges of the farmyards that were home to female dogs. Then the quietness returned until the sharp, irregular popping of an engine being started, reached her ear across the distance from John's farm. She smiled to herself, picturing the men, their senses dulled by the consumption of Mary's cooking, eaten in the over-heated kitchen, straggling somewhat reluctantly back to finish their job. She waited expectantly until she heard the steady throbbing of the motor. She was satisfied. She knew it was David running the engine; they would soon be done. Much of her well-being was restored. Then, in an instant, her serenity was shattered by the wailing, piercing shriek of the saw. She heard its wild cry, rise and fall, rending the air. She shut her eyes but she could see the round, serrated, glistening blade cutting the logs in savage precision as they were fed to it. A shudder passed over her body. It left her feeling as though a cold, clammy hand held her in a vicelike grip. Gertrude pulled the heavy shawl over her head and drew it closer about her shoulders as she hurried with lowered head to finish her task.

When she was back in the house, Gertrude shut the door quickly behind her and dropped her big armload of wood carelessly into the box beside the stove. She looked about the room. Nothing had changed, the children were playing and didn't even look up, Anna was washing dishes, humming in her own curious, tuneless way. The mound of mending and darning, which she had eyed with displeasure earlier, was still stacked neatly on the sewing machine, awaiting her attention. She walked over to it and picked out a few pieces and wondered how Arnold, her eldest, managed to wear so many holes in his overalls in so short a time. She sat down in her rocker and began energetically to ply her needle, but her fingers slackened gradually, then fell idly to her lap.

How long Gertrude had been so engrossed, when the ringing of the phone penetrated her senses, she did not know. She had not heard it until one of the children called her attention to it. Her mending fell unnoticed to the floor as she rose to answer it.

She lifted the receiver off its cradle and put it to her ear. She pulled the mouth piece down. David always turned it up to speak into it but even so he still had to bend to it, she thought irrelevantly.

"Hello," she spoke into it, but there was no answer, then she called louder, "hello.....hello?" her voice became urgent.

"Gertrude," a small voice came across the wire, "Gertrude?"

"Oh, Mary," Gertrude forced herself to speak more calmly, "yes, Mary, this is Gertrude, you sound so far away."

"We've sent one of the boys over to get you," Mary said abruptly, without preamble.

"But, Mary," Gertrude protested. "I....."

"No, Gertrude, no, you must come," Mary's voice rose in high, bleak despair, then she stopped and Gertrude could hear her take a deep breath, before she went on, "Gertrude, there's been an accident." The line crackled and hummed between them. " Gertrude? Gertrude..... are you still there?"

"It's David," Gertrude said quietly. She Knew. She had known the moment the bell had sounded. "What happened?" Gertrude clung desperately to the mouth piece for support lest her knees give way.

"David's foot got caught in the belt, and—but Gertrude," Mary said at last, "but, I don't know how bad it is. We've sent Thomas to get you," her voice came sporadically over the wire, then faded away. Gertrude dropped the receiver. She had not the presence of mind to put it back on its hook. It hung there limply by its chord, swinging back and forth, back and forth.

"What is it, Mama, what is it?" Arnold insisted anxiously. "Can we come, too?" Helen begged, with Elma adding her plea as they watched their mother put on her coat. Knowing instinctively that all was not well, they ceased their chatter.

"Not today, you can't come today," Gertrude said woodenly. "You have to stay here with Anna. Be good, mind what she says. I have to go to Papa—Papa needs me." She stooped to give each one a hurried kiss. "I'll hurry home," she promised automatically.

Anna had stopped her work and was wiping her hands on her apron. "Something has happened. Something has happened to David, Anna. I must go to him," Gertrude spoke quietly as though all emotion had already drained from her.

"Oh," Anna gasped, "oh, my," but she did not press her mistress for further information. Gertrude's controlled, pale demeanour told her that this was no small matter. She turned to the small ones, their bereft expressions beseeching her without words.

Gertrude hurried out the door and waited at the gate. The small hope that she would hear the wail of the saw again, died quickly for she knew that she would not. She leaned on the gate and for a moment put her hands over her ears to shut out the thunder of the silence which surrounded her and reached into eternity. Then the tiny sound of the clinking harness rings reached her ears.

A bright sound, usually associated with the mundane progress of uneventful daily travel, was now an assault to her being as it rapidly became louder and louder. The hooves of the single horse, pulling the buggy, sank deep into the ooze of winter's withdrawal but John's eldest son gave them no time to settle into difficulty as he mercilessly slapped the reins to hurry the horse on.

Thomas jumped down and assisted his aunt onto the seat. With no time for the horse to catch its breath, they were on their way. Neither of them spoke. Thomas was vainly attempting to suppress and hide his emotions and Gertrude shrank from what he might say if she questioned him. She remained silent.

Thomas goaded the horse to a gallop, the muddy water splashing wildly from the wheels but the minutes it took them to make the trip were endless. Not before they careened around the corner of the barn, did they see the cluster of people standing about, not moving—each one a figure of loneliness, frozen, motionless—too stunned to share their grief with each other, not yet ready to reach through the turbulent darkness of disbelief and incomprehension that surrounded them. Once their tongues were loosened to speak of it, each would dwell upon his own reaction and shock and his own part in the tragedy.

Had Gertrude been capable, she would have seen the stark disbelief, the horror chiselled on the pale, stone faces of the still figures about her, but she saw only David, lying on the cold ground. She ran swiftly toward him but with each step she seemed suspended in endless time with no sensation of her feet touching the ground. In her panic, she felt she would never reach him. Unseen hands were grappling at her, trying to hold her from him. Someone hastily threw a coat over David but not before she had seen his broken body, twisted out of shape—the white bone protruding from his hip where his overalls were torn. The belt had begun to slip off the engine's flywheel. David had kicked it in an attempt to slide it back into place. His foot got caught between the wheel and the belt. Instantly, he was dragged into the circular motion of the wheel. It captured him for an instant and then spit his mangled body out onto the ground. He had died instantly.

She fell to her knees beside him and lifted his head on her arm and cradled it in her lap. "David, David," she crooned softly, "don't leave me—please, please. David—can't you hear me?" She caressed his cheek, brushed the hair from his eyes. His cheek was still warm but he did not answer. Gently, she traced her trembling finger tips across his forehead, along his nose, over his beautiful lips, as if to commit to memory what she knew was hers to touch no more. "Why, David, why?—can't you take me with you? Oh please." His lips were still. "You know I have no place to go without you. You know it," she said almost accusingly, her teeth grinding. Quickly she was contrite for she saw that his cheeks were wet with tears. She brushed futilely at them, not aware that they were spilling from her own eyes. Firm, but gentle hands took Gertrude away from David. As the tears were drying on her cheeks, she walked into the world of her stony, quiet grief.

Chapter Twenty

If they had not told her, Gertrude would not have known it was the day of the funeral. She groped her way through the hours, barely able to distinguish between day and night. She was hearing the slow, steady rain on the roof, the rain which had begun to fall the day David died and had not ceased. She walked to the window and drew aside the curtain, the window wept she thought listlessly, but *her* eyes were dry. She rested her forehead against the cool windowpane. The others had made the arrangements and only at their insistence had she taken any part—his favourite hymn—his favourite psalm. One thing Gertrude had been adamant about. The coffin was to remain closed and draped in flowers. She would spare David from the prying eyes of the throng. John saw to it that those who came for a viewing, prior to the service, did so by invitation only.

John also arranged for their itinerant minister, John Zacharias, to travel to Rosenort to conduct the service. John knew that the attendance would be large, more than just the small number that belonged to their new church. The

Holdemans would be there from both sides of the river too. John's father had offered the use of the Holdeman church but after some discussion they decided to hold the service in the Rosenort school house which was slightly larger. It wasn't necessary for John to add that his father's church was too fraught with negative memories for Gertrude to tolerate having the service there. Father Enns understood.

John and Neil had a discussion about transportation. Neil suggested they bring the Model T's out of storage. Up until now they had not been driven while there was still snow on the ground but Neil knew from some of his friends that the cars were capable of managing reasonably well in snow. The rain that had been falling mingled with the snow into a mushy mixture of snow and mud making the use of sleighs or wagons less than ideal so they decided to give the cars a try. The day before the funeral, they were taken down frown their winter blocks, the tires were duly inflated, the radiators filled and after a bit of coaxing with the crank, the spark leaver and a few other minor adjustments they both, in turn, came to life. With the tops up and the side curtains in place they would afford the passengers some privacy as well as keep them dry if the rain persisted.

The school house was filled to capacity with mourners and the inevitably curious. Some were even forced to remain outside milling about during the service. A stillness fell as Gertrude, on the arm of Father Enns, entered the room. Anna and Neil, tending to Arnold, Helen, Elma and Benjamin came next, followed by Agnes and the John Enns family. Their desolation was palpable as they moved to their seats at the front.

The minister's words washed over Gertrude in waves and only a few passages reached her through the throbbing deluge—

'He maketh me to lie down in green pastures.....

'He leadeth me beside still waters.....'

She was transported into the past and it was David reading the passages as he had often done. She had always pictured herself and David walking hand in hand surrounded by beauty everywhere when she heard the lines—

'Yea though I walk through the valley of death.....'

But now, he was walking there alone, he had not waited for her. The beauty had vanished. She saw only barren, lonely emptiness.

When the service was over, John and Mary's oldest sons, along with members of their new church carried the coffin out of the building, followed by the minister, Gertrude, Father Enns and the rest of the entourage. The congregation remained respectively in place making no attempt to approach any of the mourners. The private graveside service was to be at the Enns family cemetery located on Father Enns's farm. They climbed into their waiting cars. Neil drove Gertrude's car and Anna supervised the children during the drive. Father Enns, John Zacharias and Agnes went with John and Mary in their car. John and Mary's remaining children drove themselves in one of their buggies. The coffin along with the pallbearers were transported by horse and wagon. Following the interment, the Reverend Zacharias returned with John and Mary to their farm. He was to spend the night with them before returning to Saskatchewan where he had his base of operation. No one else, other than Gertrude, was invited for the customary post funeral get together.

Annie, Jennie and their husbands were staying with Katie and George. Isaac and his wife had returned to Blumenort right after the service. Abram and his wife Martha who had married four years ago joined them after the funeral. Martha was a younger daughter in the Enns family. She and Abram had purchased a farm just half a mile west and half a mile south of George and Katie's farm. Three families of married Enns and Penner children now owned farms within a radius of one mile of each other. They were sitting around drinking coffee. "What shall we do?" Katie asked of no one in particular. "Gertrude looked like she didn't know where she was. Before they were thrown out of church, I told her God was going to punish her if she didn't repent. Now my words have come true." She stopped. Then she blurted out, "Maybe if I hadn't said that this wouldn't have—," but her despair prevented her from finishing her horrifying thought. She had put down her coffee cup and was pacing about the room. "Oh, how can I comfort her and help her to see that now she must come back to us? I wasn't even invited to look at David." No Holdemans were invited to the viewing except for Father Enns and out of respect for his father, John had also included George and Martha but none of the Penners. The graveside service was for Father Enns and the members of their new church only.

"I don't think any of us have any obligation to try and comfort Gertrude," Jennie retorted, her voice breaking with unusual emotion. "She has made it very clear that she doesn't want to share her grief with any of us. And just look how far she has fallen. The things that so called minister said that had nothing to do with the bible, keeping the coffin closed during the service and flowers on top of the casket! I couldn't believe what I was hearing and seeing."

Annie felt she should say something. After all she was the eldest, but she couldn't find the words that would help bring them together so she remained silent, not even able to retreat into her usual refuge of tears.

Then, quietly, from the corner of the room Abram spoke. "She doesn't know what she is doing. We will have to forgive her and wait for her to come back to her senses. She's my big sister. She has always treated me kindly." And I love her still, he thought, but didn't have the courage to say so out loud. Martha, who adored her brother David, gave Abram's arm a reassuring squeeze.

"I agree," Katie said as she slowed her pace, thinking about what Abram had just said. "Yes, we'll give her some time, and then we'll approach her," knowing now that she had an ally in Abram.

The days passed into weeks and the weeks into months. Life had not stopped around Gertrude but she had barely noticed. Neil had hired two extra men to work with him putting in the crop. John's older sons lent a hand when John could spare them. Anna had taken the responsibility of running the household on her capable shoulders. Gertrude went through the motions of living, working but with no interest in what she was doing. The children had ceased begging her to take them for a ride in the car. The car had been put back into storage after the funeral and she had not taken it out since.

* * * * *

Father Enns had come early in the evening and had played with the children. It was the month of June and the days were at their longest. Though it was not yet dark, the children had now been sent to bed, much to their displeasure. But Father Enns had stayed on. He had been coming often and did not hurry away as had been his way in earlier, happier days. He would talk to Gertrude and she answered him but there were many silences. He did not mind and she seemed not to notice the lapses.

Gertrude sat motionless in her chair for some time before she looked up to see Father Enns standing and looking out the window. His figure was silhouetted against the dusk and she was struck by the naked sorrow that she saw in the bent figure and bowed head. "Oh Father," she burst out. He was taken aback by the pain in her cry. He hurried to her side.

"What is it Gertrude? What is it?"

"Oh Father!" She repeated again, "Oh Father I have been so blind! I haven't seen how much you miss him too."

He sat down beside her and took her hand in his. "Yes, Gertrude, I do. I miss him too." Gertrude searched his face. The lines there had deepened, his hair had more grey than she remembered. He had aged, oh, how he had aged since last she had really looked at him.

"How selfish I have been. I have thought only of myself." Her reserve was beginning to give way. In her agitation she stood, then turned and looked down at him. "He was your son and you loved him and you lost him, just like I did." Her tears began to fall. She dropped to her knees and buried her face in his lap. Her sobs came slowly from deep inside, then tore wildly at her defenceless, thin body, releasing all her pent grief.

"There, there my child, cry—cry—you have needed to cry for so long, so long. You'll feel better—." He stroked her hair, soothing her, murmuring to her just as he had, many times, comforted his young daughters when they had come to him with their grief after their mother died. "Yes, I loved him," he spoke as her weeping grew less. "Not only because he was my son, but for many other reasons."

"He thought so much of you too. He almost worshiped you," Gertrude said after she could speak. "You'll never know how unhappy it made him to have to hurt you so, when we left the church. He would have done almost anything to spare you, anything except that one thing. He had to do it. He always hoped that you would understand."

"I do understand. You may not believe it but I did, even then, even in the beginning. And Gertrude, I wanted to tell him that, many times, especially in the last while before he died. But I didn't and now I can't find any excuses good enough for my having put it off. I wanted to tell him that he wasn't wrong if he had found a different way from that of our people. I wanted to tell him that we all serve the same God and that there are many pathways to Him. But now," he said desolately, "now it's too late."

Gertrude look up at him. His words reminded her of some of the things her Aunt Kathryne had said during their last meeting so long ago. He looked sad and forlorn. It was almost more than she could bear. Then her face brightened a little, "No, no, it can't be too late. It's *not* too late. You're telling *me.* Don't you see Father, you're telling *me!* Don't you see that it means as much to me as it would have to David? It's almost like your are telling him!"

Father Enns could feel some of the fatigue that had consumed his being for so long ease a little. "Thank you, Gertrude. You don't know how much better it makes me feel to hear you say that. I didn't think it was possible for me to feel better anymore. For these three months I have been coming, hoping to comfort you, maybe even to find some comfort for myself. When I'm with your children I almost forget for a time. Arnold is the image of David. They show me that life must go on and must be lived. They need you very much."

"Oh, my poor children!" Her heart began to pound in her chest. "I've got to make it up to them. They must be feeling like little orphans. Oh, how well I know that feeling! I'll—I'll start first thing tomorrow. We have to start putting our lives back together. But you—all this time, you never stopped coming. You never lost patience."

"We all knew it would take time."

"I just couldn't feel. I knew it was wrong but I just couldn't help myself. I'm so ashamed. Oh David, what must you think of me? I'll try so hard. I don't know how I'll get along without you but I know I must. I'll try hard. I've kept telling myself that I must now be both mother and father to our children but I haven't been listening."

Silence swirled around the room for a time.

"We were so happy together," she said with distant yearning. "We had so much fun. He loved our children so much." Suddenly she was flooded with wonderful memories. She knew that she had been truly loved and that she had been able to return that love with all of her being.

"Now that you can talk about it, it will help. You're strong. You have always come out on top. You will again. I know you will."

The next morning she was eating breakfast with her family. She stopped eating and just looked at them for a while. They were eating quietly with down cast eyes. Her heart sank. What had she done to them? She knew that they must have been cautioned many times not to disturb their mother. Though they had tried to come to her for their childish wants, they had turned more and more to Anna. Arnold and Helen had understood, in their limited way, that their father was not coming back and they had made some adjustments. But Elma had not understood. She grieved for her father and would still ask from time to time, when is Papa coming home? Gertrude didn't know how to answer. All she could do was hold her close and rock her. Now Gertrude asked herself, had that been enough? And Benjamin, he had long since forgotten his first word, 'Papa'. She would have to do everything she could to keep David's memory alive for him—tell him stories—create pictures that would serve as memories of his Papa.

Gertrude pulled herself together and with all the enthusiasm she could muster, said, "Arnold, Helen." They looked up at her with bland, polite faces. Her children were treating her like a stranger! She looked at the other two. They were smiling. It gave her the courage to go on. "How would you like to go for a ride today in the Model T?" The older two, registered disbelief but the suggestion brought happy yes, yes, yes's from Elma. Benjamin, always ready to follow Elma's lead joined in, pounding the table with his spoon, splattering his porridge with great glee. Helen didn't know what to say or do and Arnold bent to his food.

"No, I really mean it. Wouldn't you like to go for a ride, today? As soon as you're finished, Arnold, run and tell Neil to get the car out." Arnold, now understanding that his mother was serious, could not contain himself. He dropped his spoon and ran out on his errand, slamming the door behind him. Helen winced and looked at her mother with a worried expression on her face. "Never mind Helen. This is a happy day," and for the first time Helen, too, smiled. "We'll all come out and help get the car ready," Gertrude called after Arnold but he was already out of sight.

"Can Anna come too?" Helen sang out excitedly.

"Yes, yes, we'll all go. We'll even take Neil in case we have a flat," Gertrude added laughingly. There was an awkward pause when everyone stopped and looked at her in surprise. Her laugh sounded strange, even to herself. It had been so long a time since she had laughed. The frozen moment passed and they all broke into gales of laughter. "I'm sure we need something from the store, don't we Anna?"

"Yes indeed," Anna replied happily.

"Can we get some candy?" Elma asked hopefully. When Gertrude nodded she asked, "Can I hold the bag?" They were not allowed candy very often but when they did get some, it was a special treat and it was of the utmost importance who was to hold the bag. It was generally decided that they would take turns unless, of course, one of them had earned a special reward.

"Of course, Elma. In fact, I'll tell you what we'll do. We'll get a bag for each one of us! Now let's go out there and help Neil get the car going. The tires will all need to be pumped up so we'll take turns. It's been sitting for a long time."

So off the little group drove to Rosenort to buy some candy. They were still on edge, not quite sure of their new footing but eager to show each other how willing they were to come back to life. It would take time to fully escape from the leaden, weightlessness of the purgatory they had been living in for the last three months.

That night, in bed, Gertrude breathed a deep sigh of relief and exhaustion. Today had taken all of her energy. I hope I have the strength and the wisdom to make a good life for us. Father Enns said I did. I hope he is right.

Chapter Twenty-One

As Gertrude began to come out of her mourning, they came—those who had so adroitly, in recent years, denied her the right to follow the dictates of her own conscience. With their coming, unfolded the design to bring Gertrude back to their ways. At first the campaign was subtle—gentle, friendly overtures, often expressed in small deeds of kindness from those who had loved her in the past. Katie came to help, maybe with some baking or house cleaning, any job that needed doing but making sure not to linger too long after the tasks at hand were finished. Abram too, lent a helping hand around the farm yard from time to time. He would stay and talk for a while before returning to his farm. Abram had less experience with big farming than Gertrude so he often asked her advice—still the big sister. Gertrude was touched by their efforts. She knew they were sincere and well intentioned. As for the other Holdemans that surfaced on her farm, she only gave them token acknowledgement, quickly learning how to make it clear that their stay would be short. During this phase, there was no direct mention by anyone of her returning to the church.

By the time the fall work was done it was time to intensify their approach.

"I think it's time that we start talking to Gertrude about coming back to the church." Katie had invited Abram and Martha over after their Sunday service. "We have given her lots of time to regain her senses. It's time we let her know that she would be welcomed back."

Abram wasn't so sure. "Gertrude has always been so strong minded. She doesn't really like it when people try to tell her what to do."

From George; "She has never forgiven me for speaking up at the council meeting when they were expelled. She would probably scoff at an invitation from me to come back to the church ."

"Well, as usual, I guess it's me who must take the bull by the horns. I've been going over to help a little with this and that so she is used to me stopping by. Next time, I'll see if I can talk to her about this."

Over the summer, Gertrude had taken full responsibility for managing her farm. With Neil at her side, they had completed the harvest, hiring the extra men needed to get the crop cut, stooked, gathered, threshed and transported to the railway station. It had been one of the most abundant yields in her memory. After discussions with John, she made plans to purchase four more horses and a second binder. Next year they would operate two binders in tandem to cut and tie the grain into sheaves ready for stooking. It was obvious that she needed full time help year round now, so she made arrangements with Anna and Neil. They both said they would stay full time for the next year. Anna had been woking as part of the cleaning staff in one of the large bank buildings on Winnipeg's Main Street during the off season when she wasn't needed on the Enns farm. She was a good worker and the bank was always happy to take her back on, whenever she was available. Neil preferred his nomadic life, working as an itinerant farm worker in the spring, summer and fall and then occupying his winters with work in the lumber camps to the north. This was referred to as 'working in the bush'. But he liked working for Gertrude and knew that he was needed. Gertrude paid them both well and all agreed to review the situation again next fall.

It was time to put the car away for the winter. She would miss it. She had discovered that when the demands of managing the farm, the house and caring for the children all on her own, threatened to overwhelm her, a solitary drive in her car helped to clear her thoughts and regain her equilibrium. Anna came to anticipate when the children were not to be included and made sure that Gertrude was able to crank up the Model T and leave the farm yard without pleas from the children to go with her. Gertrude, driving on her own with apparently no specific destination in mind, a cloud of dust behind her, didn't even cause much talk anymore among her neighbours. They were past being surprised by Gertrude Enns. As she enjoyed the power of the car propelling her down the roads, she found she could talk to herself about the issues needing her attention. What seemed muddled and unsolvable, would often get sorted out in her mind. She would drive back into her yard feeling rejuvenated.

It was late morning and she had just come back from her last drive of the fall. She parked the car in the garage.

Neil would put it up on blocks later. As she was walking toward the house she saw Katie's rig coming down the road. She waited for Katie to pull up in front of the house. "I've just put the car away for the winter. It was a beautiful fall day for a drive. The fall colours are at their best." All the farm yards now had wind breaks of mature trees protecting them from the prevailing north westerly winds.

"You do seem to spend a lot of time driving that machine around the countryside don't you?" Katie at her brusk self. Gertrude tensed ever so slightly. Katie made a big show of tethering her horse to the fence in front of the house, then pausing to pat her horse's nose and say a few quiet words. "Do you have time for a coffee? I need to talk to you."

Oh, oh, Gertrude said to herself as they walked into the house. And then—"Yes, I'll move the kettle to the front of the stove." She busied herself preparing the coffee and setting out some bread and butter. Katie busied herself in the front room looking over all the trappings of the sinful life that Gertrude and David had acquired since leaving the Holdemans. Gertrude brought in the refreshments on a tray and served, making sure no one could mistakenly think they were eating from a shared table. You can't be too careful Gertrude thought, sharing a private smile with herself.

Katie's first sip was followed by a clearing of her throat. "I'll get straight to the point. It's been, what, almost seven months now since David's death?" Gertrude still flinched at those words. "I've talked to Annie and Abram and we all think and hope that you will reconsider and come back to our church. We want to have you back so much." Gertrude took a breath, about to speak. "No, wait—it must be so lonely for you. You need our fellowship and if you won't think about your *own* salvation, at least you should be thinking about your children. They need to become full members of our community in order to prepare them to join the church."

This time, Gertrude put up her hand to stop Katie and with the other hand deliberately put down her coffee cup. "Katie—Katie, you just don't understand do you? My children will never join the Holdeman church. They have been baptized into our new church and receive regular Sunday school lessons from me and from the Reverend Zacharias when he comes through. And as for me, I have never felt as close to God as I have since I left your church." Gertrude was wondering how much she should say. David had once said that it was like talking to the wind. They have all the answers so there is no discussion. Changing her tack, she continued. "I want more opportunities for my children than you or I ever had. Get more of an education than grade seven or eight. Experience the world beyond Rosenort and the Holdemans. Maybe find ways other than farming to make a living. I don't know, and I don't know yet how I'm going to accomplish all this. All I know is that I will."

"Gertrude, you have always been reaching for pie in the sky," some frustration and irritation beginning to show in Katie's voice in spite of herself. "Now that you are on your own again it's time to come back down to earth. You have one of the most successful farms in the area right now but how long do you think you can keep this up—a woman alone? You need a man. You need more sons. You'll never find another man unless you come back to the church."

The thought of 'another man' was horrifying to Gertrude. Indignation was rising in her throat. It tasted like bile. What could Katie be thinking to misjudge her situation so totally? Gertrude rose from her chair, walked to the window and looked out at the dying fall landscape, calming herself. Then she turned. She spoke slowly and quietly, carefully considering each word.

"Katie, I don't want to ever hear from you again about my rejoining your church or about me finding another man. Never again. For as long as we live. Never! I know you think you have the right to say these things to me because we are sisters. I also can still understand that you think you are speaking in my best interests. But I can't allow myself to care about that anymore. If I did, it would tear me to pieces. David and I fought for a new life. We got what we fought for. My children and I still have that new life and we will keep it. We will build on it. Sister or not, you are not in a position to question that any more. Neither are any of the other members of our family. I want very much to keep our friendship if we can but, if we do, we have to understand where the boundaries are." Gertrude came back to her chair. Katie knew her sister well enough to know that her outward calm was belied by the pale colour in her face.

"What a thing to say. We both know where the boundaries are. They are set by our church. The rules on shunning are very clear and I have stuck to those from the beginning."

"Again, I don't think you understand what I am saying. I'm not talking about the shunning rules, I'm talking about you and me—our love as sisters—not trying to make each other into the person that we think the other should be—just accepting each other. We're not children anymore. We've both changed."

"You'll get no argument from me on that one. We both have a lot to think about. Annie should know about this but I know that I wouldn't be able to repeat most of what you have just said. I couldn't do it. Now I'm going to untie Nellie and go home." Gertrude didn't get up from her chair. She let Katie see herself out.

She went to the kitchen to reheat the coffee, poured another cup and sat down near the heat of the stove. She was feeling cold. As though it were yesterday, she was remembering a talk she and David had had some months before his death.

* * * * *

They had been sitting together in the gathering dusk of evening watching the twilight fall. Neither of them had spoken but Gertrude was looking closely at David who was lost in thought. "Gertrude," he said finally with an unusually solemn note in his voice. "Gertrude, if something should happen to me….."

"David!" Gertrude immediately interrupted, startled. "Hush, David, nothing is going to happen to you. What a thing to say!"

"Yes, I know, but we never know what is in store for us. I guess that's a good thing," he mused for a second, then continued, "but if it did, say, just for a moment, suppose it did, what would you do?" he persisted.

"Why, I suppose I would go on just like now—keep the

farm going. But I've never thought about it and I refuse to now," she added vehemently.

"We should think about things, though Gertrude. I know you would manage in that way. You know just as much about farming as I do." He paused. Then he said, "That's not what I meant actually. Gertrude—"

"Then what, David?"

"If you were alone, things could be much easier for you if, if, " then he blurted it out. "If you went back to the old church."

"David!"

"You would have your family and old friends back and—" For the first time David found himself at a loss for words in explaining himself to Gertrude.

"David stop. Stop right now! Don't say any more. Listen to me. I would never, never go back! Why, it would be like….., what would it be like?" She searched for words. "It would be like jumping back into a deep, dark well after having struggled so long to escape."

David's face brightened. "It's been on my mind for some time now. I know that if something did happen to me, they would try to persuade you to go back to them. I also know they would try to make it difficult for you. I wouldn't want the memory of me to hold you back from anything you might decide to do that would make life easier for you. But I'm so relieved, even though I knew what you were going to say." Filled with admiration, he looked into the beautiful eyes of the woman he loved. "How could I have been so lucky?"

Gertrude reached and caressed his cheek. "I'm the lucky one." They rose from their chairs, David stoked the fire and they went hand in hand to their bedroom.

* * * * *

It had been a warning. 'They would make it hard for you.' Katie is trying to make it hard for me not to follow her advice. Advice that she thinks would make things easier for me. Thank goodness the rest of them have been pretty quiet. None of them have anything to offer me and it looks like they understand that now.

* * * * *

"I chose this afternoon to have my talk with Gertrude. I put our case to her just like we had agreed." Instead of going straight home, Katie had detoured over to Abram's farm. "I failed. I told her how much we wanted her back. That she would be welcome. That got me nowhere. So I tried to show her that she couldn't manage running the farm by herself. That she needed a man. That made it even worse. There is only one thing left. The church elders must put pressure on her. Must tell her that we all know David's death was her punishment from God. I tried to warn her about that before they got kicked out of church. It's not up to me to bring it up again now. I'm going to talk to George about talking to the council."

"I'm not so sure that that's a good idea Katie." Abram was doubtful. "Can we really say that we know God has punished her? Maybe God thinks she has a right to……"

"Abram! Not you too! Are you starting to think—?"

"No, no. I know what she has done is wrong. I just don't know if it's up to us to try and set her straight."

"Well, I can't give up until we've tried everything. I'm going to talk to George."

The final phase of the campaign kicked into motion with George doing as he was told. He talked to Henry Essau who said a council meeting was not necessary. He would make the arrangements for a group of elders from both sides of the river to visit Gertrude. It would take him a couple of weeks to get it set up.

A few days later, George was at Abram's farm helping clean the chicken coop. While they were chatting he told Abram about the plan. A delegation would be put together. They would soon be visiting Gertrude. It had been decided to include her brother in law, Jacob Unger. She had worked for him years ago so he knew Gertrude better than the others. They talked about including Annie too but decided against it. She might complicate things. It was to be men only. That way they could keep control and their message would be focused and forceful.

Later, after George had left, Abram went to find Martha. "I'm going to saddle up Star and ride to Gertrude's. George told me about the plan to have the elders pay a call on Gertrude and I think I should warn her, but I'm not going to tell her that Katie and George are responsible for setting this up."

"Okay, but don't stay too long."

It was a Sunday afternoon. Gertrude had finished doing the Sunday school lesson with her children and John and Mary's youngest. All the children had gone back to John's farm to play and Gertrude was getting caught up with some of her knitting. She heard the clatter of horses coming onto the yard. She got up to see who had arrived and saw three buggies, two men per buggy, pulling up in front of the house. So, they have arrived, she thought. Well, I'm ready for them. Albert Bartel and Jacob Unger stepped down from the lead buggy. Albert approached first. Why does Albert keep showing up in my life?

"We-e-ell Gertrude," immediately starting himself off on the wrong foot.

"We-e-ll Albert, and what brings you to this side of the river? When our paths cross it's usually unpleasant. But oh, yes, there was that one funny time when you lectured us about appropriate lady's undergarments. Do you remember?" As Gertrude knew, that was the last thing Albert wanted to be reminded of. He shot Gertrude what was meant to be a withering look, but she had already turned to Jacob. "Jacob—what a surprise to see you. And where is Annie?"

Jacob, never being good at eye contact, mumbled something about Annie being too busy to make the trip but Gertrude, not pausing to listen to his reply was moving away to acknowledge the others. Then she asked if they intended to come into the house. They did. She led them in. Anna was in the kitchen starting supper preparations. "Anna, we have guests. Would you set out some coffee and biscuits on the table so that people can help themselves?" Anna gave Gertrude a knowing look and nodded.

The discussion began. Each of the men spoke in turn, clearly having rehearsed what each would say. They started with generalities, expressing their condolences, their hope that she was managing and not finding running the farm too difficult. When they had covered all the preplanned niceties they moved to the real reason for their visit, stating that they knew she must be thinking about returning to the church and that they would help her with the things she would need to do in order to prepare herself to come back.

Jacob spoke at length of her need to reread the scriptures and reacquaint herself with the teachings of John Holdeman. They were so sure of themselves.

Gertrude was silent.

Then Henry Essau, an elder from the Rosenort congregation, talked about the difficulties of running a large farm operation. "A few weeks ago one of our members, who has recently lost his wife, came to me and asked my opinion about approaching you with a marriage proposal. He has three growing sons and two daughters. A nice group to fit in with your family. Then two days ago another member talked to me about the same thing. I said that I would think about approaching you. We all agreed, of course, that any future marriage would depend on your willingness to rejoin the church."

They want my soul and now they want my farm too. Gertrude had covered all of this ground with Katie. Katie still mattered to her so she had made the effort to say things that she hoped would help her to understand. But these people meant nothing to her. She was quite willing to remain silent.

Her lack of response was starting to unnerve the group. Henry began to suspect they might be losing the upper hand, not realizing that they had never had it in the first place. He wasn't used to women meeting his words with stony silence. Some were fidgeting ever so slightly but Jacob, never one to miss an opportunity for refreshments, got up noisily and helped himself to coffee and biscuits, returning to his seat balancing his coffee cup in one hand and a plate of biscuits in the other. Crumbs began to scatter about him, the detritus from his impromptu snack and his clumsy life.

It was left to Albert to make the last appeal. "We hoped that we wouldn't have to remind you of what we are sure you already know. God has punished you. He has chosen to take David away from you and sentenced him to burn in hell for eternity." He rose from his chair and pointed his finger at Gertrude. "He has done this to show you the error of your ways and to give you and your children a chance to save yourselves from the same eternal damnation." Albert was red in the face. Gertrude rose from her chair and stood, her face barely inches from his. She hoped her voice would remain steady. It did.

"I no longer believe in a God that punishes us for misdeeds by casting us into your kind of hell but I assure you, that if such a place *did* exist it would be filled with men just like you." Albert backed away. Even Jacob stopped eating his biscuit and stared, open mouthed at Gertrude. "Now, I'm going to ask all of you to leave my house and to leave *my* farm." She walked to the door, opened it, stepped outside, continuing to hold it open as they filed out. She then followed them to the gate and watched as they drove away. No one waved. It wouldn't be until decades later that Gertrude was to learn from Abram about the role Katie played in setting up this meeting.

"Now, Anna, let's clean up this mess, pour their coffee into the slop pail and start over again, make a new pot, sit down and talk about what we have to do this week."

After their talk in June, Father Enns had continued to come by as usual but now they were able to talk about David unselfconsciously, sharing memories, learning things about David from each other that they hadn't known. Gertrude couldn't help but see that his vitality was gradually failing.

She was preparing herself for the inevitable. He no longer walked with long striding steps across the fields to look in on his neighbours. Now he hitched his old mare, Daisy to his one-horse buggy and they made their rounds companionably, unhurriedly, together. For some time Daisy had been too old to work the fields or to foal but he had not had the heart to destroy her. Like old friends, they understood and looked after each other.

One day in late fall, just before the first snow began to fly, Daisy took him home. She stopped at the front gate and whinnied, her master was still sitting in his seat but his head was slumped over on his chest. His heart had simply stopped beating.

No one would ever know how great a loss Father Enns's death was to Gertrude. Without him she wasn't sure whether she would ever have been able to get her grief under control and start living again. She knew that David's death had been a mortal blow to him but how like Father Enns to delay his departure until he knew that she was strong enough to go on without him.

Now she felt more alone than ever. John and Mary were the only true family she had left. All the rest of them, except Agnes, were Holdemans. And Agnes. In spite of their shared religion, they had never succeeded in being close. Gertrude refused to succumb to Agnes's need to dominate. That was something Agnes wasn't used to and could not tolerate well. Thinking she recognized a week spot in Gertrude's armour, Agnes took every opportunity to remind Gertrude that she had been smart enough to never join the Holdeman Church in the first place so wasn't subjected to all the indignities of the shunning. Gertrude was forced to accept that they would never find enough common ground to have a real friendship—to feel like sisters. Then there was Peter. Her friendship with him dissolved immediately after she refused his proposal. Peter's pride had been badly injured. Four years ago, he had purchased land in northern Alberta where a small Holdeman congregation was getting established. He had married a woman from that community. Katie and Abram were keeping their distance as their church required. Annie? They had gone separate ways long ago. Jennie—the lost soul. She and David hadn't even been invited to attend her marriage to Margaret Fehr's brother Edward. Margaret Fehr! Their friendship had died an unnatural death. Not wanting to put Margaret in a compromising position after excommunication, Gertrude thought it best not to try to stay in touch. Oh, how she missed Margaret and longed to share a cup of tea with her once again! Isaac had attended David's funeral but she hadn't spoken with him at the time or seen him since.

So, what was left? Gertrude, John, Mary and their children along with the Eidse family, kept their regular church meetings and social outings going but they weren't the same without David. Sometimes she even thought that it was during these church activities that she missed David most. When she was alone, David was always with her. When she was in these groups he was gone. Nothing could fill the void left by his absence. Now with Father Enns gone too, Gertrude felt her world getting smaller and smaller.

It had been a draining summer and fall. Her first harvest season without David, and now the fall work done. Thank goodness Anna and Neil had agreed to work full time for the next year. All the mental and physical strain had kept her from dwelling on her loneliness. She looked out of her kitchen window at the dreary landscape. The splendour of the yearly crop, which gave it a short lived gracefulness, had succumbed to the hands of the reaper. Now the earth lay there in black, ugly lumps, turned by the shiny bright plough shares, waiting to be covered by snow. She pictured the hordes of gulls that always follow the fall ploughs, greedily devouring insects—the earth's last bounty of the season—before starting their journey south for the winter. In the spring, they would be back and just like the farmers, doing the same thing all over again and again and again. She looked down the road. Arnold would soon be walking home from school. She had endured alone, the misgivings of sending her oldest child to school for the first time. Mary had been right in her prediction that a farm in their school district would be put up for sale and probably bought by a Holdeman family. They had enrolled their four children this fall and the Friesen's first child would be of school age next fall with three more children following quickly. At the moment their school consisted of nine children from the Lutheran families who farmed to the north, Arnold, three of John and Mary's children plus the four new Holdeman children so the Holdemans were still in the minority. Katie's and Abram's farms were not in the same school district. Their children attended a school to the south. But nevertheless, Arnold would now start mingling with the children of the very people who were estranged from them. Would they be allowed to accept him or would their parents have already cast a negative influence on their attitude toward Arnold. After all, it was one thing to go to school with Lutheran children but a child of Gertrude Enns?

As she looked out the window she saw some snow flakes starting to flutter in the wind. The first snows rarely stayed so there probably would be some respite before the permanent blanket covered the land. When that happened, John provided a sleigh and horse for his children to take to school and this year Arnold would be included. They will pass through Gertrude's yard, pick Arnold up and continue across the field to school. By going over the field instead of following the section roads, the distance was cut down from two miles to about a mile and a quarter. Other children came by horse and sleigh too. The barn on the school yard was adequate to house the horses during the day. The onset of winter had always been a difficult time for Gertrude. The dread that came with the first snows had all but disappeared from her life during the happy years with David. Now it threatened to envelop her again. She must not let it. She forced herself to think about what they had been doing this time last year. They were busy planning the new house that was to have been built this last summer.

Ah, yes. Yes, of course, the house! She felt a small thrill of the old excitement. She would build it. She must build it! She knew David would want her to do it. It would ease the poignancy of the memories which filled the little house from corner to corner. They had long needed the extra space and even more so now that she would always need extra help.

Gertrude turned away from the window and went slowly to the bureau and pulled out the drawer where the plans over which she and David had spent so many happy hours were kept. They had lain there untouched and for a time forgotten. She felt a reluctance at disturbing them. She was filled with misgivings. It would be so much easier just to leave them. She and the children could make do in this house. Then quickly her hands swept them up and she clutched them to her breast. She took them to the window, to the better light, and sat down in a chair. She began to study them as though she had never seen them before. Soundlessly and unexpectedly, an envelope slipped from between the sheets into her lap. She looked at it wonderingly—her name was on it in David's handwriting. She held it thoughtfully for some moments, somehow loath to open it. And when she did, she saw that it was a short note. 'Dearest Gertrude,' it read. 'Whatever may happen, I want you to go ahead with our plans and build this house. We planned it together. It has been our dream for a long time. Do not think of what others might say. I want you to do it. It is for you and our children. Just remember the love I hold for you.' And it was signed, simply 'David.'

Gertrude held the letter for a long time her eyes staring unseeingly into space. Why, why had David written this? He must have had a very strong premonition that things were not to go on as they were. Shortly after his death, she had found an envelope addressed to his brother John with a small sum of money which he had owed him for a time. Now as she thought back, she could think of innumerable times when he had seemed to prepare her for the future, but a future without him. He had shown her how to do many little things about the place, things which he always had done himself. Their spirits were like one. Was it that their love was too ideal to last in this world of imperfections? He had left everything in order, everything but her shattered life. She would never be able to tell anyone about David's note and she must not dwell on it any longer. She must bury it deeply. But she would go on with their plans. She would no longer hesitate. She would build the house. She must build it.

Christmas came. She could not stop it. She went through all the motions to make it a happy one for her family. Christmas eve, she left the children to finish their supper while she went into the room where she had set up a tree and brought out the presents which she had hidden for some time. After supper, as had been their custom, the children rushed in and opened their gifts. It pleased Gertrude to see their joy as they unwrapped and played with their new dolls, trains and other things. But she felt empty. Tomorrow would have been their ninth wedding anniversary.

After inquiries during the winter, Gertrude found a young man whom she felt was trustworthy, to build the house. He would buy all the materials and hire the men to work for him. She and Anna would have to feed them. She saw a summer filled with activity and she looked forward to the challenge. She spent many hours scanning the Eaton's catalogue and made two trips to the store itself in Winnipeg, looking for the furnishings she would need. She furnished the house many times over before making up her mind what to order. And so the winter wore slowly on and brought them, at last, to the reality of building the house.

Chapter Twenty-Two

The long summer was almost over and the house was built and furnished. All that remained for Gertrude was to move their personal effects into the new house. The little house was going to be used to accommodate the hired men. The third floor of the new house had two large rooms. One for Anna and the second could house up to two other girls as needed. Gertrude was standing in the middle of the yard with John and Mary. How huge it looked she thought. It had two full size stories and a large third floor with dormer windows. Green shingles covered the top part from the eaves to the base of the second floor. The main floor was clothed in horizontal wood siding painted white. She had insisted on porches which she felt softened the lines and she had four. The back one was the largest and built like a lean-to. This porch was big enough to house the cream separator and a large sink for washing milk pails and storing them before they were taken to the barn. The entrance was at ground level. Inside, on the right, were three steps leading up to a landing and the door into the kitchen, Another door on the left, at floor level, opened to a stairway leading down to the basement which housed all the machinery and equipment needed to operate the house; the generation and storage of the electric power, the heating and storage of the hot water, the pressure pump to take the hot and cold water up to the kitchen and bathroom, the coal and wood burning furnace that heated all three floors.

The front porch opened into the front hall and front staircase. The side porch was actually two porches, one on top of the other. One opened into the dining room on the main floor and the one above it was accessible from one of the bedrooms on the second floor. She had always dreamed of having a house in which she could walk out of her dining room directly into her garden, the garden which was yet to be. David had planted the required wind breaks along the outer perimeter of the farm yard right after he bought the land. Gertrude's garden was off to the other side of the little house. This new house, standing alone, looked stark and imposing against the empty sky and plain landscape. It looked lonely. Had she built her loneliness into the house? She would plant many trees and bushes for it to nestle into and age gracefully. Gertrude stood looking at her house, deep in thought.

John and Mary, sensing that Gertrude wanted to be alone took their leave. They walked slowly down the well worn little road connecting their two farms. It was a lovely evening. It was still warm though there was the feel of fall in the air. They felt no need to hurry. "The house is beautiful, isn't it John, but I can't help feel as though she shouldn't have built it." Mary stopped.

"No, I think she did the right thing to go ahead with it," John picked up her train of thought. "You see, David often talked about a new house the winter before he died. They were going to build it last summer."

"Oh, I didn't know that." Mary showed her surprise. "Of course I knew they wanted to build but last summer? Oh my goodness! That's awful. It was a lost summer for all of us." Mary spoke sadly, in a moment of rare lucidity. As close as they were, Mary felt there was always a certain distance between Gertrude and her. From time to time it rankled Mary that John was closer to Gertrude than she. John and David had been as close as two brothers could be so when David married Gertrude, John was automatically drawn into friendship with her. The three of them, along with Agnes, shared the same strong motivation to learn all there was to know about the Swedenborg religion. Mary, on the other hand, had never been as keen on exploring what this new religion had to offer. After David's death, the bond between Gertrude and John became even stronger. It helped them to survive their loss. Mary understood all of this and being preoccupied with raising her large family, she never dwelt on the situation for long.

"It must be wonderful to walk into a new house, like Gertrude is doing right now and know that it is all yours—to have everything just like you've always wanted," Mary voiced her thoughts, not realizing the transparency of her yearning.

John, getting her drift said, "Yes, I believe it would, maybe we can some day." There was little conviction in John's voice. Mary could have said more but thought better of it. She, at times could become quite petulant and impatient with John. She knew that he would never build such a house. John was too much of a dreamer to make a real success of his farming. David was different. He had been a very efficient man. She was sure he had laid by all the money for the house, which indeed was true, although Mary only surmised as much. She envied Gertrude, even now. Gertrude had always had things nicer than she.

Gertrude walked in through the porch and door leading into the dining room. She wandered among the beautiful rooms admiring the staircase, the windows, the woodwork, the large, up to date kitchen. There would be no problem now, cooking for the large harvest gangs. And washing up would be so easy; just turn the tap and all the hot water that was needed came gushing out! There was a second stair off the kitchen. As well as leading to the second floor, it provided the only access to the third floor. She switched several of the electric lights on and off as she walked through the house. I'll never have to clean another lamp chimney as long as I live. Although not as grand as her former employer's house, her memory of the Stanton home had served as inspiration while she and David worked on designing their own house. It's done David, just like we planned it. I did it and now I have to see what life will be like living in it. I can see you right now coming down the staircase with a big smile on your beautiful face. Gertrude felt a sharp ache from deep inside. Her grief now came in unexpected waves. In between the waves she went about life day by day much like everyone else. When it hit she felt weak and lost. It took a few minutes and all of her strength to pull herself back to the road ahead.

There was still one piece of unfinished business which had been on her mind all summer. Having been married in the Holdeman Church, she of course, could not receive a wedding ring. Finger rings were a badge, signalling to the world that you had given in to the influences of evil. One Sunday, the summer before David died, after spending the afternoon working on the plans for their new house, David was in the barn doing the evening chores. Anna was in the house with the children reading to them and Gertrude was strolling in the vegetable garden looking dolefully at the weeds. David, having finished his work, left the barn looking for Gertrude. He spotted her in the garden. He liked to come up quietly behind her and take her waist in his hands and give her a gentle squeeze. It never failed to prompt a squeal of surprise form Gertrude. He did that now and got the desired result. She ran from his grasp and he started chasing her. They ran, Gertrude screeching, David laughing, dodging in and out and jumping over the rows of vegetables until she threw herself down on a patch of grass, laughing helplessly. He lay down beside her, resting on his elbow. They caught their breath. He leaned over and kissed her. "I want to give you a wedding ring!" Gertrude was so taken by surprise that she was at a loss for words. Although she now did own some jewellery, she had never thought of a wedding ring. For a long time they just looked into each other's eyes not saying a word. Their adoration was palpable.

When she was able to speak she sat up, "Oh David, how wonderful that would be. What a lovely way to put the finishing touch to our new life." They agreed to make a special trip to Winnipeg to buy it. However, with all the frantic farm activity of the summer and fall, winter was upon them before they knew it. They decided that they wanted to make an event of it and that late May —early June, when the new leaves were out and the early flowers were in bloom, would be a perfect time of year. They would buy the ring, stroll around the city, have an evening dinner at one of their favourite restaurants and spend the night at a hotel before returning to the farm. They would go after next year's spring rush was over.

It was while the house was under construction that she remembered about the ring. She would go to Winnipeg and pick out the ring that David would have given her. A few weeks after they had moved into the new house, Neil drove her to catch the morning train to Winnipeg. The trip was now routine. She had done it so many times. She went straight to Birks jewellery store on Portage Avenue. Gertrude had decided on a plain, wide, gold band so she wasn't interested when the clerk offered to show her a selection of other types of wedding rings. The clerk remained professionally pleasant even though she thought it strange that an unaccompanied woman was buying a woman's wedding ring. She brought out the plain gold bands. Gertrude hadn't fully anticipated how painful this was turning out to be. A couple of times her voice faltered. She chose the one that was 24 carat gold and just the right width. She asked to have it put in the beautiful blue box. The clerk suggested she slip the ring on Gertrude's finger to make doubly sure that it was the right size but Gertrude refused. Putting on the ring for the first time was to be a private moment, for David and her alone. She put the box in her purse and walked out of the store in a haze of loneliness and grief. She bumped into a man coming toward her. He apologized. She had planned to do some more shopping before catching the train home later in the afternoon. She didn't have the heart. In days to come, she didn't have a clear recollection of how she had spent the remaining hours before she caught the train. She did have the presence of mind to pick up the promised trinkets, one for each of the children. Other than that, all she could remember was stopping in at a tea room and sipping on a cup of tea.

Neil picked her up at the station as planned. It was an established tradition to bring home some sort of treat for the children after a day in Winnipeg. She was so glad that she had remembered. After much excitement over the little gifts, Gertrude sat down to enjoy a cup of coffee while she watched the children settle down to their bedtime snack. They all looked so healthy. It soothed her tired heart. After bedtime prayers, she said goodnight and went on to her room.

Her bed was always beautifully made up for two. She sat up in her side of the bed, holding the ring box. She opened it carefully. The gold glinted in the light from her bedside table lamp. The moment had come. She lifted the ring from its box and slid it onto the fourth finger of her left hand. She imagined the shy happy look that would have been on David's face.

I built our house and now I have your ring. The last two things that we planned together. A single tear escaped and ran down her cheek. She put the empty box carefully on the table beside her. She wiped away the tear. After a few minutes she put out the light. She turned onto her side. She reached over for David's pillow and pulled it close to her breast. She fell into a deep sleep.

They settled into the first winter in their new house with the novelty of all its conveniences. The flush toilet in the upstairs bathroom particularly intrigued the children. They had never seen one before. The winter passed quickly and by February Gertrude and Neil were discussing what preparations were needed to put in the next crop. Neil had already indicated that he would not be staying after the fall work was done. He was eager to return to his itinerant life. He knew of several men who were looking for more permanent work and who he knew would do a good job. He would arrange for Gertrude to meet some likely candidates and if they found someone they both thought was suitable, Gertrude would hire him on a yearly basis starting in March. Neil would have from March until the end of October to supervise the new man. Gertrude would miss Neil. Without him, she doubted if she could have kept the farm going these last two years.

Even though Gertrude was innocent of exactly what part Katie and George had played in the invasion of the elders, they had seen very little of each other since that meeting. It had been another watershed event separating Gertrude even further from her people. She knew that the views expressed by Albert Bartel and Henry Essau were shared by her sisters and brothers. When she did come for short visits, Katie made no secret of her disapproval of the new house. Howard had let slip to Arnold that his mother said, Aunt Gertrude's house is 'pure sin'. Arnold, in turn, told his mother and asked her to explain what that meant. Gertrude tried to explain to him that Holdemans had a different idea of what sin was.

Gertrude had taken several of her solitary car rides during this summer of 1918. Sunday afternoons were a good time. In the mornings they had a church service at one of their houses—John and Mary's, Gertrude's or at the Eidses. Occasionally, when they were joined by one or more of the New Church families from the south, they would picnic. On Sundays when it was just the three local families, the service would be followed by Sunday school lessons for the children and the afternoons would be free. That is when Gertrude would take her car out and talk to herself.

I'm operating a successful farm. I'm financially secure. My children are growing up. I hardly ever see Katie and Abram anymore. I can't remember the last time I've been to Blumenort. Neil is leaving this fall. Tom is good. It won't be the same but I will be able to work with him. Helen is starting school this fall so I'll be bundling up another of my babies and sending them out into the freezing cold every morning. My children have no future in this school. They must have more. I want to be able to drive my car all year round. I am so lonesome. I want to be out in the big world again. I want to meet people who don't even know what a Holdeman is. The life that was so perfect for David and me is not the life for me without him.

In the fall, when she put the car away, she felt she had a much clearer sense of what needed to change in the lives of her and her children. She knew that she and her Model T had made a good start at seeing things more realistically. It was time to stop clinging to a romanticized picture of the past, face up to the facts and start doing something about it. Now she had the entire winter ahead of her to start putting together a plan for their future.

Chapter Twenty-Three

The onset of winter was a good motivator for Gertrude to move ahead with her planing. For as long as she could remember, she looked to the coming of winter with a certain amount of dread, even more so after her children started school and had constantly to battle the elements to get there. She would be happy to never see snow again. She was going to leave the farm, leave Manitoba but now she was faced with a host of questions for which she needed to find answers. How far south should she go? How would she earn a living? Other than housework and farming, she had no work experience. Her reading and writing skills were all self taught. Were they strong enough to enable her to take some sort of training? The thought scared her. A decision would have to be made whether to sell the farm or rent it out. Whether she sold or rented, she did have enough money to get established and support her children for a time but eventually she would need to find work. The yearly income she would receive from renting the farm would help to supplement the money she would be able to earn by working. That made it an attractive option.

As she was mulling all these considerations over in her mind, she happened to see a notice in the Winnipeg Free Press from a Texas real-estate company. It stated that there were citrus orchard opportunities to be had in southern Texas. They were inviting people to attend an information meeting which was to be held in ten days. She thought about it for a few days and decided that she had nothing to lose by going to the meeting. But she thought she would have a talk with John and Mary before she went. Maybe they would be interested in going too.

The three were sitting in Gertrude's living room having a cup of tea. "This is the advertisement that I want to show you." She handed the clipping to John and Mary. "I saw it in Saturday's paper and have been thinking about it ever since. We've mentioned, in passing, a number of times the possibility of moving out of this community. I think going to this meeting could be a start."

John and Mary studied the advertisement before John spoke. "This looks interesting. But I don't know. Texas is a long way away. When I've thought of moving, it's mainly been about finding a non-Holdeman community somewhere else in the Canadian west. I don't know about the United States."

"I can't imagine moving to such a far-off place. Texas! What do we know about growing oranges? Besides, that would mean hardly ever seeing my family again—maybe *never* seeing them again," Mary interjected wistfully.

Gertrude was grateful to hear their skepticism. They were making good points. She would have to decide if they applied to her. They talked a while longer and then Gertrude asked if they would like to go to the meeting with her. "We've been talking as though by going to this meeting, we would be making a commitment to go to Texas," she laughed. "Why don't we just think of it as an enjoyable outing to Winnipeg. We can get information and have some fun at the same time."

John and Mary did decide to go to the meeting with Gertrude. The presentation was full of information about the geography and climate of southern Texas as well as detailed descriptions of the operation of citrus orchards. They passed out brochures with pictures of existing orchards and of land ready to be developed. The company was offering excursions—all expenses paid, by train from Winnipeg to Corpus Christi. From there they would take local transportation to look at sites and meet some of the local people.

On the train ride back to Rosenort, little was said. Everyone was lost in their own thoughts about what they had just seen and whether there could be a future for them in Texas. One of John's older boys was waiting at the train station. Small clouds of steam gushed out of the horses nostrils as they tossed their heads and gave a welcoming nicker, signalling their readiness to get underway and back to the comfort of their barn. They bundled up for the ride home. They drove through John and Mary's yard first. They stepped out of the sleigh said good night and Thomas then continued on to take Gertrude to her farm. Thomas took these few minutes to question Gertrude about what they had learned at the meeting.

"What did you find out, Aunt Gertrude? Does Texas really look like a place that you could live? I wish I had gone to the meeting too. I want so badly to get out of this place. What did my parents think?"

"Your Mom and Dad are pretty sceptical at this point. They may not be ready to commit to the next stage of actually visiting Texas but I've made up my mind to take the excursion and I'll tell you all about it when I get back."

"I'll really be looking forward to hearing what you have to say. Maybe my parents will be more interested when they hear what you learned from being there." Thomas hesitated, then said, "If you move to Texas and they decide to stay here, maybe I can come and live with you." Gertrude felt the desperation that was lurking behind the open, searching look and shy smile that he gave her.

Sensing a kindred spirit, Gertrude was touched. "What I've been learning these days, Thomas, is that anything is possible. Let's take this one step at a time and see where we get." She returned his smile and gave his arm a reassuring squeeze. Thomas helped her out of the sleigh and said good night. Gertrude thought she saw a brightness in his face that she hadn't see for some time. She understood all too well Thomas' need for something more.

John and Mary clearly were not ready to take any further action. Gertrude, on the other hand, knowing that she was getting caught up in a momentum that she did not want to lose, had, as she told Thomas, made up her mind. She signed up for the next excursion which was to leave for Corpus Christi in three weeks. That would allow her to be back home in plenty of time for Christmas. She had no qualms about leaving the children and farm in the capable hands of Anna and Tom.

* * * * *

"Well, I've bought an orchard." Gertrude was with John and Mary and some of their children at their kitchen table enjoying a mid morning snack. She had just got back from her trip to Texas and was readjusting to the cold. She was surprised at how easy it had been to get used to the warmth of the Texas winter sun. John and Mary were taken aback by the speed of her decision. They had expected Gertrude to return with information that might lead to a move sometime in the distant future.

Not so.

"That was fast," was all John could manage to say. Mary was speechless.

"If you think about it, my decision wasn't as fast as it seems. David and I often talked about eventually leaving this Holdeman community. We knew that the world here was too small and we both wanted to provide our children with more opportunity than they could ever have here. We just weren't ready to take action. Now I am ready."

"Yes," John agreed. "I used to talk to David about the same thing."

"My orchard is part of a beautiful community and only a few miles from the ocean. One hasn't really lived until they have seen the ocean and stepped into its water. I can still hear the sound of the waves lapping the shore which has a beach with the most wonderful soft sand. Padre Island is just off the coast of the mainland with more beaches. We'll be an hour by car from Corpus Christi which has a population of about 10,000, much smaller than Winnipeg, but it has a variety of stores, a couple of theatres, a library, a small college, a large hospital and all the professional services are available there. It already has a busy port but the city has plans for greatly enlarging it in the next few years which will create additional jobs and prosperity for the area. My local town which is much smaller than Corpus Christi and only two miles down the road from my orchard, has the essential services and a good school that goes from grade one to grade twelve. All kinds of interesting things are grown there—even cotton and something called mesquite. There are lots of palm trees and cactus and one of the most beautiful flowers I've ever seen called bougainvillea."

"Oh my word, the way you are describing Texas.....it sounds like another world!" exclaimed Mary.

Gertrude agreed. "It is, Mary. It is. That's what we need—you, John, me and our children. That's just what we need, a different world than what we have here."

Thomas, Margaret, Peter and Edward who were at the table were hanging on Gertrude's every word, Margaret wondering if you could actually swim in the ocean. "Is the water really warm?"

Thomas couldn't get enough information. The questions just tumbled out of him. "What exactly goes on in a port. Are the ships in the port really big? Where do they come from? What are they bringing in and what are they taking away? What do men who work in the port actually do? How easy is it to get a job?"

"How close will you be to Mexico?" Margaret asked. "Can Mexicans speak English? Do they look like us? It all sounds so exciting!"

Edward was more interested in the school. "I could actually go to that school right through to grade twelve?

And, oh yes, I have to tell you that I read a book on plants, animals and insects of Texas while your were away, It said they have rattle snakes and tarantulas." Gertrude was getting caught up in the children's enthusiastic curiosity and was trying her best to answer their questions. Her own children were still too young to show this kind of lively interest.

"I've brought back lots of pictures and some of the local newspapers. I'll show them to you next time you come to my place. And the food is interesting too. There are many restaurants owned by Mexicans serving Mexican food. It is very spicy but I kind of like it and think I could get quite fond of it. They eat a lot of shrimp which is brought in fresh every day."

Peter didn't know what a shrimp was. Edward, again based on his reading, explained to him about shrimp and threw in some additional information on crabs and oysters for everyone's benefit.

John and Mary were not actively participating in this part of the discussion but John was making lots of mental notes, not only about the information, but also about how his children seemed to be coming to life as they spoke with Gertrude. Now, Mary brought them back to what was on *her* mind.

"But what about your farm? What will happen to it—and your beautiful new house?" Mary asked plaintively. John looked at Gertrude as though it was he who had just asked Mary's question.

"I had several meetings with my bank manager before I left. He agreed that I had enough money to buy an established orchard without selling my farm here. He advised me to seriously consider not selling my farm at this time if I could find a suitable tenant. It would give me income and could always be sold any time in the future. It would be like money in the bank. He said he knew customers of his bank who were looking for a farm to rent. Their family farm is several miles south of mine. They have an adult son who is getting married this winter and they want to set the young couple up on a rental farm near the family homestead. He approached them for me and then I met with them."

"But what do you know about growing oranges?" This was a recurring theme with Mary.

"What I don't know, I'm going to learn. Some of it will be like running a farm but a lot of it will be quite different. The land must be irrigated. The previous owners have not finished setting up the system so that will be the first big job. There is a lot of available and affordable labour for hire locally. I met some of my nearby neighbours and they are so friendly. And they are willing to teach me some of the ropes and lend me some books. Two of the orchards near me are owned by people like me who moved from the north and started with no experience. I see the orchard as a beginning. It may or may not work out. If not, I'll find some other way to make a living. I know how to look after myself. I've been doing it ever since Mama and Papa died."

"You seem so definite about all of this. I envy your confidence," John said quietly as he took Mary's hand.

"I know you are not ready to make a decision just yet but I do hope you will consider making a similar move. Give me a year and then come for a visit. Bring some of your children. I think you would be really interested in seeing Texas first hand for yourself," she said to Thomas. "It's a long, tiring train journey but you might find it worthwhile. After I'm there, I'll find out if there are any other New Church families in south eastern Texas." The church that had been built around writings of Emanuel Swedenborg was officially known as The Church Of The New Jerusalem but commonly referred to as 'The New Church' by its members.

Now Gertrude was faced with the task of telling Katie and Abram. She drove to Katie's farm first. Katie was surprised to see Gertrude. She didn't know that Gertrude was already back from her trip to Texas. She invited Gertrude in and they made themselves comfortable in the kitchen.

"How was your trip? George and I couldn't believe it when we heard that you had left for Texas. Texas of all places! I don't even know if I could find it on the map! We wouldn't even have known you had gone if Agnes hadn't made a point of telling us. She had some time off from her job in Winnipeg and was at John's farm for a few days. He told her you had gone. It was like she couldn't wait to tell us. To think that I heard it first from Agnes of all people. But I'm getting used to being the last to know what you are up to these days."

Katie's attempt at making Gertrude feel uncomfortable had little effect. "My decision to go was made quickly and John and Mary were the only people I told." Gertrude went right to the point of her visit. "I have bought a citrus orchard about an hours drive south of a city called Corpus Christi. If you have a map I can show you."

"We don't have any maps in this house. And what about your farm? I'm afraid to ask."

"I'm renting it to a couple who are just starting out and who are being backed by the boy's parents."

"You're renting out your farm," Katie repeated flatly. Her voice was dead as she stared at her hands in her lap.

"Yes, I'm renting out my farm. The children and I will be leaving by the end of June."

"You won't be putting in a crop then."

"No."

The well of sisterly affection that had sustained them in the early days was dry. These were two women now, exchanging facts. Facts that, in former days, would have evoked a highly emotional exchange, now took on a hollow, dry, quality. The foundation of love that had supported their relationship lay in ruins, buried under years of hurt. The shadow of that love remained but now the need to protect themselves from each other was paramount.

Her next stop was Abram's farm. Abram knew of her trip to Texas from Katie and he also knew Gertrude well enough to know that she would come back with her decision made. He was not surprised but dismay was written on his face. "Was there nothing I could have done to keep you—?"

"No. Oh no." Gertrude spoke quietly but urgently.

"But, I feel as though I have failed somehow."

"No, no, Abram, what could you have done? This all started so, so, long ago—way before we got to know each other as adults. We were separated when we were so young. You need to know that my entire life has led me to this point. It had to be."

"But, you're leaving so much behind," he insisted.

"No, really—I'm leaving very little behind." She saw the anguish in his eyes. Her words had cut him deeply.

She felt sorry for what she had said but the words could not be retracted and they both knew them to be true. Suddenly, he reached out his hand. She hesitated, but only for a second, for she had not expected the gesture. It startled her but she grasped his hand firmly and put her other arm around his shoulder and hugged him to her. "We are going to have to say good-by my little brother," she whispered in his ear, pressing her cheek hard against his. The tickle of his beard against her face reminded her of Papa.

When they stepped back from one another he whispered back, "Good luck my big sister. Good luck—," his eyes brimming with tears.

* * * * *

The end of June was approaching. Gertrude had made an arrangement with her tenants which involved the new couple moving into the little house in time to put in the spring crop. They would move into the big house after Gertrude and the children left. They had also bought some of the horses and machinery and even some of the furniture in the big house. The rest had been sold at an auction sale early in the spring.

All the normal farm activity was buzzing around her. Not being part of the activity felt strange to Gertrude. Anna had left for Winnipeg. She had been hired permanently by the bank and was busy working at her new job. It had been a poignant parting. Anna had been through so much with Gertrude and the children. Gertrude paid her a generous bonus to help her get settled in Winnipeg. To cover her sadness, she jokingly told Anna that she would always have a job with her if she wanted to move to Texas. Anna understood and they shared a smile and a long embrace.

Every once in a while Gertrude was hit by the thought that maybe she was making a huge mistake. But not for long. She knew that she couldn't afford to have doubts at this stage of things so she would carefully remind herself of all the reasons that had gone into her decision to move.

Abram had bought Gertrude's car making him the first Holdeman Modle T owner in the district. Abram was not accustomed to being a trend setter but owning and driving Gertrude's car was fraught with deep meaning and emotion for him. He hadn't hesitated in making her the offer. She had taught him how to drive but she was keeping the car till their day of departure. Then he would take ownership and drive them to the railway station.

Today she was driving it for the last time. She was on her way to the Ennses' small family cemetery. Tom had brought the car out for her and put up the top. There were dark clouds forming in the west. Heat mirages tickled the horizon as she turned east onto the section road. They always passed the graveyard on their way to Rosenort but it was not her way to stop there very often. She could not bear to think of David lying there, but today she needed to sit by his grave for one last time. She saw the two half grown trees in the distance. John had planted them among the graves hoping to soften the austere picture. She slowed down, pulled over to the side of the road and set the brake. She passed through the little gate and sat down in front of David's headstone. She reached over and caressed the inscription. The stone was cold and she drew her hand away quickly. Then, picking up some of the warm earth beside her and letting it dribble slowly between her fingers, she began to feel the closeness which she had sought.

"When you left me, my darling," she began softly, "I felt that I would never be able to leave here. All our life together was here. All our hopes and dreams were built here. I thought the memories would sustain me forever. I had to go on with what we had begun, just to remain near you. But it's not that way anymore and I want you to understand. Remember," she reminded him, "how we did talk of leaving here sometime but it seemed so far in the future and we would have left together?" She paused, thinking about what else she wanted to tell him. "The place the children and I are going to is beautiful and I know you would like it. I hope you are willing to let me go." She paused again. "No. I think you *want* me to go. Yes—I can feel it! You *do!*" She sat for sometime, her still figure silhouetted against the darkening sky. In spite of being aware that she was getting wet and chilled she felt a warmth welling up inside her. She got up and stood motionless reliving the pain of David's departure while at the same time savouring their timeless love she knew would always be with her. For a time her feet were held as though anchored to David's grave. Then slowly, she felt the earth release its hold on her. 'You *must* go.'

A persuasive gust of wind propelled her into action. She picked up her skirts and ran for the car forgetting to close the gate. She revved up the idling motor and deftly swung the car around and headed for home. The rain had begun to come down in torrents and she pushed the throttle down as far as it would go The car careened madly form side to side, water and mud splashing wildly from the spinning wheels. Lightning flashed all around her, lighting up the dark sky. Rolling thunder crashed and for the first time since Papa was struck down, she didn't even care! Her clothes became soaked as the rain drove through the open sides of the car. She had said good bye and nothing, nothing could stop her now!

Epilogue

Elma before her solo piano recital at the Wichita Women's Civic Centre, 1936

Helen in Kansas, 1936

Arnold, the animal lover, back at the farm in Manitoba, 1942

RCAF Flying Officer Benjamin Enns, 1943, three months before he became a WWII fatality

Gertrude, 1945